# THE EARLY WRITINGS OF

*Alan Watts*

# THE EARLY WRITINGS OF

*Alan Watts*

## THE BRITISH YEARS: 1931–1938
## WRITINGS IN
## *BUDDHISM IN ENGLAND*

●

Edited by John Snelling,
with Mark Watts and Dennis T. Sibley

CELESTIAL ARTS   **CA**   BERKELEY, CALIFORNIA

Celestial Arts
P.O. Box 7327
Berkeley, California 94707

Published simultaneously in the United Kingdom by
Century Hutchinson Publishing Group Limited, London.

Cover design by Ken Scott
Text design by Ken Scott
Typography by HMS Typography, Inc.

**Library of Congress Cataloging-in-publication Data**

Watts, Alan, 1915-1973.
The early writings of Alan Watts.

1. Buddhism.     I. Snelling, John, 1943-
II. Sibley, Dennis T.     III. Watts, Mark.     IV. Title.
BQ4055.W36     1987          294.3          87-11756
ISBN 0-89087-480-8

Manufactured in the United States of America
First Printing, 1987

1  2  3  4  5        91  90  89  88  87

# CONTENTS

# ACKNOWLEDGEMENTS

I should like to thank the following for their kind help with the present volume: Garry Thomson and Maurice O'C Walshe, who read the typescript of the Introduction; P. Pollak of The King's School, Canterbury, for invaluable help with that phase of Alan Watts's life; Joy Buchan, Alan Watts's cousin, for talking about her memories of him and helping with photographs; Oliver Caldecott, for effecting introductions; and Mark Watts for guiding the volume to publication. The lines from "September 1, 1939" by W.H. Auden are reproduced by kind permission of the publishers, Messrs. Faber & Faber; the poem currently appears in *The English Auden, Poems, Essays and Dramatic Writings, 1927-39*, edited by Edward Mendlesohn. Finally I should like to thank Dennis T. Sibley for his long and patient support.

—John Snelling
London, August 1987

# INTRODUCTION

## by John Snelling

This first volume of the early writings of Alan Watts covers the period from 1931, when he was still a schoolboy, to 1938, when he departed from Britain for the United States with his young bride Eleanor. Besides the tail-end of his school-days, this period also encompasses that exciting phase when he was a young man about town, gaining a somewhat unusual but remarkably interesting education for himself in the esoteric and occult circles of London, which of course often ran concurrent with sections of the bohemian demi-monde of the day. It was also a period when he was working hard to develop his talents both as a writer and editor—and to great effect.

The period could be aptly called Watts' *Golden Years* or his *Years of Promise*, for there then seemed to be hardly a cloud in the blue sky of his brilliant potential. We have, however, chosen to subtitle this volume *The British Years*, for this aspect needs emphasising, because on account of his fame—some might say his *infamy*—as a luminary of the Californian Counterculture, many have come to regard Alan Watts as an essentially American phenomenon. Certainly he spent the last thirty-five years of his life in the United States and attained far greater influence and popularity there. Indeed, in his autobiography, he laments that, despite the efforts of his publishers, his books never sold as well in Britain as they did on the other side of the Atlantic. Yet it was in Britain that he was born, grew up, and received his first formative influences. As this anthology clearly demonstrates, many of those influences were lasting ones, and many of the themes that emerged in these early writings were to recur throughout his life. In fact, there is strong evidence here to support the view that most of Watts's major philosophical themes arose in these early years and that he later merely developed, refined and played variations upon them.

Alan Wilson Watts was born on January 6, 1915 at Chislehurst in Kent, the only son of Laurence Wilson Watts (1880–1974) and Emily Mary Buchan (1876?–1961). His father was by all accounts a quiet and thoughtful man, with many interests. He was particularly fond of reading (the works of Rudyard Kipling were a lifelong love) and, gifted with a very retentive memory, had acquired a large fund of knowledge. He was also a great lover of nature and gardening. His working life was spent in the City of London, working for the Michelin Tyre Company and later as a fundraiser for the Metropolitan Hospital Sunday Fund. Laurence and Alan got on famously together and shared many interests in common[1], including eventually an interest in Eastern religion. Alan's feelings for his mother, on the other hand, were not so happy. She was a schoolmistress, and repressive religious influences during early life had inculcated a certain straight-lacedness that grated on her son. Nevertheless, Laurence and Emily were a loving couple and without a shadow of a doubt wanted to do the very best they could, within their limited means, for their precious only child.

A couple of years ago I paid a visit to Chislehurst in search of Alan Watts's roots. I caught the train from Waterloo East railway station on a grey English winter morning and, having traversed the amorphous urban sprawl of south London, soon came to the suburbs. There were rather more trees here than in London proper, and in summer the area could probably be described as leafy, but now the trees were leafless, their stripped branches thin and metallic against the white sky. Not far away lurked the rolling chalk downland of the Kentish countryside: the Garden of England, as it is sometimes called. The harrassed businessmen and office-workers of London had been retreating to this area for more than a century in search of semi-rural security and tranquillity. Here they had built their brick and stucco villas: shrines to solid English Middle Class values. From here they had daily returned to the workaday fray of London, shuttled to and fro on regular British Railways commuter trains. Familiar with such stultifying rhythms from an impressionable age, Alan Watts decided early that this lifestyle was not for him—and indeed he succeeded in forging a very different one for himself.

Walking up from the little red brick railway station at Chislehurst, I realised that the area was now much more built-up than it had been in Watts's youth, yet among the faceless modern developments there still remained the substantial suburban villas that as a young man he no doubt had passed innumerable times on his way home after a fascinating evening in the esoteric salons of London, his head buzzing with new ideas. Then, he would be often walking in the dark, his way sometimes perhaps lit by a pale moon, the wind whispering in the trees.

I eventually managed to locate Holbrook Lane, where he had been born and brought up. This is also where he had lived until he was twenty-two or twenty-three years old, so the bulk of the items collected in this volume were written while this was still his home. A row of semi-detached cottages presented themselves to me, the lower storey of each built of good red brick, the upper storey pebble-dashed. Each also had a trim pocket-handkerchief front garden secluded from the road by a wooden fence. They were neat and respectable, but very small, tiny in fact, and easily dwarfed by their more imposing neighbours.

Holbrook Lane had also been built up since Watts's boyhood and the houses had been renumbered, so I found it difficult to locate what used to be Number 3: Rowan Tree Cottage. I knocked on various doors and asked if anyone knew the precise house in which Alan Watts, the well-known writer on religious subjects, had lived. Each time I was greeted with a blank expression and "Never heard of him. . . ." I reflected on the irony of this; had I mentioned the name in the appropriate parts of San Francisco, say, it would have elicited a far more positive response.

Eventually I did manage to work out which was the former Number 3. The rowan tree in the front garden had gone, and there was no way I could see the long back garden that had been Laurence Watts's pride and joy, and which Alan, who as a boy had frolicked by the hour in its herbaceous abundance, described in his autobiography as "flutant with birdsong." It used to back onto a girls' school (and still does, I fancy).

From Chislehurst, I caught a local bus to nearby Bromley, where I had an appointment to meet Alan's cousin and boyhood playmate Joy Buchan. Bromley is one of those suburban dormitory towns that lack all colour and character, as though, in its insatiable hunger, the nearby metropolis has syphoned off all its potential along with the energy of the bulk of its inhabitants. It is a place one passes through; not the sort of place one visits.

Alan Watts and his parents had in fact been obliged to move to Bromley when for a short time they had fallen into financial difficulties. Harry Buchan, Joy's father, owned some property, and he let them have the use of a house here, so Rowan Tree Cottage was temporarily let, and Emily did embroidery work to support the three of them. During this period, a regular Sunday ritual was a visit to Joy's family home for tea and supper. There would also be singing—both hymns and secular songs—in which one and all would take part.

"Both my uncle and his son had fine voices and I can hear them now singing *Rejoice in the Lord Alway* and my uncle singing Kipling songs as well," Joy has written in a memoir of Laurence Watts.

It was during these soirées *that Joy Buchan got to know her cousin Alan. She remembers him as a quiet boy at first, but fun-loving—full of tricks and always ready to entertain.*

*"He was very clever with drawing," Joy told me. "He could have a book with him and he'd just sort of start drawing animals or all sorts of pin men. He could make them really come alive. He didn't copy anything; he did it all out of his head. I just sat there fascinated. . . . And he used to be very keen on ju-jitsu too. He used to try things out on me, trying to make me completely powerless—but I managed to get out of the vice sometimes!"*

*Even as a child, enjoyment of life was a priority for Alan: "I can see him in the cottage at Chislehurst, just letting off steam. He'd sing quite off the cuff; all sorts of ditties and things. A lot of nonsense rhymes, really. They were really fun. He made them fun. . . ."*

Alan was also always very kind to Joy. One day, for instance, she suffered an accident. He told her to relax on the sofa and not to worry—"he was very, very good . . . ." She experienced this kindness again when she did secretarial work for him in London after his marriage to Eleanor Everett in 1938, and yet again when she was their guest in the United States at the time when Alan was Chaplain at Northwestern University in Evanston.

Joy also recalled seeing oriental art objects in Rowan Tree Cottage, which we know were influential upon Alan's development: "It had a lot of Eastern hangings and china. In the sitting room they got those big vases—some of them were Chinese and Japanese. And they had a little tiny dressing-room that my uncle and Alan used to use, and there was a little Buddha on the mantlepiece in there. They also used to have joss-sticks and incense, I think . . . ."

Joy Buchan was a kind and hospitable person, and it was a benign portrait of Alan Watts that she painted. There was something a little incongruous, however, about the memorabilia that she brought out: the American editions of his books—and the gramophone records that he had made, the sleeves of some of them designed in dated psychedelic graphics that evoked associations of California and the fast-fading hippie culture of the sixties (echoes of Jimi Hendrix and the Grateful Dead). How far away all that was from Joy's comfortable but very English and respectable drawing room in suburban Bromley; but in a way it also spoke eloquently of the contrasts that Alan's life embraced and demonstrated how far he travelled from his origins.

Alan's education began at a kindergarten situated quite near the family home at Chislehurst. Then, in 1922, he became a boarder at St. Hugh's, Bickley. His development, however, undoubtedly underwent a great leap forward when, in the autumn of 1929, he went to King's School, Canterbury on a scholarship. King's is reckoned to be the oldest and one of the most prestigious public schools in the land, and everything about it smacks of quality and tradition. Its very situation is a remarkable one; it stands within the hallowed precincts of Canterbury Cathedral, the very heart of established religion in England. All around there is soaring Gothic architecture at its most impressive: towers, pinnacles, flying buttresses, vaulted crypt and cloister; and the very stone gives off a musty antique aroma that has taken centuries to culture. No school is more saturated in history.

Now, the myth has arisen in the popular mind that English public schools, with their bullying all-boy atmospheres, sporting obsessions and spartan regimes, are awful places: forcing-houses devoted to the mass-production of authoritarian brutes and to crushing the spirits of the sensitive and the creative. Probably they are not ideal places for producing the most emotionally well-balanced people, but they do foster talent and it is usually possible for those not so inclined to find subtle ways of opting out of the prevailing sporting ethos and of developing their own interests. Indeed, if their interests are cultural, artistic, or spiritual, kindred spirits can usually be found among the teachers and the other pupils: sympathetic, well-informed, and/or talented souls ready to actively encourage and assist the flowering of individual potential.

Thus it was in Watts's case. Like another distinguished old boy of King's, the writer Somerset Maugham, he has the standard disparaging things to say about the place in his autobiography, but in fact being there gave him a new confidence, and his interest in the spiritual traditions of the orient became something really strong in the quasi-ecclesiastical atmosphere of the place.

We have mentioned how oriental artefacts back home in Chislehurst helped to foster this special interest in the young Alan Watts. Later, reading the Fu Manchu novels of Sax Rohmer and Lafcadio Hearn's literary gleanings in Buddha-Fields[2] quickened it. It was further encouraged by Francis Croshaw, the urbane father of a boyhood chum, and by other friends. Then quite by chance Alan one day opened a book that Croshaw had lent him,[3] and in it he discovered something that was to alter the course of his life. It was a yellow pamphlet published by a group in London that called itself the Buddhist Lodge. He promptly wrote off to the Lodge, became a member, and began to subscribe to its journal, *Buddhism in England* (now *The Middle Way*). This was in 1930. In the same year, he formally declared himself to be a Buddhist. Far from being horrified and rushing to extirpate this pernicious Eastern infection, the staff and boys at King's (Patrick Leigh Fermor, the war-hero and writer was one of them[4]) took the whole thing perfectly in their stride—but then, it's considered healthy for an English gentleman to cultivate a few eccentricities—they add colour to his character. He even got encouragement. When in 1932 the powers-that-be at King's were asked to send two representatives to a religious conference to be held in Hayward's Heath in Sussex, they selected a chap with the highly appropriate name of Parsons *and . . . Alan Watts.*

Watts began his remarkable lifelong career writing upon oriental spirituality while still at King's School. In 1931, his very first article (with which we begin this anthology) appeared in *Buddhism in England.* Unfortunately, however, we have not been able to trace any unpublished material dating from this very early period. Nor have we been able to find items bearing Watts's name in any King's School publications. He appears to have been more active there as a public speaker than as a writer. He held the post of Hon. Secretary of the Debating Society and also of the Caterpillars Club, the junior branch of the Marlowe Society.

The Buddhist Lodge, of which Alan Watts was now a member, had been founded in 1924 by an eminent English barrister named Christmas Humphreys (1901–1983), the author of that fateful yellow pamphlet, and his future wife Aileen—or Toby and Puck as they were affectionately known. At first it had come under the umbrella of the Madame Blavatsky's Theosophical Society, but later it took on an autonomous life of its own. It became the Buddhist Society, London in 1943, and then in 1952 contracted its name to simply The Buddhist Society. As such it is known to this day.

Travers Christmas Humphreys was a tall and imposing figure with a distinguished beak of a nose and an authoritative voice that he had moulded into a marvellous oratorical tool. He had won national fame for himself in the Old Bailey, London's principal criminal court, as a leading prosecuting counsel in many important murder trials. In those days, of course, the Death Penalty was still in force, and so the shadow of the gallows loomed over and intensified the drama of these proceedings. Yet, incongruously enough, this barrister who in his professional life often found himself dealing with the sinister—and often gory—details of violent crime was also the country's leading Buddhist and personally against execution as a form of punishment. Many have found this apparent contradiction hard to explain, but Toby himself managed to work it out. Broadly he would argue that someone had to do the job, and he tried to do it fairly. If there was any doubt about a man's guilt, then he would not push the case; and always he tried to look coolly at the facts and not be swayed by emotion.

It was the First World War and the trauma of a beloved elder brother's death in action that precipitated Toby on the religious search that soon brought him to Buddhism via Theosophy. He was always very much a Theosophist at heart, however, and his Buddhism was of a rather intellectual sort. He laid particular stress on the notion of rebirth, which, no doubt, helped ease the pain of his brother's death: it allowed Toby to believe that he had not been utterly annihilated but would return to the world again in a new body.

I had the pleasure and honour of working with Toby Humphreys during the last three years of his long and productive life, and I remember once asking him about Alan Watts—did he remember him first coming to the Lodge?

"Oh, yes, indeed," he replied, settling back in his chair in the inner office at 58 Eccleston Square, the Society's headquarters in London. "He was quite remarkable. We first heard about him when he wrote to us from King's School. We assumed from the tone and content of his letters that he must be a senior master *at least*. But then when he at last showed up at a meeting with his father—that would have been around 1932—we were surprised to see that he was still not out of his teens . . . *but he was actually talking Zen. . . .*"

Toby laid special emphasis on the last words and shot

me a penetrating look that intimated that I was to understand that the young Watts had not been talking *about* Zen: Zen itself had been issuing from his lips.

Watts was clearly a kind of *wunderkind* and right from the start of his association with the Lodge he displayed both an almost uncanny talent for understanding highly elusive oriental spiritual ideas and a comparable talent for putting those ideas across to Westerners in ways that made them readily comprehensible. Toby could only account for these precocious talents by appealing to the notion that Watts had developed his intuition, a faculty which Toby believed enabled a person to have insight into the most profound matters, in previous incarnations. He had thus arrived in the world already highly developed spiritually.

So Watts began turning out a steady stream of articles and pamphlets, and at twenty produced a full-length book, *The Spirit of Zen*, which was the first of a long line of titles that sold remarkably well, though mainly on the other side of the Atlantic—in America. Toby Humphreys was a fine writer, too, with a similar talent for stating religious ideas simply and clearly, and also for making them come alive for the ordinary reader. He wrote many books that brought a great many people into initial contact with Buddhism. This, plus his activities as a speaker and broadcaster, made him a great *Dharma*-spreader: a disseminator of Buddhist ideas.

Alan Watts very much followed in Toby Humphreys's footsteps as a great *Dharma*-spreader—and herein lies their special historical importance. Over the next fifty years, tens of thousands of Westerners were to come to take a serious interest in Buddhism after reading a book by either one or the other of them. America was Watts's particular sphere of influence; as the late Edward Conze, the Anglo-German Buddhist scholar, remarked in his memoirs (though with a critical edge):

*Most of my American students first became interested in Buddhism through Alan Watts. It is true that they had to unlearn most of what they had learnt. It is equally true that he put out the net that caught them in the first place.*[5]

Watts has other claims to distinction. He was well ahead of time in seeing the virtues of Buddhism and Eastern spirituality generally; also in advocating a return to the mystical roots of spirituality, and the integration of sex and spirituality. He also saw where useful cross-connections might be made between religion and psychotherapy. He was a professed pacifist too, and he showed great courage by attempting to live out his spiritual convictions in his own life at a time when the world, monolithically materialistic as it then was, was by no means sympathetic to what he was trying to do. He was indeed a sort of natural priest, but one who sought original ways of discharging his vocation (or *dharma*). Perhaps he did not get things entirely right, but then how many pioneers ever do? And is there not great virtue anyway in just having made the attempt?

When Alan Watts left King's School in 1932, he did not go on to Oxford or Cambridge as would have been the normal course for a public school boy. Instead his father pulled a few strings and got him a bread-and-butter job with the Metropolitan Hospital Sunday Fund. In his spare time, however, he set about getting an offbeat education for himself. He made numerous friends in the Buddhist world of London and around its fringes and inveigled himself into a coterie or two. It is probably fair to say, however, that the Buddhist Lodge was his spiritual home.

In those days, Buddhist Lodge meetings were held in the Humphreys's London house, Number 37 South Eaton Place, about five minutes' walk from Victoria Station in the prestigious Belgravia district with its imposing stucco facades and columned entrances. Toby and his wife Puck were charming and hospitable hosts, and together had created an elegant environment furnished with all manner of tasteful oriental bric-a-brac that the young Alan Watts found quite fascinating. In Toby Humphreys he also found a significant guru-figure, though his influence was not only religious. The two of them had cultural interests in common too and, for instance, used to like to toff themselves up in cloaks and white gloves and strut off together to the ballet at Covent Garden toting silver-topped canes. "The mind boggles at this couple of show-offs making their way through life," snaps the acerbic Dr. Conze[6]; but there is no doubt some truth in it. Humphreys and Watts were both endowed with more than a touch of the showman (Toby's London club was the Garrick)—but then that helped them enormously in their respective vocations as disseminators of oriental spiritual ideas.

Vasa Lindwall, who attended the Lodge at the time, recalls Watts coming to meetings at South Eaton Place. He was often accompanied by his father, who himself became Treasurer of the Lodge, and was invariably well-dressed and well-mannered. This accords with a photograph taken of him at the time which shows him as very much the dapper young-man-about-town, a sparse moustache on his upper lip, urbane cigarette in hand and well-cut suit (no trace whatsoever of the latent bohemian that was to subsequently emerge in California). Mr. Lindwall also recalls that he spoke quietly but with great authority for his tender years, and personally gave him one piece of sound advice that he valued greatly: "Don't jump out of the Christian box only to get trapped in the Buddhist box."

The years immediately following 1932 were golden ones for Alan Watts. He went on from one triumph to another, producing articles, pamphlets, and books with seemingly effortless brilliance. He was also a remarkable public speaker. In short, his trajectory seemed set for the very highest achievements. The year 1936 was undoubtedly his *annus mirabilis*—'that year of true grace in my life'', he calls it in his autobiography. His first book came out then; he attended the World Congress of Faiths and met Dr. D. T. Suzuki for the first time; and he took over the editorship of *Buddhism in England* from the journal's founder, Arthur C. March. He was then still only twenty-one years old. He retained that editorship until he left British shores two years later in 1938.

All but a couple of the works reprinted here first appeared in *Buddhism in England*. Spanning in all about seven highly creative years, this represents a very substantial body of work, for besides major articles, some of which were thematically linked and later reissued as pamphlets. Watts also published editorials, book reviews, poems, news reports, and much else besides. Not all of his contributions to the journal can be definitely attributed to him, for he did not sign all his pieces, and he also used pseudonyms, such as "Interpreter" and "Ronin".

Despite the substantial nature of this body of work, it does not by any means constitute *all* of Watts's literary output during the period. He also contributed articles and book reviews to *The Modern Mystic, The Occult Review,* and *The Sufi*; also to Dmitrije Mitrinovic's *New Britain* and *The Eleventh Hour.* A volume is in preparation that will comprehensively anthologise these.

## NOTES

*1. Joy Buchan recalls that Watts's senior and junior were at one time very keen on collecting butterflies. Buddhism, with its injunction against killing, put a stop to that.*

*2. Lafcadio Hearn (1850-1904) was born on a Greek island of an Irish father and a Greek mother. He came to the United States before he was twenty, gravitated to printing and journalism and in 1890 went to Japan on an assignment for* Harper's. *An existing interest in Buddhism was intensified; he also became interested in Shinto. He made Japan his home for the rest of his life, married a Japanese lady and in 1895 took Japanese citizenship. He delighted in Japanese folklore, particularly in stories of the supernatural. His books include:* Kwaidan; Kotto; Gleanings in Buddha-Fields; *and* Glimpses of Unfamiliar Japan.

3. *Specifically this book was Edmond Holmes's* The Creed of the Buddha; *the yellow pamphlet was by Christmas Humphreys; ref. the 1973 Vintage Books paperback edition of Watts's autobiography, p. 84.*

4. *Patrick Leigh Fermor was about a year younger than Watts and was eventually sacked (expelled) from Kings for walking out with a girl—a crime no doubt compounded by the fact that she was of low social status (viz, a greengrocer's daughter). There are numerous mentions of him in Watts's autobiography, notably on pp. 118-119 of the paperback edition mentioned above.*

5. *Edward Conze,* Memoirs of a Modern Gnostic. *Sherborne, Dorset, 1979, volume 1, p. 74n.*

6. *ibid. p. 74n.*

# PART ONE

# A BUDDHIST
# IN THE
# PRECINCTS

# PART ONE

The piece with which we begin this anthology, "Ultimate Reality," appeared under Watts's name in the January 1931 issue of *Buddhism in England*. It is, so far as we have been able to find out, his first published article and must have been actually written in 1930, when he was a mere fifteen. Although at the time he was a cloistered scholar living in the shadow of the great Bell Harry Tower of Canterbury Cathedral, the piece clearly shows that he has already become totally disillusioned with Christianity and hardened against its central notions of a personal God and an eternal soul. He in fact goes so far as to draw up his "case against God," basing his indictments largely upon what he calls "the conclusions of modern philosophy and science." He also passionately attacks the trivial manner in which religious matters are treated in the contemporary West. But if things are amiss, from which direction will redemption come? There is no doubt here: from the East, where an "unknown reality" has been discovered. This is that "unborn, unoriginated, uncreated, unformed" of which the Buddha spoke— and what is more, there is a way of approaching it. That he exclusively credits the East for this discovery shows that as yet Watts knows little or nothing of the English mystics.

"Ultimate Reality" is in fact a spirited little piece, naive in parts perhaps, but quite remarkable to have been written by so very young a person. There are inevitably suggestions of influence here and there—of Theosophy, for instance— and an impressive array of writers and thinkers, both Eastern and Western, are referred to or quoted—a useful device for adding authority to the piece. All in all it shows Watts to be quite amazingly well-informed and insightful—and vastly ahead of his time.

We know from Watts's own account that early encounters with examples of oriental art were a vital formative influence. His mother had obtained a few pieces through her work at a school for missionaries' children in Sevenoaks (county of Kent), and her son's interest developed from there, amplified by his reading of Lafcadio Hearn and other writers. The first record of a public talk that has come into our hands informs us that on November 27, 1929, when he was fourteen, he delivered a paper to the Caterpillars Club at King's (of which he was also Hon. Secretary) on the subject of "The Romance of Japanese Culture." Apparently, "He dealt with Japanese religious manners and customs, and *especially with their art*, and provoked a lively discussion," [italics mine][1]. This took place in the room of Watts's housemaster, Alec Macdonald, the deviser of a system of musical notation "similar to the Hindu" of whom Watts writes very enthusiastically in his autobiography. Then two years later, in October 1931, he was expatiating to the members of the Marlowe Society on the Zen poet Basho in a paper entitled "Two Eastern Poets," which also included reference to Omar Khayyam. Both poets believed in an Impersonal God, Watts contended, but "while Omar Khayyam regarded this God as a hard master to be forgotten in the wine-cup, Basho preferred to realize it in himself—to tune his soul to the Rhythm of the Universe, and so to attain to perfect happiness."[2] Watts also touched on the technique of Japanese verse and the various emotions that it is intended to convey.

But even before he read this paper to the Marlowe Society, another major article on the same theme had appeared in the February 1931 issue of *Buddhism in England* under Watts's name. It was entitled "The Influence of Buddhism upon Japanese Art," and is reprinted in this section. What is astonishing about this particular piece is that the young Watts contrives to write with such unwavering assurance and authority—the veritable young expert!— about things that he only knew about from pictures and books. And he ends with such a flourish too: a vivid purple passage delivered with all the stops out that evokes the scene in an Eastern temple. It is an arresting little cameo but overcharged with a spirit of high romance that gives it away at once as the work of a young writer. A pleasant touch is the edifying little story of Rikiu's hand-washing bowl that he drops into the essay earlier on. To convey a point by means of a concrete illustration rather than risk losing it in airy abstraction is a very Zen device; the skilful use of such devices was to become an important aspect of his literary style.

It is undoubtedly true that besides having a very genuine priestly vocation, Watts also had a highly developed aesthetic side to his nature. He was, in short, something of an artist. Words of course were his principal medium, both written and spoken; but he was also an accomplished calligrapher in both the Eastern and the Western styles. Endowed in this way with a fusion of religious and artistic talents, he was very well qualified to appreciate the relationship between religion and art: how the two spring ultimately from a common source and how, therefore, art, in the right hands, can be a truly religious activity and can fully express the deepest truths of religion.

After the piece on Japanese art, there was a long hiatus of nearly two years before Watts again published anything substantial in *Buddhism in England*. In the interim he did, however, participate in a debate that took place in *Our Forum,* the correspondence column of the journal. Dr. G. E. Halstead had contributed a long and thoughtful article entitled "A Rationalist View of Buddhism" to the October 1931 issue. The Editor, A. C. March, invited readers to send in criticisms of this, and Watts duly took up the invitation and contributed the letter that is reprinted in this section. In a subsequent issue, A. C. March himself entered the fray, commenting at length on Halstead's article and also taking issue with a couple of points that Watts had made in his letter:

*And Mr. Alan Watts echoes the same question when he says that Ultimate Reality is beyond human standards of justice. But we are not assuming "human standards of justice" when we assert that a Law of unerring justice rules the universe?*

*What we are asserting is that the universe is a cosmos not a chaos, that it is ruled by inviolable Law and not by the arbitrary decrees of a personal and therefore fallible deity. . . .*

And:

*. . . when Mr. Watts asks, "Who am I that I should attain Nirvana?" he fails to realize that the "I" that attains is the outcome of aeons of striving.*

A second letter from Watts, also reprinted in this section, appeared in the March/April 1932 issue of the journal in response to these cavils. Both this and the earlier letter are very insightful. They cut through all the prevailing waffle and home in on the central issue: that in absolute terms there is really no "I," no personal entity here. If a person has seen this fact, then he will not waste his time worrying about rebirth and attaining Nirvana. This of course is the classic stance of the Zen school as it came to its first great flowering in China: the central experience of Enlightenment is all-important, for like a great sword it slices cleanly through the Gordian knot of mental agitation, and at once the practitioner is liberated.

The pamphlet, *An Outline of Zen*, was published by the now defunct Golden Vista Press in 1933. Against Watts's signature to the Preface the name "Canterbury" appears, so we have included it in this section of King's School writings. It represents the first of what Watts himself termed his "impudent" attempts to "clarify and popularise" the Zen writings of D. T. Suzuki. The First Series of Suzuki's *Essays in Zen Buddhism* had been published in London by Luzac in 1927 and *Studies in the Lankavatara Sutra* followed in 1930, the year in which Watts says that Christmas Humphreys introduced him to the writings of this venerable Japanese sage. This introduction must have been by correspondence, as the two did not actually meet until 1933, when Watts began attending Buddhist Lodge meetings.[3] Watts did not meet Suzuki until the session of the World Congress of Faiths held at London University in 1936.

Watts was, in time, to disown this little pamphlet as one of the less successful creations of his salad days, later writing that it was then "happily out of print" and elsewhere that it was both "out of print and out of date." It was subsequently superceded by his first full-length book, *The Spirit of Zen*, published by John Murray in 1936, and in 1947 by another pamphlet published by the Buddhist Society, *Zen Buddhism: A New Outline and Introduction*. Then of course in 1957 came his most influential book on the Zen school of Buddhism, *The Way of Zen*.

We have also included in this section an exuberant piece on the same subject, "The Essence of Zen," which is an attempt to strike at the heart of this notoriously elusive subject by means of high-spirited flourishes. It is idealistic, romantic, unmistakably a piece of juvenilia. Perhaps Watts strove when writing it to adopt what he felt to be the true Zen spirit: wholehearted, unhesitating, more in tune with the heart than with the critical thinking mind. It rather reads like that now. There are also, however, indications here of themes that were to be developed later: that religion is about Life (Watts himself uses the capital L) and that in his unredeemed (i.e. unenlightened) state, man is the victim of the "warring opposites" within his own nature. This suggests that he had already been exploring the new psychological notions that were being discussed in the intellectual circles of the day. These were to increasingly engage his interest—and indeed one of the great projects of his life was to integrate the two: the religious notions of the East and the psychology and psychotherapy of the West. Although "The Essence of Zen" did not appear in *Buddhism in England* until the January/February 1933 issue, it must have been written during the previous year, possibly before he left King's. We have, therefore, included it in this section.

The poem "Shambhala" appeared in the December 1932 issue of *The Cantuarian*, the King's School magazine, under the pseudonym, "Ronin"—*ronin* being a Japanese word signifying a masterless samurai.[4] We know for certain that Watts is the author, because he later reprinted the poem in *Buddhism in England* under his own name. Shambhala is a mysterious Buddhist kingdom mentioned in Tibetan Buddhist texts and associated with the *Kalachakra Tantra* and the related Initiation. Tibetan Buddhists regard the Kalachakra as the apogee of the Buddha's teaching, and an aura of great esoteric secrecy and redemptive anticipation surrounds it. Thus Shambhala is charged with powerful mythological associations. Some Theosophists and other romantic esotericists and occultists were greatly enamoured of the idea of Shambhala in the early part of this century, and it is perhaps from their writings that Watts came to know about it.

This concludes the section of Watts's early writings drawn from his King's School period. We have, however, also included in the Appendices to this volume the report published in *Buddhism in England* of the religious conference for public schools that took place at Hayward's Heath in Sussex in 1932. Watts attended this as one of the two representatives of the King's School, his companion being a pious boy with the very appropriate name of Parsons, who, as though to confirm his priestly vocation, used illicitly to indulge in a smoking mixture named Parson's Pleasure. The conference was presided over by no less a person than William Temple, then Archbishop of York, later of Canterbury. The report that we reprint gives a verbatim account of Watts's contribution to the proceedings.

## NOTES

*1.* The Cantuarian, *December 1929. p.150.*

*2. ibid. December, 1931. p.459.*

*3. The earliest entry in the Buddhist Lodge Visitor's Book bears the date 30/3/33. A strange address is given: River Cottages—and an undecipherable name, possibly Chipstead. In the Membership Book, Watts is recorded as having joined the Lodge on 19/5/30 and his father on 11/4/32.*

*4. A* ronin *might be a samurai whose clan lord had died or who had been expelled. Unlike other samurai, who wore their hair in topknots, he let his hair hang down. Nowadays the word is used for students who fail their final exams and business executives who go commuting from company to company without having any special loyalties.*

# ULTIMATE REALITY

From *Buddhism in England*
*January, 1931*

●

*"Expenditure of force leads to outward decay,*
*Spiritual existence means inward fulness.*
*Let us revert to Nothing and enter the Absolute,*
*Hoarding up strength for energy.*
*Freighted with eternal principles,*
*Athwart the mighty void,*
*Where cloud-masses darken*
*And the wind blows ceaseless around*
*Beyond the range of conceptions.*
*Let us gain the Centre,*
*And there hold fast without violence,*
*Fed from an inexhaustible supply."*

Ssu K'ung-T'u

We are not beings, but becomings. The aim and end of becoming is being; being is real, becoming transitory. Yet in becoming there is Being; Being is the ultimate; Being is pure; Being evolves; becoming is evolution.

We are now in an age of change, when old beliefs are passing away and giving place to the conclusions of modern philosophy and science. "Orthodox" religion is tottering under the blows of research, both mental and physical, and each year more and more men and women begin to realize the impossibility of their old faiths in personal deities and immortal souls. It may be asked what leads philosophy and science to abandon these beliefs; the answer is simple. There are three great objections put forward by philosophy and science against the idea of a personal, loving, ruling God: first, why should He allow such a catastrophe as the Great War or cause hurricanes to destroy thousands of lives?—second, a belief in a ruling diety must necessitate the belief that he causes rain, thunder, drought and other natural phenomena, but science shows that such phenomena are caused by high or low pressure systems which also have natural causes, so cause follows cause in natural order; no power intervenes to change their course. The third and last great objection is this: a personal God must have endless faculties among which he must be able to foretell the future. Now, if he knows what is going to happen, the course of events must be fixed, and to admit this would be to admit oneself a fatalist. Surely the future is open for every man to do as he will in as far as Karma permits him? The whole idea of a personal God is anthropomorphic; can the Infinite be personified? Now as regards the belief in an immortal soul, science shows that we have no souls but our characters, which are based on physical organs; they are not immortal, for they are subject to continual change and at death they cease to exist—in a certain sense. When re-birth takes place, nothing passes from body to body except Karma; in the next body, Karma regenerates a similar character and consciousness. "Character is immortal—not the same identical character, but the result of conduct in character—good or bad—ever tending to the ultimate character of unalloyed and simple goodness." [Professor Beal.]

The trend of modern philosophy is to show that in this Universe there is but One Reality which is Being; all else is becoming, for everything is continually changing, and, very slowly, all is moving to good. This is evolution. It is a scientific fact that everything progresses, however slow may be its advance, and one may well ask why this is so. It is because we are all manifestations of Being, only we do not realize it; our separate, craving "self" is not our real "Self." Our real "Self" is impersonal, infinite, and one with the real "Self" of all becomings; it is the very Norm of existence; it is that of which the Universe is the outward expression. This unknown Reality is like Lao-Tzu's Tao—evolutionary yet effortless, passionless and impersonal; it is just the essence of the Universe.

> *"Before beginning, and without an end,*
> *As space eternal and as surety sure,*
> *Is fixed a power divine which moves to good,*
> *Only its Laws endure.*
> *It will not be contemned of anyone,*
> *Who thwarts it loses, and who serves it*
> *gains,*
> *The hidden good it pays with bliss,*
> *The hidden ill with pains."*
>
> [Arnold: *Light of Asia.*]

He who acts against the progress of evolution must suffer, he who acts with it must progress accordingly.

Finally we may say that the material Universe has no absolute existence. Matter is the sum of our sensations, which are phenomena of Mind. Scientists are beginning to see that matter is a conglomeration of forces—*these forces are moral.* The Universe is an emanation of the Universal Mind, our minds contribute to it, our actions contribute to it even as do the atoms of our bodies contribute to our bodies.

> *"What you call atoms are really combinations,*
> *unstable aggregates, essentially impermanent,*
> *and therefore, essentially unreal. Atoms are but*
> *Karma."* [Lafcadio Hearn.]

> *"The aggregate actions of all sentient beings*
> *give birth to the varieties of mountains, rivers,*
> *countries, etc. . . . Their eyes, nostrils, ears,*
> *tongues, bodies,—as well as their gardens,*

*woods, farms, residences, servants, and*
*maids,—men imagine to be their own posses-*
*sions, but they are, in truth, only results*
*produced by innumerable actions."*
[Kuroda: *Outlines of the Mahayana.*]

Above are two quotations which show that the material Universe is but Karma and that "burnt-out suns are rekindled by the passions of men."

The idea of the Unknown Reality is new to the West; it is found in the ideas of recent philosophers such as Herbert Spencer; Emerson hints at it*; but it was known in the East over two thousand years ago; it was a favourite theme of the *Upanishads* of Ancient India. The West is only just beginning to see it has yet much to learn, especially at the feet of Sakyamuni, the Great Sage—the Buddha.

One of the West's great faults is that it is too trivial, especially over religious matters. They must needs bother about all manner of myths connected with Jesus and consider belief in them of the utmost importance, while they pay little attention to what is really important and that is His teaching. As if some august deity chose to reveal a special, absolute and authoritative law to men, or rather, to only a *small part of mankind!* When will they soar above this blindness? When will they be reasonable enough to cast off a belief which only brings bigotry and persecution in its wake? As if it matters what a man believes as long as he lives well—and Buddha taught that he who lived well would realize Truth. That Truth cannot be described with words, and those who have realized it intuitively have left such small inklings of it as what is written above—not as conclusions, but as convictions.

*See "Xenophanes" and "The Over-Soul."*

"There is, O Bhikkus, an unborn, unoriginated, uncreated, unformed. Were there not, there would be no escape from the world of the born, the originated, the created, the formed." [*Iti-vuttaka.*]

Mahayana Buddhism has divided the approach to Nirvana into several stages which it calls heavens. They are not heavens in the Western sense of the word, but rather states of mind and meditation. The first of these stages is known as "Luminous Observation of Existence and Calm Meditation upon Existence." Observation is luminous in the sense of throwing light upon Existence. Passing through this stage the thinker enters into the sphere of "Luminous Observation of Non-Existence and of Calm Meditation upon Non-Existence." The thinker is as yet in supersensuous realms, he must ever strive higher through the state of "Meditation upon the Abandonment of Joy." Thence it is only a short step to the state of "Calm Meditation upon the Abandonment of all Joy and Pleasure," and it is here that the supersensuous spheres end. But he has not yet reached Nirvana, for he must abandon all ideas of personality, and in doing so he enters the state in which only the idea of "Infinite Space" survives; again, "Infinite Space" melts into the idea of "Infinite Reason," but even this idea is illusion. There follows the idea of "Infinite Nothingness," but even this stage has been attained by means of personal thought; Nirvana is yet to come. With the entry into the state called "Neither nameless nor not nameless," personality vanishes and with it all ideas; the candle of Karma flickers and dies out, the becoming ceases to become: it is absorbed into the Ultimate Reality, into the "Peace which passeth all understanding."

*"Om, mani padme, om!* The Dewdrop slips into the shining sea!"

# THE INFLUENCE OF BUDDHISM UPON JAPANESE ART

From *Buddhism in England*
*February, 1931*

●

Of all religions, Buddhism is the greatest promotor of art. The glorious achievements of Chinese and Japanese artists have been inspired by Buddhism; the wonderful pictures of Wu-Taotzu, depicting Amida looking down upon the world with passionless tenderness, will never be forgotten as long as there is any love for art.

Buddhism came from China to Japan in the sixth century C.E. Japan had not produced any artists of note before this time, and with the coming of Bhikkhus and Bhikkhunis from China, the Japanese, who have great talent for learning, began to learn how to draw and paint in the Chinese style. The finest Japanese works of Buddhist art are done in what is known as the "classical style."

Close by the sea among the ruins of an old temple in Japan sits a mighty figure of Amida. As he sits he smiles the smile of Perfect Peace. The Ultimate Reality is personified by Amida, and in this beautiful image we see the pure nature of the Noumenon. The face of this Buddha is set in an expression of passionless tenderness, for the Ultimate is a "Power which moves to good," all things are manifestations of it and it is, like the Chinese Tao, devoid of passion. In this way the *Bhutatathata* may be compared with Tao. Once a temple sheltered the Buddha, but now it has been swept away by earthquakes and tidal waves, but the Daibutsu still sits inwrapt in the Peace which passeth all understanding.

Looking upon the scene, the sage would say: "Transient are all component things, but Reality shall not pass away, therefore know Reality and be no longer subject to decay."

Japanese Art ever expresses the Noumenal by means of the phenomenal, so that the common people can understand the Truths of Buddhism. The deepest Truths can also be read from this Art. Christians may assert that Amida is a gilded idol, but in reality he is the symbol of "Suchness," the actual image is merely an illusion, a personification of the impersonal. All Japanese Buddhas are seen sitting or standing upon lotus flowers, for the lotus is the symbol of the "Wheel of the Law." This flower is a predominant feature of Japanese Art, for, runs the proverb: "The wise man born in a poor man's hovel shall be liked unto the lotus which groweth out of the mud."

Japan is famous for paintings, carving, ceramics, gardening, architecture and sculpture: all of these arts have either come from China with Buddhism or else have been deeply influenced by Buddhism. However, there is still an art not so widely known in the West because no European has ever understood it: the art of the tea-ceremony (*cha-no-yu*). When tea was first imported from China it was used by the Zen (Dhyana) priests to keep themselves awake during their midnight meditations. It also became at a later date the subject of this most wonderful aesthetic ceremony. The *cha-no-yu* takes place in a tea-house (*chaseki*), which is a small, frail, one-roomed building, usually set in the middle of a garden. In the tea-house is hung a *kakemono* (hanging scroll), on which has been pasted some wonderful picture or a specimen of calligraphy; on a small table at the foot of the *kakemono* is placed a flower or some object of real art which is to be the object of the guests' silent admiration. When all is prepared, the guests come to the house and drink tea in the manner which the rules of the ceremony prescribe, and then they meditate in silence upon their aesthetic surroundings and go away feeling better men for their spiritual exercise. No soldier might take his sword into the peaceful tea-house, for all was to be of the good, the beautiful and the true. The pathway up to a tea-house is described thus in a Japanese poem:

> *"A cluster of summer trees,*
> *A bit of the sea,*
> *A pale evening moon."*

Japanese gardens owe much of their beauty to Buddhism. The priests and garden artists of old used to express moral ideals in the arrangement of gardens. Rikiu, the great tea-master, had a garden by the sea; when showing his guests to the tea-house, they would pass through the garden, but the sea was carefully concealed from them until they reached a small stone bowl where they washed their hands before the ceremony. The sudden sight of the vast and silvery sea contrasted with the sight of the small bowl in which they were about to wash, and they consequently thought of a similar contrast between themselves and the vast Cosmos.

Some Japanese pictures which appear at first sight to be drawn in the ordinary manner with bold strokes of the brush are really made up of minute ideographs—the words *"Namu Amida Butsu!"* repeated over and over again, here massed, here scattered, to represent shade and light. "Is our universe so composed?—an endless phantasmagory made only by combinations. . .of units finding quality and form through unimaginable affinities;—now thickly massed in solid glooms; now palpitating in tremulosities of light and colour. . .yet each unit in itself a symbol only, a character, a single ideograph of the undecipherable text of the Infinite Riddle?"* There is one such picture of Amida standing upon clouds, with the moon at the back of his head forming an aureole. Such work must have taken hours of painstaking labour by loving hands in some temple—long ago.

---

* *Lafcadio Hearn:* Gleanings in Buddha Fields.

In the Buddhist temples of Japan are to be seen many marvelous *kakemono*, screens and carvings; the temples are veritable treasure-houses of Buddhist Art, especially those of Kyoto where is the famous temple of Nishi Hongwanji. The whole building is marvellously adorned with beautiful *kakemono*, sliding screens, coffered ceilings, fantastic wood carvings and floral designs upon the paper walls— all made up of the familiar lotus flowers, plum trees, pines, bamboos, peonies, birds, chrysanthemums, peacocks, fans, landscapes by famous painters, and dragons among clouds. In some temples are to be found pictures showing events in Sakyamuni's life, carried out in marvellous detail; there are paintings of the Nehanzo (entry into Nirvana), where crowds of men and animals are seen weeping—every face is drawn in detail—and great is their grief. Then there are pictures of the various hells and heavens, and the tortures for the wicked are inconceivably horrible. Yet all the heavens, hells, angels, devils, gods and goddesses with which Buddhism abounds are but personifications or symbols of states of mind and of good and evil principles. To condemn developed Buddhism on the ground that its numerous "deities" are hopelessly polytheistic and idolatrous is merely to show ignorance. Maybe these personifications have fallen into abuse, yet it must ever be borne in mind that truth is to be found in all this seeming unintelligible mass of corruption. Personification of this kind is almost certain to fall into abuse, yet it has offered countless subjects for Japanese Art, and let us remember when we next look upon any of these beautiful images or fantastic pictures that they are full of spiritual meaning if only we are willing to look for it. Amida stands for Ultimate Reality, Shaka (Gautama) for the historical founder of Buddhism, Kwannon for Mercy, Fudo (Achala) for Wisdom, and Jizo for Love; all are manifestations of Amida, the Supreme Buddha.

Far-Eastern Art is essentially "spiritual"; to Western eyes it usually appears "unreal"—but it must be remembered that the artist does not draw the actual object before him, but the "spirit" of it. To use a slang phrase, he "catches the spirit of it." Hiroshige never drew an actual representation of a landscape, but his colour prints give the same aesthetic impression as the landscapes to which they belong. This refers chiefly to painting, for the Japanese can make models of animals which are so realistic that they are often mistaken for the actual animal. So it is with the religious side of Japanese Art; all the drawings of Buddhas are but "catchings of spirit," and they truly represent that state of Perfect Peace putting upon their countenances that sublime expression of passionless tenderness which is characteristic of Japanese Buddhas.

In all countries the best art is devoted to religion, and it is only in the East that a philosophical religion and a spiritual art meet: witness the effect!

The last boom of the great bronze bell has died away, and from without in the stone-flagged temple court can be seen the candles flickering on the altar. Above are the sweeping copper roofs overshadowed by a great gnarled pine; on all sides rise mighty trees shutting off the sanctuary from the outer world. There comes the elusive smell of incense and from within is heard the weird, measured chant:

"When every phase of our mind shall be in accord with the mind of Buddha, . . . then there will not be even one particle of dust that does not enter into Buddhahood.* *Namu Amida Butsu!*"

The temple fades, the Buddha sits alone smiling on his lotus, he too fades, and then comes emptiness and yet not emptiness—an unutterable feeling of void.

* *Engaku-Sho.*

# TWO LETTERS

From *Buddhism in England*
*Nov.–Dec., 1931*

●

To the Editor of "Buddhism in England."

Sir,

The article in your last issue by Dr. Halstead raises some points which, especially to the student of Zen, are of great interest. He writes: "The conviction that Justice is at the heart of the Universe would be for mankind a comforting one; but is there the faintest reason for thinking that it is a correct conception?" My interpretation of the Zen idea has not led me to think so; I understand the Ultimate Reality to be something quite beyond these human standards of justice and injustice, good and evil. Karma is not necessarily just, according to our ideas; Karma is merely the fact of cause and effect and in its *ultimate sense* is Buddha. Everything is transient except Karma, which is the direct manifestation of Reality. For though "things" change they are aspects of the Eternal Karma which has nothing to do with good or evil.

But now we come on to the question of Rebirth; this is something about which we know absolutely nothing, and Dr. Halstead is rash to be so dogmatic about it. Science is not yet in a position to make any decisions upon these things. But, in any case, no true Buddhist should worry himself about such matters. Supposing my personal existence does not continue, what of it? The only possible answer to this is: "Oh, but I shall not have a chance of attaining to Nirvana." Here I will quote Dr. Halstead again: "Nature herself is both path and goal, method and end." Does this not remind us of the words of Dhyana Master Hakuin (*Cloud Men of Yamato*): "How wondrous! How wondrous! There is no birth-and-death from which one has to escape, nor is there any supreme knowledge after which one has to strive"? What am I that *I* should attain to Nirvana? The whole point of Buddhism is to concentrate upon Nirvana—to actualize the fact by treating all things as Buddha—and to eliminate the consideration of "I" altogether.

Alan W. Watts

To the Editor, "Buddhism in England."

Sir,

Over one point, at any rate, the difference between us seems to be a matter of words. You say that in asserting that justice is at the heart of the Universe you are not assuming human standards of justice; the difficulty lies in the word "justice"—whether we take it to mean action in accordance with human standards of right and wrong (there can be no other standards for the two are purely relative), or whether we take it to mean action in accordance with the Law of Cause and Effect, namely, that any event must result from and give rise to other events. I assume that you conform to the latter interpretation—so do I, and we may agree, I hope, that on this point the difference between us is cleared up.

But then you go on to say that I fail to realize that the being which attains to Nirvana is the outcome of aeons of striving towards that end. I am not quite sure whether you have understood me here, so let us go through the argument leading up to those words of mine: "Who am I that I should attain to Nirvana?" I pointed out that Dr. Halstead was rash to reject the doctrine of rebirth as science was not really in a position to speak on this subject, and I went on to say that no Buddhist should trouble himself over the question as to whether he would be reborn or no. The state of mind of one who worries about rebirth is this: "I am as yet an imperfect being; supposing that when I die I be utterly annihilated, I shall never be able to attain to Nirvana." This state of mind is highly dangerous in that it constitutes personal and selfish desire for Nirvana. The Buddhist should concentrate on the fact that Nirvana, Buddha, the Infinite, Reality or whatever you like to call it—*is*. He should not worry about being reborn that *he* may attain to it, because *there is no "he" that can attain to it*—there is just Buddha. If only he could see the fact, he has attained to it already; let him put all his faith in Reality and in so doing lose all sense of self within the Eternal Peace of the Infinite. Let him say to the Buddha-nature:

> Shine forth thy light that I may truly know that ev'rything encompassed by Infinity is but a transient aspect of the Mighty Whole. . . . That soon I lose the sense of self within the all-embracing Peace of God, and act the while rememb'ring that whate'er I touch or see is but the Infinite enclosed in finite form.

I remain yours,
Alan W. Watts

# AN OUTLINE OF ZEN BUDDHISM

*Published in London:*
*THE GOLDEN VISTA PRESS*
*Fetter House, Fetter Lane, E.C.4*

●

### Preface

During the last few years there has been an increasing interest in the West in that branch of Buddhism known as

Zen. This cult whose name is quite unknown to the vast majority of Europeans and Americans has been one of the most potent influences in moulding all that is best in the cultures of China and Japan, and it is amazing that it is not even mentioned in some of the histories of those countries. It is almost as great a mistake to leave out the consideration of Zen in a history of Japan as to omit Christianity in a history of England. The reason for this ignorance is that until quite recently the exponents of Zen were averse to spreading their doctrine abroad in the written word, for the religion is based entirely upon personal experience and no real idea of its truths can be given in words. Recently, however, various Far-Eastern writers—among them the noted Dr. Suzuki—have made known the methods of this remarkable Way of Life which is responsible for many of those things which amaze Westerners from *ju-jutsu* to that exquisite taste which characterises Chinese and Japanese art.

Many hold Zen to be the root of all religion, for it is a cult devoid of specified rites and ceremonies, all the usual impedimenta of organised worship being quite foreign to it. Zen centres around the basic fact of all mysticism—the oneness of life and the inward, as opposed to the outward, existence of God. But the word God is misleading, because, as will be seen, the Western conception of a Deity is also foreign to Zen.

The aim of this booklet is firstly to act as a guide to the Western student who desires to form some idea of the basic principles of Zen before going on to read the larger works on the subject, of which a list is given at the end. And secondly it is to point out the way, to offer the rudiments of the Path, to those whose search for Truth has been blinded by the dogmas, creeds, systems and ceremonies which choke the road of true religion.

Alan W. Watts
*Canterbury*, 1932

# ORIGINS

Zen is the Japanese form of the Chinese *Ch'an*—a corruption of *Dhyana*, a Sanskrit word whose nearest English equivalent is Meditation. This is hardly a correct translation of *Dhyana* as interpreted by the exponents of Zen, who regard Meditation as a constant attitude of mind rather than a contemplative exercise, this latter coming under the heading of *za-zen*—a practice for the cultivation of the intuition.

The cult was brought from India to China by Bódhidharma in the sixth century of the Christian Era (A.D. 527), and so came under the influence of a highly practical people who purged it of much that was unnecessary. The Chinese turned Zen into a way for everyday life, whereas it had once been confined to hermit and recluse. Its great beauty is that it can be practised in the home and requires neither priest nor rite, prayer nor ceremony. "Those who wish to train themselves spiritually," says Wei Lang, "may do so at home. There is no need for them to stay in monasteries."[1] Yet there are certain aspects of Zen which require personal contact with a master and these will be dealt with later.

## TEACHINGS

What is Zen? There can be no final and satisfactory answer to this question in intelligible words. Zen is the conquest of dualism and the inward realisation of the Buddha-nature which is the *raison d'être* of all things. Zen has been summed up thus:

> *"A special transmission (of knowledge)*
> *outside the Scriptures;*
> *No dependence upon words and letters;*
> *Direct pointing to the soul of man;*
> *Seeing into one's own nature."*

[1]*From* The Sutra of Wei Lang (Hui-neng).

The true essence of all things is the Eternal Principle of which all phenomena are manifestations—in Sanskrit it is called *Tathata* (Suchness) and it is quite impossible to apply to it any form of logical analysis. It is recorded in the *Vimalakirti Sutra* that a company of Bódhisattvas were invited by Vimalakirti to express their views on this Ultimate Reality. Many ideas were put forward, until Manjusri, one of the company, asked the host for his view. The answer was complete silence, whereupon Manjusri exclaimed: "Well done! Well done! The Principle of Non-duality is truly beyond letters and words." Again we are told of a certain teacher who was about to preach a sermon when a bird started singing nearby: when it had finished he announced that his sermon had been preached and went away. On another occasion a wise Confucian visited a master of Zen and asked for an introduction to Buddhism. He received only vague replies and on questioning further the teacher said "I am keeping nothing back from you." The Confucian was sorely puzzled, but sometime later he was walking with this same teacher in a garden, and as they passed some beautiful flowers the master said: "Isn't the scent glorious, can you smell it?" "Yes." "You see," said he, "I have kept nothing back from you." The purpose of this terse mode of teaching is to show how ridiculous it is to seek Reality outside the universe—outside our everyday concerns. Why? Because it is manifest in *every single thing*! All component things—men, mountains, rivers, flowers, trees—all are fleeting as dreams and empty as shadows. This arises, that becomes and then crumbles away into dust; one thing remains and that is the Law of Karma—the Law of coming and going—of Cause and Effect. All that ever was has been and shall be, proceeded from a cause and gave birth to an effect—this is Karma—all is Karma, and Karma is the direct manifestation of the Eternal Principle. Don't look for God above the skies or fast within the walls of monasteries—He is here, there, everywhere—in part as well as in whole. Buddha-nature[1] is just as much on the point of a pin as in the greatest of mountains. "That subtle Being of whom the whole universe is composed, *tat tvam asi*—That art thou!" But how is this to be turned from a mere theory into a living fact?

True meditation is a constant attitude of mind—not an exercise occupying only a few moments of the day; this is the teaching of Zen. Ideas alone are profitless; they must be tried in the fire of everyday realities, thus it has been said that he who talks much about the Law and makes no effort to put it into practice is no better than the cowherd who counts only the cattle of others. Zen is not a theory, not a religion in the ordinary sense of the word—it is an experience—a way for everyday life, and in the practice of it we are not concerned with such misleading conceptions as those of "self," of "merit" or of "attainment." He understands Zen who can live without thought of self, who has given up all attachment to things; when he walks he reflects: "There is a walking"; when he works he considers: "There is a working"; in this manner he cultivates the universal as opposed to the personal attitude to life. To regard Existence from this impersonal point of view is the essence of Wisdom, for it leads to calm and to knowledge of That which is. The mind is no longer swayed by selfish desires, and thus it resorts to that Inner Principle which dwells in all things; to the Awakened. It is all in all, found by the giving up of self and by the cultivation of this universal attitude towards life. It is by attachment to things that misery arises, and he that wishes to tread the Path must know that they are unreal—transient and fleeting. Thus he will regard them impersonally, the while reflecting: "This arises, that becomes, yet in essence all remain unchanged, for their Inner Principle, being universal, can never be said to come or to

[1] *The word "Buddha" in this use does not refer to the historical personage; it is rather the Heart of Buddha or The Eternal Principle.*

go." All the while It stays unmoved, and so it is that the sage comes to identify himself with It, for by adopting this frame of mind he naturally reverts to his true nature. And so he passes beyond both good and evil, joy and pain; his outlook, being impersonal, is not fettered by false ideas. It is from the personal outlook that illusions arise. The quality of All never changes, neither does the quality of him who has passed beyond self. And what is this Inner Principle? It is the All, the Real, the Veiled—understood only by the Awakened; vain is it for those still in the bonds of illusion to discuss It. Know then: you have that Principle—universal in character—within you; release It and you will understand: this is the secret of Zen.

The truth of what is said here cannot be proved by reason and logic; experience is the only proof—therefore let us give up all selfish attachments and put our ideas to the test, otherwise they are worthless—fit only to be cast upon the dung-heap. Above all let us not mistake the written word for the object of our search—it is only a finger pointing the Way; let us not mistake the finger for the Way.

Zen teaches us to face the facts of life—pleasant and unpleasant—with supreme equanimity. We are told to fear nothing—to be disturbed by nothing. Prepare for the event by all means; make sure that you act rightly under the circumstances—but regard it impersonally and so penetrate to the true nature of things which is beyond all dualisms. Says Shakespeare: "There's nothing good or ill but thinking makes it so." It is only when we consider the effects an event has upon ourselves that we begin to think of it as good or evil, as pleasant or unpleasant; this is the root of selfishness.

## ZEN METHODS

"Thou thyself must tread the Path; Buddhas do but point the Way." It is for this reason that Zen places no trust in the written word; Enlightenment can only be gained by personal experience and no amount of intellectual puzzling will ever bring us to the Goal. The *Dhammapada* says: "Purity and impurity are personal concerns; no one can purify another." It would be utterly futile to try to explain the glories of a sunset to one born blind, so to those who ask: "What is Reality?" the answer must be "Silence—and a finger pointing the Way."

There is a Zen saying: "Buddha or Devil—ignore him just the same"—nothing must stand in the way of the seeker after Enlightenment. To become attached to a Buddha is just as foolish as to become attached to a demon. Zen master Rinzai, in a famous sermon, said:

> *"O you followers of Truth, if you wish to obtain an orthodox understanding (of Zen), do not be deceived by others. Inwardly or outwardly, if you encounter any obstacles kill them right away. If you encounter the Buddha, kill him; if you encounter the Patriarch, kill him; . . . kill them all without hesitation, for this is the only way to deliverance. Do not get yourselves entangled with any object, but stand above, pass on, and be free."*[1]

Ananda, the most intimate of the Buddha's disciples, was one of the last to attain to Enlightenment because he was so attached to the person of his master. Rinzai exhorts us to kill that attachment by looking at life impersonally, thus identifying ourselves with the universal Buddha-nature.

Hence the insistence of Zen upon the "direct method" of teaching, that disciples may not become attached to words and letters. In the *Diamond Sutra*[2] the Buddha points out that things are not really things, they are only called "things"; words are only embodied ideas—they are not facts.

[1]Essays in Zen Buddhism, *by D.T. Suzuki.*
[2]Prajna Paramita Sutra. *English translation, by Wm. Gemmell.*

Zen aims at establishing contact with the facts without allowing "ideas" to slip in between. Once we start thinking of the effects of an event upon our persons we begin to regard it selfishly; as soon as this tendency is conquered the Buddha-nature becomes to us a reality—we realise it within ourselves. In the *Tao-teh-King* we read: "Aim at being impersonal and maintain the greatest equanimity," and again in the *Sutra of Wei Lang*: "Our essence of mind is intrinsically pure; all things, good or evil, are only its manifestations, and good deeds and evil deeds are only the result of good thoughts and evil thoughts respectively." And again: "*Dhyana* means to be free from attachment to all outer objects and *Samadhi* means to attain to the inner peace." Don't stop to argue about life—that's not the way to understand it; all the time you've been thinking it has slipped away from you; jump into the stream and flow with it; cultivate the impersonal serenity of the Buddha-nature and so become that Buddha-nature. And yet you are really Buddha-nature all the time!

## PARADOX

Zen abounds with paradoxes of this kind—"Enter Nirvana, but you are really there already!" They are confusing to the uninitiated, but a little "meditation" will soon show things in a different light and then, after much practice, will come the flash of *satori*[1] —the foretaste of Nirvana. Once you try to express the truths of Zen in logical terms there arise paradoxes and seemingly nonsensical sayings. Here is an example: "A student once asked the Patriarch (Wei Lang) what sort of man could get the keynote of the teaching of Wong Mui (the fifth Patriarch). 'He who understands the Buddhist Dharma,' replied the Patriarch. 'Have you, sir, got it then?' asked the student. 'I do not know the Buddhist Dharma,' was his reply." (Quoted from the *Sutra of Wei*

[1]*See below.*

*Lang*). An Emperor of China once asked the Bódhidharma what was the main principle of his holy doctrine. The sage replied:

> *"In vast emptiness there is nothing holy."*
> *The Emperor was highly puzzled and said:*
> *"Who is it then that stands before me?"*
> *"I don't know."*

Even more perplexing is the "sermon" of Dhyana-master Goso, who, having taken his seat in the hall (*zen-do*), looked over one shoulder then over the other, held up his staff and cried: "Only one foot long!" "What's in a name?" the Truth is there whatever you say!

## SATORI

By far the most important event in the life of Gautama the Buddha was his Enlightenment under the Bó tree (528 B.C.). Here he received that flash of spiritual illumination which in Zen is called *satori*—a sudden awakening of the intuition to Ultimate Truth. The religious history of China and Japan abounds with instances of *satori*, but for all that it is by no means easy to realise. A famous instance is of a monk, who, worried by the lack of any convincing realisation, retired to a lonely cottage to work contentedly in a small garden. One day while he was at work a stone flew up and hit a bamboo: suddenly the whole Truth dawned upon him and he went back to his teacher who was overjoyed at his success.

A favourite answer of the Zen masters to a question on Buddhism is a slap on the face, dealt not out of anger or contempt, but in the hope that it will induce the flash of *satori*. It may be the most trivial incident that lights the flame—the sound of a bell, toothache, an itch, a clock striking—anything that rouses the receptive mind trained by meditation. When the mind has cultivated the habit of regarding things impersonally such trivial happenings will form the climax of the exercise; they will finish off and fix the experience gained in a position whence nothing can remove it; the soul is tuned to the Eternal Rhythm, and passes beyond life and death, beyond all the pairs of opposites. *And yet the man loses none of his faculties*: this has been proved by long experience.

## ZA-ZEN

The nearest equivalent in Zen to meditation as understood in the West is the practice of *za-zen*—a form of intense concentration upon various problems (*ko-ans*). Westerners will probably prefer to use more straightforward types of *ko-ans* than those used in the East. A typical example of the latter is this problem: "You clap your hands; it makes a sound. What is the sound made by the clapping of one hand?" Another: "If the many are reduced to the One, to what is the One to be reduced?" Yet another famous *ko-an* is that known as Joshu's *Mu*: "What is no-thing-ness: that which is devoid of all differentiation?" But something of this kind will be found more suitable for Europeans: "Foregoing self, the universe grows I." Or: "The Mind is the great slayer of the Real. Let the disciple slay the Slayer." These *ko-ans* should not be considered intellectually; their purpose is to cultivate the use of the intuition. Instead of meditating upon them with the reason one should rather "soak" in them—use them as rungs upon which to climb to higher understanding. Do not worry out their truth, but accepting them as final see what consequences they involve; look at them from every point of view until the mind is thoroughly saturated in them. Then will come the flash of intuition showing the problem in a clearer light.

When meditating the spine must always be held erect, the legs crossed and the hands touching; these three factors are absolutely essential. There is no need to acquire the correct lotus-posture (sitting with feet placed on the thighs, soles upwards), for the practiser may either sit or kneel—

but the spine *must* be erect, the legs crossed and the hands touching. The position must be comfortable so that nothing can disturb the exercise of concentration. Let go all worries and excitements; shut yourself completely off from the outer world and give yourself up to perfect equanimity. When the mind has thus been brought under control, take up the *ko-an* and begin to consider it. Each one must find his own way of "concentrating" on the *ko-an*; it is only by practice that "results" can be obtained.

## A WARNING

The Western student is advised to avoid all Raja or Hatha Yoga practices in meditation unless he is under the guidance of a properly qualified master. *Pranayama* or breath control is highly dangerous to anyone attempting to practise it on his own; the usual fate of such people is *madness*. Many of the asylums are filled with those who have taken up dangerous spiritual and physical exercises; avoid all practices the result of which you cannot reasonably foresee, and be warned never to meditate in order to gain personal power or for the sake of self-aggrandisement. The motives of the Zen student must be absolutely unselfish, and it is essential that he be living an absolutely pure life, otherwise his efforts will result in libertinism or antinomianism. The only kind of Yoga in which unguided Westerners should indulge is Karma Yoga—the Path of Action whereby the disciple is taught to do good deeds without any personal motive. In all Zen monasteries the discipline is almost militaristic in order that strict morality may be ensured.

## LIFE IN A ZEN MONASTERY

The motto of the Zen monasteries is "no working, no eating"; for the monks are engaged for much of their time in agricultural operations. Attached to most institutions is a farm where all work, even the masters, for in Zen manual labour is regarded as an important element in meditation. Besides this it helps to keep the monks from moral degeneration and laziness—the curse of monasticism. The result is that the inmates are happy and contented; they are simple industrious people—not religious maniacs who seek only that "other world" and are blind to the beauties of this. The Zen monk is not afraid to laugh—not afraid to enjoy life in a reasonable way; nor does he shrink from contact with the unenlightened, shutting himself away from "this world of vanities"—he goes on living right in the midst of it, yet remains supremely unattached and pure. His life is not wrapped up in the solemn pomp of religious rites, nor in the repeating of endless prayers; it is the simple, hardworking existence of the poor farmer or woodman who at the same time does his best to act as "guide, philosopher and friend" to the rest of the world.

The routine of work is broken by special periods for hearing sermons from the master and for *za-zen*, which is usually practised in the dormitory. The presiding monk—or it may be the master—lights a stick of incense to help him keep an eye on the time and at a given signal, after the reciting of a sutra, *za-zen* begins. Should any monk fall asleep during the exercise he is woken by a smack on the back from an attendant! A signal is then given for relaxation and another period may be begun after a few minutes.

During the day there are three meals: breakfast, which is held early in the morning, lunch, held at about ten o'clock, and medicinal food in the evening. Students are not really supposed to eat after mid-day, but climatic conditions in China and Japan render it necessary. Meals are eaten in silence, being accompanied by special meditations; they are characteristically Zen and have something in common with the famous Tea Ceremony (*cha-no-yu*) of old Japan. The whole meal is conducted in the spirit of: "There is an eating"—"There is enjoyment," etc., the notion of "I" being carefully avoided.

At times the master interviews each monk separately to give him instructions or to set him *ko-ans* upon which to meditate. There is no regard paid to ceremony once the monk is in the presence of the master, who will resort to blows if necessary; he will seldom waste words. But this system is more suited to the Eastern temperament than to the Western, and most Europeans will consider it somewhat out of date. But as long as the four principles quoted under the heading of "teachings" are adhered to almost any system will do; Western students will have to make up one for themselves. But let no one consider the life in a Zen monastery to be pure drudgery; it is not all working at crops, for it has produced great artists and poets. Zen encourages almost every trade; while in primitive communities these may take the form of agriculture, manufacture of household utensils, painting or carving; there is no reason why the Zen method should not be extended to engineering, medicine, scientific research or "office work." Moreover it is possible to introduce Zen into almost every form of sport as in the cases of *ju-jutsu* and *kendo* (Japanese fencing); though both these sports are really practice in fighting, Zen does not regard them as such but treats them purely as exercises. The core of Japanese chivalry (*bushido*) was Zen; it made the soldier fearless in the face of death, and when he had to kill the action would be treated as a duty—without any ridiculous emotion and without personal hate. But because of this let no one think that Zen encourages fighting; it comes into a world where wars exist, treats them as a temporarily necessary evil and teaches men how to fight that their mental equanimity may not be disturbed. Yet the true disciple of Zen will abstain from all bloodshed.

## ZEN AND ART

Zen Buddhism is responsible for much of that exquisite taste which characterises the art of China and Japan; for that quiet blending of colours so restful to the eye, and for that charm of design which seems to catch the spirit of nature better than any Western realisms. And this form of art has a deeper lesson to teach than that which attempts to copy nature or to suffuse her forms with strange, fantastic, ideas. We find hints of *satori* in Japanese poetry—as in this epigram of Basho's (1644-94):

> *"The mountain is cool,*
> *The moon in the water,*
> *The depth of my soul!"*

Just three elusive ideas, perhaps without much meaning for us, but full of the deepest wisdom for one who has had a like experience. These three lines will compare with a poem by Kobori Enshiu describing a garden:

> *"A cluster of summer trees,*
> *A bit of the sea,*
> *A pale evening moon."*

We have all seen it pictured thousands of times on lacquer boxes, hanging pictures, delicate vases and massive screens—but next time we see these things let us remember something which will make them infinitely more interesting. Remember that the artists of China and Japan painted each flower, each bird, each mountain, each as a symbol of the nameless Reality manifest in Karma. They knew that it was impossible to convey any real idea of the Ultimate with words, so they covered their plates and vases with exquisite symbols of It. These great artist and poet philosophers—cloud-men as they called themselves— finding that all things were, in themselves, symbols of the Unknown Reality, tuned their hearts to the rhythm of the waterfall's song, to the beat of the passing seasons, to the Eternal Law of the circling stars.

## EAST AND WEST

Though the East has much to learn from the West in

the way of science and commerce, the West has much to learn from the East in the realms of religion. We have in our search for Truth contented ourselves with plunging into the depths of complicated metaphysics—a *cul-de-sac* which has led, and will lead, us nowhere. As soon as one metaphysician produces a theory another disproves it and no one is any the better. What has the world to gain from all the Berkeleys, Hegels and Bradleys of the West? They lead people into a maze of conflicting propositions, which, though interesting, are only fit for use as mental exercises. On the other hand the East has to offer us a set of philosophers— mystics if you like—who are all agreed upon one central fact and who are thoroughly and honestly convinced of its Truth. This central fact can only be understood by experience— and when that experience has been felt, he who has felt and understood it always leads a beautiful life thereafter. Zen does not lose itself in unprofitable arguments

> "Of Providence, Foreknowledge, Will and
>     Fate,
> Fixed fate, free will, foreknowledge absolute."

Western metaphysicians are trying to untie a veritable Gordian Knot—perhaps they will one day realise that they are wrestling with the wrong knot after all and might as well begin all over again. Only a few—among them Bergson— have seen that the intuition is to be looked to for all real knowledge of ultimates. Did not the Buddha discourage all the metaphysical speculation which flourished throughout India in his time; he said "Nirvana *is*"—realise this for yourselves by becoming unattached, for that is the only way to Understanding.

The West is sorely in need of a really practical religion—even if only for the few. If the many must still worship at the altars of superstition one can only hope that better education will, in time, bring them to a state when they can look to higher things. Many there are whom the Christian

Churches have ceased to satisfy and they have had to with-draw from communal religion altogether failing to find any sect good enough to meet their needs. To such people the East offers the Art of Zen—not really a sect, not "yet another 'ism,'" but what many hold to be the root of all religious experience. Zen is practical mysticism, incorporating none of those unhealthy sex emotions found in some Christian and Hindu cults. Zen loves not the shade of the cloisters but the fresh air of the mountain tops.

## THE PURPOSE OF ZEN

Yet what is the purpose of religion? What is the use of all these labours to eliminate selfishness? How often is it asked: "Why should I be good? Why can't I enjoy myself while there's life and leave the rest to chance?" In answer to this question the Buddha bade us look at the world around—at the world where selfish craving is worshipped as a god. However optimistic we are we must admit that Life is certainly not as good and free from Suffering as it might be; yet the optimist, though he has been able to con-quer sorrow to some degree, is yet inclined to see no mis-ery where in truth it abounds. He often tries to make out that life is not so bad after all, but in so doing he attempts to gloss over facts which must be faced if happiness is to be found for the majority of mankind. Moreover his out-look is essentially selfish, as he takes only his own attitude to life into consideration. But there are two kinds of optimists: he who is really blind to the facts of life and rejoices in his own smug, self-satisfaction, and he who has the strength of will to smile under all difficulties. This last kind of man does not try to make out that life is really lovely and pleasant—he knows it is not, but he also knows that

> *"The mind is its own place, and of itself*
> *Can make a hell of heav'n, a heav'n of hell."*

The true optimist is filled with compassion for his fellow beings whom he knows to be burdened under the weight of events which he himself has learnt to throw off. Let those who think that life is really "quite a pleasant show" travel about outside the sphere of their daily concerns; let them learn to understand the lot of those less fortunate than themselves and to have compassion; in so doing they will learn the great truth of Buddhism that life is filled with Suffering which arises out of selfish craving. It is from this that Zen seeks to deliver us—from the ceaseless round of birth and death lasting throughout enormous periods of time. For the Awakened have passed beyond the concepts of Space and Time into "Nirvana, where the Silence ends." It is written: "He who hath overcome Time in the past and in the future must be of exceedingly pure understanding."

The attainment of Enlightenment and Buddhahood is not a means to an end; It is the End itself—the very highest Goal to be reached by cosmic evolution; It is the Alpha and the Omega of Existence, beyond change and decay, good and ill, Space and Time. When thou canst see the Whole as if thou wert that Whole, then shalt thou understand.

### BIBLIOGRAPHY

*The Religion of the Samurin*, KAITEN NUKARIYA. Luzac, 1913. IOS.

*Essays in Zen Buddhism*, D.T. SUZUKI. Luzac, London, 1930. 17s. 6d.

*The Sutra of Wei Lang (Hui-neng)*. Yu Ching Press, 1930, Shanghai. Limited edition. 3s. 6d.

*Studies in the Lankavatara Sutra*, D.T. SUZUKI. Kegan Paul, London, 1930. 20s.

*The Buddha's Golden Path*, DWIGHT GODDARD. Luzac, London, 1930. 4s.

*The Garden of Vision*, ADAMS BECK (Fiction). 10s. 6d.

*The Japanese Spirit*, Y. OKAKURA.

*The Cloud-men of Yamato*, GATENBY. Murray. 3s. 6d.

*Zen, der lebendige Buddhismus in Japan*, OHASAMA and FAUST.

Also articles in the following periodicals:

*Buddhism in England; The Eastern Buddhist; The Hawaiian Buddhist Annual; The Aryan Path*, etc.

# THE ESSENCE OF ZEN

From *Buddhism in England*
*Jan.–Feb., 1933*

●

The essence of Zen lies in one's attitude to Life. Most people adopt what may be called the personal attitude—they look upon events with reference to themselves; they call things good or bad simply because they affect their persons in such and such a way. But the Zenshuist looks at Life impersonally; he sees things as things—that is all there is to it! It is only when we consider the effect an event has upon our lower, personal selves, that we call it pleasant or unpleasant, good or ill, but the Zenshuist does not consider things in this way. He finds the Buddha-nature by giving himself up to supreme equanimity—that calm, balanced and unruffled state of mind wherein all the "pairs of opposites" merge into One; wherein the distinction between "self" and "not-self" vanishes and all things are seen as being just so. For him events just happen—they are *thus*—he is concerned only with facts, not with ideas about facts. He at-ones himself with the stream of Life and does not attach to any particular wave in that stream. Why strive after a part when you have the Whole? When he does anything he merely sees that there is a doing of it; he does not separate himself from Existence by thinking "I do"; all actions, whether his own or other people's, just happen—they are perfectly natural. He moves: there is movement; a bird moves: there is movement. So the teaching of Zen about the Kosmos may be summed up in the words "There is." And seeing thus the Buddha-nature of things the Zenshuist treats all with love, reverence and respect, humbling himself in the presence of the Universe. He gives up all idea of self: there is just Reality—his own person is of no account—, and in this supreme act of self-surrender he realizes that state of spiritual freedom which is Nirvana. "Nothing is mine—not even myself—all belongs to the Universe." In this way he cultivates the impersonal attitude to Life, beyond "I" and "not I," good and evil, joy and pain. For once you annihilate the distinction between subject and object, once you pass beyond the "pairs of opposites" and see all things in terms of Reality—as being just so, then you find that peace of soul called Samadhi—that sense of sublime non-attachment and selflessness which lies at the heart of Zen.

# SHAMBHALA

From *The Cantuarian*
*December, 1932*

●

Let the Past be forgotten as a long-vanished cloud,
And the wrong of former years be buried in the shade
Of Long Ago. Let us waken to the Future's trumpet-call,
And shout a mighty challenge to the stars, and ride
To the Kingdom of Shambhala with the banner of the Just.
Take heart, O Blessed Conquerors, the Advent is at hand
When Maitreya shall lay his hand upon the world and sooth
The troubled hearts of living things with messages of Peace.

Rônin

# PART TWO

# YOUNG BRAHMIN
# ABOUT TOWN

# PART TWO

This part anthologises the writings that Watts contributed to *Buddhism in England* after he had left King's School in 1932, down to the middle of 1936, when he assumed the editorship of the journal himself. During this period, he was working in the daytime in the City of London for the Metropolitan Hospitals Sunday Fund, but the evenings were his own, and he was then free to pursue his own interests in religion, psychology, and allied subjects. By his own account—see the "My Own University" chapter of his autobiography—he put his spare time to good account. Like Cinderella, however, late each evening he had to leave whatever fascinating situation he might be in and hurry to catch the last train back to Chislehurst, for he was still living at his parents' home.

The first piece in this section, "The Buddha's Path to Reality," appeared in the March/April 1933 issue of *Buddhism in England*. It has a trace of romanticism about it, but the bulk of its propositions are reiterations of accepted, mainstream Buddhist teachings: that the Buddha always maintained a proverbial "noble silence" when asked about the nature of "Ultimate Truth;" that this Reality is to be found within ourselves, in the quiet mind—did the young Watts always heed his own injunctions?—and not by means of intellectual speculation. Nothing strikingly new or creative is encountered, however, until about three-quarters of the way through he embarks upon an extended poetic analogy of the religious life being like the ascent of a high mountain. The climber leaves behind "the lowlands of Desire" and at last reaches the peak, where he bathes in "the boundless blue of Eternity." Presumably, during the course of the climb, he has sloughed off the trammels of personal attachment that in mundane existence made him feel separate from the rest of life. Christmas Humphreys was much enamoured of this analogy. It crops up a lot in his writings; for instance:

> *I dislike flat walking on a Way. I prefer to climb. I want the wider view, the selfless air, the light* (reference lost).

He also used to have an enlargement of an early photograph of the North Col of Mount Everest hanging prominently in his bedroom at his home in St. John's Wood in north London, and he even called his last anthology of poems *The Mountain Side.*

The last part of "The Buddha's Path to Reality" is a rather youthful and idealized evocation of the equanimity of buddhas—not of course to be confused with mere coldness or indifference—as they sit "undisturbed amid the turmoil and conflict of existence . . . all idea of self . . . set aside. . . ." Watts even has the audacity to commandeer the great fifty-two foot high bronze Buddha of Kamakura, the *Daibutsu,* in order to enhance the aesthetic effect of this section.

"The Sutra of Wei Lang" appeared in July/August 1933 as the fifth in a series of articles on the Buddhist scriptures then being published in *Buddhism in England.* "Wei Lang" is in fact the Canton dialect form of "Hui Neng," the name of the great Sixth Patriarch of Zen Buddhism, who lived in China C.E. 637–713. His "Sudden" school is to be distinguished from the "Gradual" school of Shen-hsiu, his fellow pupil under Master Hung-jen. Shen-hsiu's school soon went the way of all flesh, but the two major schools of Zen Buddhism surviving in Japan down to the present time— the Soto and the Rinzai—both trace their lineages back to Hui Neng. The title of Watts's article is in fact identical with that of an English translation of the sutra (also known as *The Platform Sutra*) that was made by Wong Mou-lam and published in Shanghai in 1930. Copies of this were imported throughout the 1930s by The Buddhist Lodge, which eventually brought out a revised version of its own with a new title in 1940. It was undoubtedly this translation that Watts used.

The first part of this piece is a straightforward exposition of fact, which Watts does with characteristic lucidity and skill. A little later on, however, he launches into rather highfalutin prose, and, to this writer at any rate, there are passages here that read like quintessential Christmas Humphreys, especially when claims that the *sutra* is essentially a work for the intuition that "cannot be understood by the application of logical and ratiocinative methods," and that it is really a vast *koan* in which the reader must saturate himself until at last, in a blinding flash of Truth, the meaning is revealed.

The last part of the article basically recapitulates many notions that we have already encountered elsewhere in Watts's early writings on Zen: the need to cultivate dispassion and generally to take things "as they come—quietly and naturally." This is in fact the only way to live: free of self. The closing remarks are very much Watts: Enlightenment is not to be gained by fleeing from the world into trance states or quietism but through "a certain attitude to life" which can be applied in all situations. The final quotation reveals what this open secret is:

> *Whether you are in activity or under rest,*
> *abide your mind nowhere. . . .*

The September/October 1933 issue of *Buddhism in England* published the first part of Watts's first major series for the journal: "Buddhism in the Modern World." In this and the three subsequent issues, Watts addressed himself to what he regarded as four topics of vital contemporary importance: humour (or the lack of it), politics, sex (something taken far too seriously, he contended) and war. In 1934, John M. Watkins[1] of the famous religious and occult bookshop in Cecil Court, just off the Charing Cross Road in London, reissued the series in pamphlet form, though with one important deletion, which we shall consider in due course.

In his introductory remarks to the series, Watts sounds an apocalyptic note. Civilization has lost its way and the babble of conflicting voices propounding all sorts of "new-fangled beliefs and opinions" threatens to lead the world into an "orgy of moral conflicts and religious strife." All hope is not lost, however. If men would only heed the teachings of Buddhism—and put them into practice—then salvation is possible. By "Buddhism" Watts does not so much mean the religion as conventionally understood, but rather the "age-old Wisdom Religion" preached by the line of buddhas stretching back into the mists of time. This wisdom is by no means obsolete. Quite the contrary, in fact; it is still very much a living force and highly relevant to the modern age. Indeed, men ignore it at their peril.

In a sense Watts is writing here very much as a child of his time. Grim memories of the dreadful events of World War I haunted the contemporary consciousness, which at the same time had to witness the inexorable build-up towards the second conflagration. To paraphrase Carl Gustav Jung: the whole world longed for peace and yet the whole world prepared for war; mankind seemed powerless against mankind—and the gods merely showed the way of Fate. In other words, the old optimistic Victorian belief in the essential goodness of the human race and the ability of Progress to solve all problems had been smashed. Mankind was in the grip of dark forces that it neither understood nor could control. Economic depression contributed additionally to the prevailing sense of doom.

How timely, therefore, that a young philosopher like Watts should address himself to four of the key "problems" of the day—and how ahead of his time for him to take a spiritual perspective and to argue that Buddhism might contain keys to "solutions." As he makes clear in his introductory remarks, however, he is well aware of the enormity of the task that he is taking on. He also seems concerned to preempt the critics who might leap to challenge his credentials or take issue with him for being over-dogmatic or over-critical, for exaggerating or failing to be "sweetly reasonable." All of which suggests that some sympathetic friend, Christmas Humphreys, perhaps, or A. C. March, the editor of the journal, may have taken young Watts aside and, in a kindly way, suggested that he restrain his literary panache a little. And Watts has listened. But having done so, he is still determined to go ahead and say what he has to say, for "Buddhism is not a religion of compromise." Rather, it is a religion that is prepared to really lay the hard truth of any matter on the line.

A strange line at the end of the first paragraph of the introductory remarks talks of "that inevitably far-off time when the Universe shall enter Nirvana." Strictly speaking, the Universe never left Nirvana. Nor did human beings ever do so. It is only because we are deluded that we believe that we have. Moreover, as Nirvana is timeless, it is nonsensical to talk of a "time" when the Universe shall be restored to it.

"Buddhism and the Need for a Sense of Humour," the first part of the series, is an early recital of what was to become a major Watts theme, one to which he was to return again and again throughout his life. Essentially it is a critique of the puritan disposition, which in the West at any rate has come to dominate most of religious life. It was also one of the personal struggles of Watts's own life to throw off the incubus of puritanism and break through to a lightness and sheer joy in living that seemed not merely to have been lost but to be actively resisted by many dominant elements in Western society. But he is cautious here. It is not his intention, he reassures his readers, to advocate a swing to the opposite extreme. He is not recommending frivolity or licentiousness. Rather, he is for steering a middle course between "Grundyism"[2], on the one hand, and "unrestrained self-expression" on the other. Is he really being frank here, one wonders, or merely keeping a certain diplomatic distance from the proponents of "self-expression"—presumably the new breed of psychoanalysts—so as not to alienate the readership?

The burden of the item is that humour is vital to the religious life because it confers a sense of proportion, in particular a sense of proportion as regards the importance of the individual self, the 'I'. Puritans, on the other hand, are po-faced precisely because they are so anxious about their own individual salvation. This is at once both highly egotistical and highly absurd: "I" want to save myself, whereas, in fact, salvation consists precisely in being relieved of the burden of that "I" that wishes to be saved. Humour then, used in a kindly way, can be a marvellously liberating and spiritually healthy tool.

And so to Part 2: the item on politics. Here Watts adopts the classic Western Buddhist stance that Buddhism is primarily concerned with spiritual rather than worldly matters; strictly-speaking, therefore, politics lies outside its ambit. That having been said, Watts goes on to argue that what really matters anyway is the spiritual quality of the individuals who collectively constitute a particular state, not the system by which that state is organised. Effective solutions to the world's problems can, therefore, only be effectively approached on the individual level: by each person undertaking spiritual work on themselves. To approach from the other level, from the mass or "sociological" level, by making changes in the machinery of state, is not only useless but often counter-productive. The more state machinery, in fact, the more the individual is enslaved; also, the less able to order his own life effectively, thus requiring more interfering state agencies to organise his life. The item ends with a clarion call to one and all to begin treading the Buddha's path to "self-mastery," for "if Buddhism can only teach us to rise superior to mere organisation and machinery, it will have done much to resolve the political and economic problems of today."

Unfortunately, in the first paragraph, Watts rashly asserts that it would be perfectly possible to adhere to fascism, among the other political *-isms*, without being out of accord with the Buddha's teachings. This elicited a sharp rebuke in the next issue of the journal from a reader who quoted a nastily bellicose statement by Benito Mussolini to prove that Buddhism and Fascism were not as happily compatible as Watts had maintained. Printing the letter, the editor, A. C. March, invited Watts to comment, adding that "Perhaps he would also include the political ideals of the Nazi and Soviet regimes in his explanation." Watts, in a subsequent letter, declined to do so, however, on the grounds of insufficient knowledge, adding:

> *If the ideals of Herr Hitler and Stalin are sincere and just they will have their reward; if not—well, it must be left to Karma. It is not our business to judge or "punish" them.*

He was, however, obliged to concede the main point of the reader's letter; he had been, he said, under the impression that Signor Mussolini's ideas were "moderately sane" but the quotation had dispelled that illusion. He thanked the reader for "adding to my knowledge of world affairs," and then went on:

> *I understood Fascism as a political system embodying the corporate state and the office of dictator, and it must surely be true that in a country of practising Buddhists, ruled by a practising Buddhist, this system would work perfectly well.*

However, he had not intended the article to imply that Buddhism was compatible with "any of the queer forms of political lunacy which from time to time blight the minds of men":

*For instance, it would be absurd to say that
Buddhism is compatible with a policy whereby
citizens were forced to be injected with typhoid
microbes to give unemployed doctors something to do, compelled to eat enormous quantities of cheese every morning to get rid of a
cheese "glut," to rob and murder to give work
to the police, or to dance the polka in public
halls all night in aid of the Unemployed Dancing Mistresses Union. Anyone introducing such
a system would be called mad, but I think his
scheme would be a good deal saner than that
of anyone who set up war (or to give it its
proper name, "Mass Murder of Civilians") as
a noble ideal. War wasn't so bad in the days
of chivalry, but nowadays statesmen have no
sense of sportsmanship[3] in their dealings with
other countries and can never be relied upon
to "keep the rules."*

Watts concluded his letter of reply by quoting
Christmas Humphreys and Lao Tzu in support of the general
pacifist line of argument that had evolved as he had gone
along.

Many might be surprised at the extent to which the
young Watts shows himself—indeed openly *declares*—
himself to be politically uninformed and innocent in this
last letter. But then, his general lifelong stance was an apolitical one. He knew that every kind of state was basically
unsympathetic to the kind of man he was: one who wants
to heed his own counsel and generally go "in my own way."
On the other hand, he was at this time either involved with
Dmitrije Mitrinovic, or about to become involved with him.
Mitrinovic was a Yugoslav then living in the Bloomsbury
area of London who was one of Watts's early gurus. Specifically, Watts classifies him as a "rascal-guru" of the same

ilk as G. I. Gurdjieff.[4] He was a great occultist and esotericist, with ancillary interests in psychology. But he also had strong political and social ideas as well, and he went so far as to set up a movement, the New Britain Movement, and to start two journals—*New Britain* and *The Eleventh Hour*—to advance those ideas. "The historical importance of Mitrinovic was that he tried to save Europe from Nazism and economic insanity," Watts wrote. On the face, it seems uncharacteristic of the essentially apolitical Watts to have worked on both these journals and to have tried to sell them on the streets of London—unless he was prepared to buy into the whole package for pragmatic rather than ideological reasons.

The minor flurry that the item on politics sparked off in the correspondence columns of *Buddhism in England* was a storm in a teacup compared with the controversy occasioned by the next installment of "Buddhism in the Modern World." But then, who would have been surprised? The title of the item was "Buddhism and Sex."

The important thing to bear in mind when reading this piece is that Watts, like so many of the young men of this less permissive era, passionately wished for an erotic consummation that proved to be frustratingly elusive. By his own account, it was at least three years more before he at last achieved it. What he has to say here is, therefore, informed more by theory than by practice—but then, as we have seen, Alan Watts never found himself overly inhibited by such limitations.

In the main, "Buddhism and Sex" deals quite skilfully with what was at that time a very sensitive subject. Watts again argues for a sensible middle way course: one that avoids the dangers of repression on the one hand and of overindulgence on the other. He both castigates his times for its obsession with sex and also takes a characteristic sideswipe at the puritans. He furthermore wisely defers to the

Buddha's requirement of celibacy for monks and nuns, conceding that such a course might indeed be necessary on the higher stages of the Path; and it is not repression but *sublimation*, hence perfectly healthy. On the lower stages of the Path, however, some form of sexual expression may be quite in order, even beneficial, and he cites those ancient myths that see in it the authentic pursuit of a kind of wholeness.

So far so good. Nothing to bring a blush to even the most modest cheek. But then in the final paragraph he overplays his hand rather when he praises the oriental attitude to prostitution—or at least his somewhat idealized fantasy of what that attitude might be. This rather ill-conceived little sally prompted a spirited lady of marked feminist tendencies named A. Beresford Holmes (with whom Watts crossed swords on more than one occasion in the columns of *Buddhism in England*) to take up her pen and compose an outraged letter of reply which appeared in the next issue of the journal. Mr. Watts, with his "typically masculine view," had, she contended, been tempted to "view everything Eastern in a rosy light." In the West, reasonable efforts had been made towards the emancipation of women by gradually equalizing their position *vis-a-vis* men, but in the East, the position was infinitely worse: there women were "sexual slaves." Mrs. Holmes went on:

> One hears many excuses for prostitution, but it is a new one on me that it is done artistically in the East, and is, therefore, less pernicious. Vice is vice, and I do not see how anyone professing Buddhist ideals can advocate or see anything artistic in prostitution, which degrades both women and men. . . .

And she concludes:

> For my part, I prefer to place my reliance upon the teachings of the Buddha. . . . There is a

*wholesomeness about Buddhism, a refreshing cleanness and absence of eroticism. So many religions become tainted with sex feeling, some become distinctly phallic, but Buddhism is singularly free from sex interests, and that is because it is essentially a* spiritual *religion. If Buddha, with his great wisdom, enforced celibacy on both Bhikkhus and Bhikkhunis, we may rest assured that he saw it was necessary for all those who really wish to live the spiritual life. As for the dilettantes and those who live the life of the ordinary householder, they will find that as their interest in spiritual truth grows in intensity, so will their lower desires become purified and attenuated until they cease to have any power over the awakened will. For those who are attempting to live the spiritual life, better, far better, that they should err on the side of starving their sex nature than by thinking it will offer them a solution of cosmic problems* (sic) *by indulging it. It is much more likely to land them in terrible difficulties.*

While a lot of Ms. Beresford Holmes's letter may strike the modern reader as rather Grundyish, some of her criticisms were quite well-aimed. A rather more shrill letter of criticism from the pseudonymous "Nemo" was also printed at the same time. It declared:

*The mass of people in India are effete and degenerate through sexual depravity, and the same is true to a great extent in China.*

*Mr. Watts should read* Cities of Sin, *by H. de Leeuw, published last year, in which a full account is given of the traffic in women in the Orient and its relation to the drug traffic. . . .*

One wonders if Watts took "Nemo's" advice and read the book—and, if he did, what he thought of it. The same correspondent also launched into a heated diatribe against the "insidious doctrines" of Freudian psychology, "which may weaken our struggle with this hydra-headed monster" (i.e. sex), He/she went on:

*The teaching that it is more dangerous to suppress one's sexual appetites rather than yield to them is the teaching of sexual perverts and is wholly contrary to the self-control taught by the Buddha. . . .*

Fortunately, the young Alan Watts was not left alone to be devoured by hostile critics for having had the audacity to speak out on the "ever-interesting topic." One broad-minded reader, H.N.M. Hardy, found his article "excellent" and commented:

*We Buddhists are taught to face the facts of life and, therefore, for us, prudery is a weakness, a form of wilful blindness, out of which we should educate ourselves.*

He did not, however, agree with Watts's assertion that the Buddha had not dealt adequately with the subject of sex, "for His very silence . . . shows . . . that He attached no special importance to it, and left the question to be settled by those concerned."

Looking back on "Buddhism and Sex" from a perspective of more than fifty years, it has to be recognised as a pioneering piece of work. For despite Mr. Hardy's contention, Buddhism offers little guidance on sexual matters, and Buddhist writers seem to have been reluctant to deal with the subject. Watts, in fact, is one of the exceptions to the rule. The truth is that Buddhism, in contrast, say, to Islam or Judaism, takes a negative view of the relationship between man and woman and broadly hints that those seriously interested in fulfilling their spiritual potential to the highest degree should cut it out of their lives completely. Thus, indeed, the monastic community, the *Sangha*, forms the core of the religion, and its members are required to be strictly celibate. It is true that there latterly arose kinds of religious who were allowed to marry—certain types of Tibetan lamas, for instance, and Japanese Zen priests—but on the whole the basic disposition of Buddhism is to polarise over the matter of sex: if one is seriously interested in living the religious life one foregoes having a sex life, if one wants a sex life one foregoes having a fully realised spiritual life. This sort of polarisation is challenged by some Western Buddhists today who would like to see both sides of human nature, the spiritual and the instinctual, given fair expression. This integration was something that Watts was to advocate in his later writings, though he seems to opt for a more orthodox position in this early essay. As a person who usually tried to carry through his intellectual convictions, he also attempted to live out this ideal in his actual life. Whether he got it right, though, is open to debate.

Finally, to return to that last controversial paragraph: when "Buddhism in the Modern World" was eventually re-released in pamphlet form, that offending item had been duly deleted, a fact welcomed by A. C. March when he reviewed the publication in *Buddhism in England*—'so no one now need hesitate to pass these views of a modern Buddhist on to their friends, whatever their age or sex may be."

The spirit of debate that "Buddhism and Sex" had sparked off in the correspondence columns of *Buddhism in England* was carried on by the next and final part of the series, "Buddhism and War," though here concord prevailed.

As we have already noted, war was a matter prominent in every thinking person's mind during that uneasy interregnum between the two devastating World Wars, and the question of pacifism inevitably became a keenly debated topic. It was even debated in the Oxford Union, where the House decided that in the event of another war its members would not fight for King and Country. While still a schoolboy at King's, Canterbury, Watts had participated in a similar debate in the Debating Society in October 1932. He spoke against the motion, *That in the opinion of this House conscientious objection to fighting for one's country is unjustifiable*. At the time he was Hon. Secretary of the Society, and said:

> *. . . that the moral victory of a community of conscientious objectors over an aggressor would be so great that it would always be remembered as one of the greatest things in History and an example to future generations. The concept to "turn the other cheek" is for the brave man, while the coward is the one who wants to "hit him back."*[4]

When the House divided, the votes fell equally for each side, but then the President used his casting vote in favour of the motion.

In "Buddhism and War," Watts again takes a pacifist line, but an extreme one that is explicitly critical of those casuists who declare themselves ideologically opposed to killing but who, when the chips actually go down, are usually able to find some high-minded reason for taking up arms against the common foe. This really will not do, Watts insists. If one is opposed to war, if one is convinced that killing does not merely solve nothing but is actually wrong in itself, then one must desist from it *absolutely* and *right now*. One cannot honestly defer one's pacifism to a hypothetical ideal time in the future when the world is ready for it.

Watts readily concedes that he is not proposing a "path of roses" but an extremely thorny one: "Safety is not offered, nor even success for those who start upon the

*The Early Writings of Alan Watts*

adventure, but only suffering, frustration, scorn and abuse."
One must be fully prepared to sacrifice one's own life, to
see one's women raped and one's children massacred—and
one must be prepared to go even further than such merely
passive acceptance: one must counter hatred with active
love. This kind of utterly selfless love alone can generate
the karmic force that, gathering momentum, will eventually overcome hatred and inaugurate the millennium of perfect peace.

The correspondents to *Buddhism in England* were
generally sympathetic to these arguments, though "S.F.W."
did believe that there was such a thing as a just war and that
it wasn't such a bad thing to want to protect one's wife and
children against atrocities. He also strongly hinted that Watts
wasn't really facing up to the "realities of life" and that he
was falling into "some delusions which theorists are apt to
fall into." In another thoughtful letter, James Tempest, while
appreciative of the article, drew attention to the root causes
of war: dark forces like "war psychosis" and "mob feeling," that lie hidden in the human heart, even in the hearts
of professed pacifists, and which only require the right combination of circumstances to bring them out.

As we shall see, Watts was to return again and again
to the theme of war during his writings in the period covered
by this volume. He remained always true to the pacifist ideals
that he had first publicly propounded in the Debating Society at King's school, and towards the end of the 1930s, when
it did appear that war was inevitable, he stood firm by his
intellectual convictions and departed for the United States
rather than face conscription and fight in a forthcoming war
against Hitler. He was criticised for this, as pacifists are
always criticised, but it is only fair to say that his action was
perfectly consistent with all his declared statements on the
subject of war.

In retrospect, we may look back on "Buddhism in the

Modern World" in its final pamphlet form as Watts's most substantial achievement down to 1934. It shows him emerging as an independent voice, confident and eloquent, able to orchestrate balanced arguments and expound them with lucidity and vigour. There are all the signs of quite amazing precocious talent here, but little giveaway tokens of immaturity, too: in particular, a natural youthful tendency to be rather airily idealistic and to say things that derive more from theory than from practice. In short, marvellously mentally agile though he is, Watts cannot completely disguise his inevitable lack of experience.

"Is Buddhism Serious" is a brief report that Watts himself submitted to *Buddhism in England* giving the gist of his address at the 1935 Wesak Meeting. This meeting was the high point of the Buddhist Lodge's annual calendar and celebrated the Birth, Enlightenment and Death of the Buddha. Based on the traditional Theravada Buddhist festivity, it was held on or as close to the date of the full moon of May as possible. In 1935, it was held on May 17 at the Caxton Hall, a municipally-owned complex of venerable wood-panelled meeting rooms of various sizes in the Westminster district of London, not far from the Houses of Parliament. The Caxton Hall is perhaps best remembered in history as the place where General Dyer, the instigator of the Amritsar Massacre, was assassinated by an Indian patriot.

At Wesak Meetings, it was usual for a shrine to be set up with a Buddha-image on it and the people attending would bring flowers to decorate this. A number of distinguished speakers would speak from the platform under the chairmanship of Christmas Humphreys. In 1935, these included a Sri Lankan gentleman named Dr. B. E. Fernando, a Mr. Charles Galloway—and Mr. Alan Watts. For some reason, however, perhaps lack of space, when the meeting was reported in *Buddhism in England*, while verbatim reports of all the other speeches were printed, similar treatment of Watts's speech was deferred until the following issue. It is actually a very lively and witty little piece that recapitulates arguments already propounded in the section on humour in "Buddhism in the Modern World." No doubt delivered from the platform with Watts's usual panache and showmanship, it probably went down very well with the audience.

I have heard it said that the young Watts was quite outstanding as a public speaker—that indeed he was second only to Christmas Humphreys himself in this respect, which is high praise indeed, for Humphreys was a past master of the art. Humphreys's style had been honed to near perfection in the courtrooms of the Old Bailey, during his time as First Treasury Counsel. On the public stage he became a kind of actor, extemporizing from rough notes in a beautifully modulated and authoritative voice, now explaining a point delicately, now putting over a persuasive argument with impeccable logic, moving into lyrical mood to introduce a quotation from one of the Masters, then quite suddenly and unexpectedly raising his voice to startle his audience into full attention for a key point. It was performance admittedly, but performance in the grand manner of an Irving or a Tree—and it always worked like magic on the audience. As Humphreys was Watts's chief guru back in the mid-30s, it is fair to assume that he was the model upon which his young and enthusiastic protege based his own oratorical technique.

The final piece in Part Two is "The Genius of China," which is a brief report on the International Exhibition of Chinese Art held in 1935 at Burlington House, London, under the auspices of the Royal Academy of Arts. We know from Watts's autobiography that he was kindly presented with an official pass for this "absolutely sensational exhibition" by his friend Robert Holland-Martin, the Chairman of Martin's Bank, and that he visited it "day after day, trying to understand and absorb the mood beneath Chinese art forms." Part of the fruit of those many hours of contemplation is presented here, and while the towering sixty foot high Buddha in the main gallery still occupied a commanding position in Watts's memory when he came to write his memoirs over thirty-five years later, this report clearly shows that, at the time, he was more deeply impressed by the spontaneity and lightness of the Sung Dynasty paintings, whose half-suggested forms were for him highly suggestive of the Golden Age of Chinese Zen art.

## NOTES

*1. Toby Humphreys introduced Watts to John M. Watkins in the early 1930s. Watkins' son, Nigel, was also active in The Buddhist Lodge at this time and became one of Watts's early mentors. As Watts wrote in his autobiography: "Nigel not only became my bibliographer on Buddhism, comparative religion and mysticism, but also my most trusted adviser on the various gurus, pundits, and psychotherapists then flourishing in London. . . . [He] is worth at least twenty academically accredited professors. Instead of giving lectures and seminars, he simply tells you what to read."*

*2. Grundyism. Mrs. Grundy is the conventional personification of Anglo-Saxon prudery.*

*3. The notion of "sportsmanship" is elemental to the English public school ethos, which essentially sees the whole of human life in terms of games, notably the game of cricket; hence come phrases like "it's not cricket" and "playing the game." A sportsman is a decent sort of chap who sticks to the rules and does not seek to gain any sort of "unfair advantage" for himself by dastardly underhand methods.*

*4. G. I. Gurdjieff was a Russian from the Caucasus who propagated a curious esoteric "system" in the West in the early part of the present century. This system was clearly based on traditional Sufi teachings and practices, with borrowings from elsewhere. Gurdjieff was highly charismatic—the writer Katherine Mansfield fell under his spell—but he was also sensual and enigmatic; hence, many find it difficult to decide whether he was an authentic spiritual teacher or some kind of opportunist or poseur exploiting the deep hunger in the West for spiritual instruction for less than pristine motives—or indeed whether he was a combination of the two.*

*The Early Writings of Alan Watts*

# THE BUDDHA'S PATH
# TO REALITY

From *Buddhism in England*
*March–April, 1933*

•

We are told that when the Buddha was questioned on points of Ultimate Truth he maintained a "noble silence"; he knew that it is one of the supreme follies of mankind which tries to limit the Eternal by expressing it in finite form, which tries to condition that which is Nameless and Formless by ideas and words. And the attempt to limit the Infinite in this way always fails. Carlyle wrote in his *Sartor Resartus:* "Man's Unhappiness, as I construe, comes of his greatness; it is because there is an Infinite in him, which with all his cleverness he cannot quite bury under the Finite." A Buddhist philosopher summed up Gautama's teaching on the Ultimate in the words "Nirvana IS," for the furthest he ever went in his definition of the Infinite was: "There is, my brothers, an Unborn, Unoriginated, Uncreated, Unformed: were there not the Unborn, Unoriginated, Uncreated, Unformed, there would be no emancipation from the world of the born, the originated, the created, the formed." He deemed it sufficient to know that Nirvana, Reality, or whatever you may call it, IS, but at the same time he emphasized that this fact cannot be appreciated until we have advanced some way on the Path.

In the few things which the Buddha said about Reality we can find no indication of the fact that he saw It as a Deity such as that preached by conventional Christianity—the personal Being who rules over the Universe as does a king over his realm; Buddhism is not a "God-fearing" religion—such would be quite incompatible with the great command: "Be ye lamps unto yourselves, be ye a refuge unto yourselves, take to yourselves no other refuge." Voltaire once made the witty observation that as God created man in his own image, so man had been returning the compliment ever since, for the personal God is a man-made idea—at best only an idea. Reality is a fact, based on experience, not primitive speculation. Sir Henry Maine writes: "It is now clearly seen by all trustworthy observers of the primitive condition of mankind, that, in the infancy of the race, men could account for sustained or periodically recurring action only by supposing a personal agent." This belief is an outcome of the instinct of fear—the fear of the cave-man who did not see in thunder and rain and wind the working of universal law, but the hand of a being like himself, only more powerful, who might be "bribed with blood" and brought to suit his actions to man's convenience. Such was the origin of selfish prayer, of which Buddhism knows nothing, for true prayer consists, not in asking for material benefits, but in tuning oneself to the Rhythm of Life.

Where is Reality to be found? Where are we to seek this Rhythm of Life? Where else but in ourselves, for the Path and the Goal are within this body of ours "six feet in length, with its sense impressions and its thoughts and ideas." All Knowledge, say the Zen masters, is in our essence of mind, all the wisdom of Buddhas past, present and future, we can find in ourselves if only we know how to get at it. And the Way to this Knowledge is simply to learn to see things as they are, in other words to know Reality. While the mind is fettered by selfish ideas we can only have distorted views of things; we think of *my* body and *your* body, whereas they do not really belong to you or me at all—they belong to the Universe, and to understand this is to free oneself from attachment. It is this idea of personal possession, this idea of attachment which is at the root of all illusion and suffering, and while it occupies our minds we can never hope to see things as they are. The Eightfold Path was constructed to show man the way to equanimity—the state which alone can contemplate Truth. All ideas of attachment are therein set aside, and the multitudinous phases of existence are seen as being *just so*—free from the illusion of self, beyond pleasure and pain, joy and sorrow. "Ignore the distinction between subject and object," says the *Sutra of Wei Lang,* "and let the essence of mind and all phenomenal objects be in a state of Thusness"—of being Real and True. And in the Tao-teh-King we read: "Thus it is that the highest form of man keeps his personality in the background, and yet it asserts itself; treats his own existence from an objective point of view, and yet preserves that existence. It is not that he possesses no individuality, but it is in this way that he is capable of developing his individuality."

Reality cannot be discussed; we cannot find out why it exists or anything about it by intellectual speculation which only leads the mind round in circles—it will never get us anywhere and in addition to this it is harmful to that tranquillity so necessary for arriving at Truth. The first step is to understand ourselves; one of Low's cartoons depicts an old scientist in a large room full of dusty books on the why and wherefore of Life, sitting in front of a mirror. And underneath is written: "The little thing that puzzles him is—himself." The Eightfold Path is the way to knowledge of self, for it teaches us our right place in the scheme of Things; it breaks us of the illusion that we are separate from the rest of Life, until we finally come to know ourselves, not as individual entities, but as aspects of the Real—'Seek in the impersonal for the Eternal Man; and having sought him out, look inward; thou art Buddha." Reality can be perceived only in the silence of the undistracted mind where no flow of jarring thoughts and ideas can cloud it from view; we must set aside all confusion and take a look round to see where we are, just as a mountaineer pauses in his climb to see where he stands; as he ascends he gets further and further from the lowlands of Desire until at last he reaches the peak and looks up into the boundless blue of Eternity; below he can see the earth laid open as a map and he understands it—how trivial and unimportant were all his fears and worries!—while above is the radiance of Nirvana, and gazing up into its awful infinitude he loses himself in the Eternal.

But the calm and disinterestedness required of Buddhists does not involve cold indifference to the sufferings of others; rather it means that we should not allow our minds to be influenced by circumstances and that we should be no "respecters of persons." Lafcadio Hearn, gazing up at the smiling faces of Buddha-figures, used to hear them say: "I have the same feeling for the high as for the low, for the moral as for the immoral, for the virtuous as for the depraved, for those holding sectarian views and false opinions as for those whose beliefs are good and true,"—the feeling of infinite compassion and understanding. At Kamakura in Japan there is a gigantic figure of the Buddha Maitreya sitting wrapt in contemplation among the ruins of a once magnificent temple. And there the Daibutsu (Great Buddha) has sat, tranquil and alone, ever since storms and earthquakes destroyed Minamoto Yoritomo's splendid capital—

> *"Above the old songs turned to ashes and*
> *pain,*
> *Under which Death enshrouds the idols and*
> *trees with mist of sigh,*
> *(Where are Kamakura's rising days and life*
> *of old?)*
> *With heart heightened to hush, the*
> *Daibutsu forever sits."*

A veritable symbol of the Buddha-calm which remains undisturbed amid the turmoil and conflict of existence. You are bereft of all your worldly possessions? What is that to you—they were never yours. You have been buffeted and shaken by the storms of Life? Yet did your heart remain unmoved; all idea of self was set aside and you had no personal feeling in the matter. You were not concerned as to whether events were good or ill, as to whether they affected you or another; you took them for what they were— universal law; you saw both the pleasant and the painful, the good and the evil, the self and the not-self without attachment, for your mind was smooth as a mirror, reflecting all but grasping nothing.

---

# THE BUDDHIST SCRIPTURES
## V. THE SUTRA OF WEI LANG

From *Buddhism in England*
*July–August, 1933*

●

The *Sutra of Wei Lang* has been called "the only *sutra* spoken by a native of China," for the designation "sutra" is, in every other case, applied only to the words of the Buddha or famous Bodhisattvas. Wei Lang, or (as usually and more correctly rendered) Hui Neng, was the thirty-third patriarch after Mahakasyapa, to whom the teaching of the Dhyana School was said to have been transmitted by the Buddha himself. This collection of his sayings is one of the most important texts of the Zen sect, which, although placing no reliance in the written word as a means of expressing Ultimate. Truth, yet recognizes the value of such a work as this as a guide to the beginner.

The Zen (Dhyana) teaching was originally brought to China by Bodhidharma in 527 C.E., and though it has now sunk into abeyance in that country, it still flourishes in Japan where it was introduced by Eisai and Dogen towards the end of the twelfth and the beginning of the thirteenth centuries.

Wei Lang (638—713) lived in the T'ang Dynasty—the Golden Age of Chinese Buddhist culture—and while he was practising the doctrines of the "Sudden School" in the South, Shang Siu was teaching the "Gradual School" in the North, but the former was the legitimate successor of Hwang Yan, the Fifth Patriarch in China, and much of the Sutra is taken up in explaining the differences between the two schools. Wei Lang spent most of his life teaching in the district of Tso Kai, using the Pao Lam Monastery as his centre, where he was accompanied by several hundred pupils under Vinaya Master Tung Yin, and all his sermons were collected together by one of his disciples—Tsung-pâo—and this collection forms the Sutra, the full title of which is: *Sutra Spoken on the High Seat of the Gem of the Law* (Nanjio's Catalogue No. 1525).

The Sutra consists of ten chapters:—Autobiography, On Prajna, Questions and Answers, Samadhi and Prajna, Dhyana, On Repentance, Dialogues of the Patriarch, the Sudden School and the Gradual School, Royal Patronage, and His Final Instructions. Selections from most of these are given at the end of this article. It would be quite impossible for anyone to understand the teaching of this remarkable work at a single reading, unless prepared by a long course of meditation; it is one of those books like the *Voice of the Silence*, the *Tao Teh King*, and the *Bhagavad Gita*, which need constant study and thought. The *Sutra of Wei Lang* is essentially a work for the intuition; it cannot be understood by the application of logical and ratiocinative methods; the whole is one vast "koan" which must be read again and again until the mind is thoroughly saturated in it, and then perhaps one single sentence from it will bring to the reader's mind a flash of Truth, shedding its light on the whole book.

It is to be regretted that there is as yet no translation of the Sutra which can conveniently be carried about in the pocket, for it is one of those works which one can study with great profit in spare moments—while in the train or waiting for an appointment—for it contains many paragraphs and sentences summing up the essence of the Zen teaching:

> *Dhyana* means, to be free from attachment to all outer objects, and *samadhi* means to attain inner peace. If we are attached to outer objects, our inner mind will be perturbed. When we are free from attachment, the mind will be at peace. Essence of mind is intrinsically pure; the reason why we are perturbed is simply because we allow ourselves to be carried away by the circumstances we are under. He who is able to keep his mind unperturbed, irrespective of circumstances, has attained real *samadhi*.

The fact that we are slaves to circumstance is the root of all our suffering, for it distorts our view of Life and clouds Reality with the illusion of "self." The idea of looking at Existence from anything but an ego-centric point of view is, to the mass of mankind, highly unfamiliar; we are used to judging events by the effects they have upon ourselves and we consider them good or evil simply because they affect our persons in such and such a way. But Buddhism wants us to learn another way of looking at Life—the impersonal way, which sees all things in terms of Reality and is not concerned with these phantasms of good and ill, joy and pain. By giving up the mind to supreme equanimity one is able to see things without attachment: one does not think of my self and your self, of my house and your house, but seeing all these things as aspects of Reality, selfishness and attachment are eliminated altogether. In other words: when everything, even ourselves, appears to us as just so—as perfectly natural—we shall no longer have any cause for attachment.

*Towards all things, good or bad, beautiful or ugly, our attitude should be the same—we should treat all of them as void; and even in times of disputes and quarrels we should treat our intimates and enemies alike and never think of retaliation. In the exercise of our thinking faculty, let the past be dead. If we allow our thoughts, the past ones, the present and the future ones, to link up in a series, we put ourselves under restraint. On the other hand, if we let our mind attach to nothing at all times and towards all things, we gain emancipation. For this reason we take "non-attachment" as our fundamental principle.*

The Zenshuist lives in the eternal; he has no regrets for the past and no fears for the future; he takes things as they come—quietly and naturally—and remains unmoved. This is the great principle of economy of mind, of concentrating on the affairs of the moment without worrying about other things. When asked what Zen was, Master Poh Chang replied: "Eat when you are hungry; sleep when you are tired. People do not simply eat at table, but think of hundreds of things; they do not simply sleep in bed, but think of thousands of things." Or, in words more familiar to the West: "Be not anxious for the morrow . . . sufficient unto the day is the evil thereof." Do not worry about what is going to happen on another day while you are engaged in the affairs of this, otherwise you put yourself under restraint.

The *Wei Lang Sutra* contains a certain amount of verse offering great opportunities for the poet translator: would that we had another Edwin Arnold to render it into English verse! Unfortunately, much of this poetry suffers from literal translation, although some fine passages may be found here and there.

*Unperturbably and passively he practises
    no virtue.
Self-possessed and dispassionate, he
    commits no sin.
Calm and silent, he gives up seeing and
    hearing
Even and straight, his mind abides
    nowhere.*

Or again:

*Buddha-seeds latent in our mind
Upon the coming of the all-pervading rain
    will sprout.
The "flower" of the doctrine having been
    intuitively grasped,
The fruit of Enlightenment one is bound to
    reap*

This time a somewhat curious passage:

*The Kingdom of Buddhism is in the world,
Within which Enlightenment is to be
    sought.
To seek Enlightenment by separating from
    this world
Is as absurd as to search for a rabbit's
    horn.*

Throughout the whole Sutra is emphasized the futility of seeking Enlightenment from outside. Wisdom is something that grows by experience; that comes as a result of putting principles into practice. It cannot be had for the asking. If you travel to the ends of the earth you will not find it; if you invoke all the gods in heaven you will not be any nearer to it, for you will be as foolish as the man who cries out for water in the middle of a river.

"The wisdom of the past, present, and future Buddhas, as well as the teaching of the twelve canons, are immanent in our mind."

We must be lamps unto ourselves and endeavour to learn by our own efforts without seeking the help of the supernatural, for, in the words of the Dhammpada: "Purity and impurity are personal concerns: no one can purify another."

> *The Three Bodies (Trikaya) are inherent in*
> *     our essence of mind,*
> *By development of which, the four Prajnas*
> *     are manifested.*
> *Thus, without shutting your eyes and ears*
> *     to keep away from the external world*
> *You may reach Buddhahood directly.*
> *Now, I have made this plain to you;*
> *And if you believe it firmly, you will for-*
> *     ever be free from delusions.*
> *Follow not those who seek Enlightenment*
> *     from without:*
> *These people talk about Bodhi all the time*
> *     (but they never find it).*
> *Bodhi is to be found within our own mind,*
> *And there is no necessity to look for mysti-*
> *     cism from without.*

Yet there is no need to shut oneself away from the world, or to indulge in the type of meditation which induces deep trances and delusive states of auto-hypnosis. Enlightenment is not to be found through quietism, through banishing all thoughts from the mind (for this only puts one on the level of an inanimate object), but through a certain attitude to life which can be preserved as well in the solitude of the mountains as in the hubbub of the market-place.

"Whether you are in activity or under rest, abide your mind nowhere. Forget the discrimination between a sage and an ordinary man. Ignore the distinction between subject and object. Let the Essence of Mind and all phenomenal objects

be in a state of Thusness. Then you will be in *samadhi* all
the time."

---

# BUDDHISM
# IN THE MODERN WORLD

From *Buddhism in England*
*Sept.–Oct., 1933*

●

## Buddhism and Humour

*Introductory Remarks.*

The West does not understand that Buddhism is a living
religion, and not a cult of interest only to students of ancient
myths and exploded philosophies. Buddhism is not to be
treated like a museum curiosity, as a relic of the Past, which
has long outworn its days and has no value for the Present.
For the religion of the Buddhas is not just "yet another
'-ism'," not one of hundreds of other creeds, but almost the
father of them all, for it is the greatest representative on earth
of the age-old Wisdom Religion which was born with Man
and will not die until that inconceivably far-off time when
the Universe shall enter into its final Nirvana. So far from
its having no value for the modern world, we of the present day will put ourselves in a perilous position if we turn
a deaf ear to our ancient Teacher, and listen only to fanatics
and humbugs whose empty talk so often passes for religion
and morals. To-day there is such a hubbub of conflicting
teachers and moralists that the world does not know which
of their many plausible philosophies to believe, with the
result that it is in danger of forsaking religion and morality

altogether or else of wasting itself away in an orgy of moral conflicts and religious strife. And if our new-fangled beliefs and opinions are leading us into such a chaos, is it not right that we should listen once again to the oldest of all the philosophies[1] and give it a fair chance by putting its precepts into practice? It is small wonder that we derive no benefit from our modern "isms" when we have never even tested our ancient Faith by applying it to life. There are many who say that Buddhism is a failure because it was unable to save the East from the pitiable plight it is in to-day; we would ask our critics to think again—which of the two is the failure, Buddhism, or Man who failed to put it into practice? And, moreover, what about the present condition of the West? Christianity was not able to save it from the War, or from its slavery to the outward forms of civilization. There is nothing to be gained by running down Buddhism, or even Christianity for that matter, for the fault is our own, and if we have disobeyed our instructors, they are hardly to blame.

The modern world has many bugbears—some of which it recognizes and calls "Problems," and some of whose existence it is ignorant—but there are four which are probably the most formidable, and it is of these that I am going to treat in a few short articles on *Buddhism in the Modern World*. They are: Too little sense of humour, politics, sex (one that is taken much too seriously), and war. These articles are written to provoke thought and discussion on subjects which at the present time must be of concern to every Buddhist. The opinions offered are only tentative, and though based on fundamental Buddhist prin-

[1]*In speaking of Buddhism as the "oldest of all the philosophies," we do not refer to the specific system laid down by Gautama so much as to the immemorial* Bodhidharma *said to have been preached by a long series of Buddhas stretching back into the remotest past. Wei Lang (Sutra of W.L., p. 71) gives the Buddhas of the present Kalpa as follows: (i) Kakusundha, (ii) Konagamana, (iii) Kassapa, and (iv) Gautama. Buddhas are supposed to arise by reason of cyclic law about every 5,000 years.—Vide Blavatsky,* Secret Doctrine *(T.P.H. edn.) i. 73*

ciples, such as "the middle way," the universal attitude to life, overcoming evil with good, and the need for mastering one's own mind, I lay no claim to the authority of Buddhism for my suggested application of these principles. For my own part, I am quite prepared, *if necessary*, to alter my views. So I trust I shall be forgiven if I seem over-dogmatic or over-critical on some points, but it will only be for the sake of emphasis. If I exaggerate and fail to be "sweetly reasonable," it will not be because I am incapable of seeing the opposite point of view, but because at all costs I wish to be clear. Buddhism is not a religion of compromise and indefinite opinions; its teaching is plain and straightforward, and it makes no attempt to serve up distasteful and bitter facts in a palatable and easily digested manner. As H.P. Blavatsky wrote in her introduction to *The Secret Doctrine* (quoting Montaigne): "'Gentlemen, I have here made only a nosegay of culled flowers, and have brought nothing of my own but the string that ties them.' Pull the 'string' to pieces and cut it up in shreds, if you will. As for the nosegay of *facts*—you will never be able to make away with these. You can only ignore them, and no more." And so when my own personal prejudices creep into what follows, as inevitably they will, the fault will be mine, and you are welcome to take them with a big grain of salt.

## I. BUDDHISM AND THE NEED FOR A SENSE OF HUMOUR

There is a regrettable tendency in the West to associate Religion with long faces, intense seriousness, gloom and morbid restrictions, with the result that Religion has generally got a bad name. One often hesitates to use the word "religion" on account of the depressing significance it carries with it, whereas in reality this negative puritanism is one of Religion's greatest enemies. This does not mean that true Religion is frivolous and imposes no restrictions whatever on man's lower nature, but rather it steers, as in Buddhism, a middle path between the extremes of "Grundy-ism" and what some modern thinkers are pleased to call "self-expression"—in other words, obeying every impulse and doing just as one likes for fear of harbouring any "repression complexes." But particularly in England and America the puritan extreme has been so much over-emphasised that we are in danger of breaking away from Religion altogether for fear of further restrictions and more "Grundyism," which are actually the outcome of taking oneself much too seriously and of failing to recognize that there is a very close connection between Wisdom and Humour.

Though Humour is a word with many shades of meaning, many of them having no reasonable connection with Wisdom, there is one particularly subtle form of humour which is, sad to say, one of the rarest virtues in life because it is the most difficult of all the arts and the greatest secret of the wise man. It is not just the knack of being comic, nor yet a mere hilarious state of mind; it is neither making fun of the oddities of other people, nor the ability to indulge in pleasantries, for, although these require a certain amount of skill, they cannot be compared to the sublime but elusive art of the real philosopher of humour. Someone has wittily observed that a sense of humour is an acute sense of proportion, and it is doubtful whether any other definition has come nearer to the truth. And this is where Humour is closely connected with Religion and Wisdom. For the Puritan's intense desire to be "saved" makes him take himself too seriously, with the result that he is willing to undergo a morbid asceticism, to submit to all manner of pains and penances, not because they are beneficial to mankind, but because they are said to be necessary for "salvation," and in so doing he loses sight of the fact not only that he is fostering an intense self-righteousness, but that the salvation of his personal self is a matter of no importance whatever. While we consider ourselves to be so important that we are ready to send all the joy out of religion in order to be "saved," we can have no true sense of proportion. For what is this personal self but a mere link in a long chain of personalities stretching from the eternal to the eternal? To be anxious for its everlasting salvation and immortality shows not only a thoroughly bad sense of proportion, but a poor sense of humour, because the first test of a humorist is that he should be able to laugh at himself, and he is unable to do this until he has in some measure stepped out of his own personality. When he realizes how wrapped up he was in that odd creature called himself, and what a "bee in his bonnet" he had about his own importance, his first reaction will surely be to laugh.

Let us take an illustration—that of a man slipping on a banana-skin and falling down in the street. Everyone enjoys the joke but himself, who, unless he has a true sense of proportion, will be annoyed at the loss of his dignity. But under the same circumstances the humorist would be able to regard himself objectively and share in the amusement, for the whole art of humour is to be able to see life whole without distorting it by imagining oneself the thing of greatest consequence. For it is impossible to laugh at anything unless it is seen from outside, and when one laughs at oneself it is the first sign that he is able to look upon himself from a more universal point of view, instead of being boxed-up in the small, cramping and humourless sphere of his own importance.

And this is just where Buddhism comes in. "Self is an error, an illusion, a dream. Open your eyes and awake. *See things as they are*, and you will be comforted." For if self is an illusion it is certainly not a thing to be taken seriously. On the one hand it is foolish to long for its salvation, and on the other it is foolish to be "terribly in earnest" about conquering it, because in so doing one treats it as a definite and important reality. In both cases one fails to see self as it is—a mere speck in the whirl of Samsara. Buddhism teaches us to burst the bonds of personality and, looking upon our own destiny with the equanimity of the Eternal, to rise above a purely personal attitude to life and to cultivate the universal attitude. To do this we must be able to stand aside from the chaos of our thoughts and emotions, to cease to identify ourselves with them, and in so doing realize a true sense of proportion. "Foregoing self, the Universe grows I."

If you walk down a crowded street and watch the faces of those that pass, you will notice that almost every face is set in an expression of intense and worried pre-occupation and you will realize that the world is full of people running round in small mental circles without fully understanding that there is an immense universe of things outside their own worries and concerns with which they have never come into contact. It is this ridiculous confinement which a Buddhist sense of humour will destroy, for it will teach us to laugh at the proud little thing which thought itself so great, at the comic bundle of worries which imagined itself the most important thing in the world—the self. For laughter is the best weapon we can use against evil, because, as the saying goes, "it bears no malice," To oppose evil with violence is only to stir it up all the more, and violence is a game that evil can play much better than we can; but laughter is disarming and baffling—not the harsh and cruel laughter of the man who takes a pleasure in vice—but the gentle, loving laughter of the sage who knows what a small thing evil is *when it is seen from outside*. It is the laughter of Understanding on seeing the confused condition of Ignorance, yet as Understanding proceeds from Ignorance no malice is born by it, for the sage does not laugh because he finds pleasure in our weaknesses, but because he wants to make us see the humorous side of them.

The modern world has a great need of laughing at itself, at a time when people are starving because there is too much food, going naked because there are too many clothes, becoming irreligious because there are too many religions, holding peace conferences and manufacturing armaments, saying one thing and doing another—never was there a more paradoxical and ludicrous state of affairs. Yet it is the old story of Trishna—selfish craving—whirling round in its small vicious circle until finally it narrows down to the centre, which is Man, and grips him in a choking ring of suffering. We have built up a civilization which we are unable to control, and, instead of being masters of our creations, our creations have become our masters.

---

# BUDDHISM IN THE MODERN WORLD

From *Buddhism in England*
*Nov.–Dec., 1933*

•

## II. Buddhism and Politics

As the chief interest of Buddhism is with spiritual rather than with temporal things, no specifically political principles are embodied in its teachings, and for this reason it must be made clear that no one has the right to express an "authoritative" opinion on the attitude of Buddhism towards this particular subject. Therefore, in writing this article I lay no claim to the authority of the Dhamma for my ideas on the problem of government. The teaching is there for us all, but as our interpretations of it are almost bound to differ, its particular applications are matters of individual responsibility, and no one is in a position to dictate another's duty in the actual practice of Buddhism. This is especially true in the sphere of politics, for Buddhism inclines neither to Despotism nor Republicanism, Constitutionalism nor

Socialism, Fascism nor Communism, Idealism nor Individualism, and one may adhere to any of these schools of political thought without being in disaccord with the Buddha's teachings. The Buddha would probably have agreed with Pope when he wrote:

> *For forms of government let fools contest,*
> *Whate'er is best administered is best,*

for it is not so much the form of state-organization that is of importance as the spiritual condition of individuals, upon which the welfare of the community depends. It is a truism that the perfect state can never be made by legislation alone, for statesmen are unable, however wise they may be, to change anything beyond the mere machinery of government, which is in itself no more than a dead system of no value without the intelligent support of the community.

It would seem that there is a tendency in human nature always to begin at the wrong end in approaching sociological problems, and this is particularly noticeable at the present time, when it is frequently imagined that an efficiently organized state is the same thing as a perfect state. Indeed, the delusion that progress is somehow inseparable from labour-saving devices, up-to-date educational establishments, super-cinemas, wireless, five-year plans, aeroplanes, town-planning, world-conferences and skyscrapers is one of the most wide-spread and absurd delusions of the modern world. Less ridiculous, but equally absurd delusions, are those which confuse peace with disarmament and leagues of nations, national prosperity with the gold-standard and credit, sound government with youth-movements and extremist dictatorships, chaos with capitalism, religion with belief, or freedom with leisure. The machine, the organization, the outward form, has so fascinated man that he has put all his faith in it, and in imagining that it can provide the solution to all the world's problems he fails to realize that he is in the lamentable position of the doctor who thought he could cure chickenpox by cutting off the spots. As Matthew Arnold wrote in *Culture and Anarchy* over sixty years ago:—

> *Faith in machinery is our besetting danger; often in machinery most absurdly disproportioned to the end which this machinery, if it is to do any good at all, is to serve; but always in machinery as if it had a value in and for itself. What is freedom but machinery?... What are railroads but machinery? What is wealth but machinery? What are, even, religious organizations but machinery? Now almost every voice in England is accustomed to speak of these things as if they were precious ends in themselves, and therefore had some of the characters of perfection indisputably joined to them.*

The state, just as the human body, works from within outwards, and it should be obvious that if man wants to control the world he must start by controlling his own mind. For man is supposed to be able to look after himself by virtue of his being a man and not a sheep—to be herded about in a senseless flock. But so long as he refuses to order his own life he must submit to the clumsy, inefficient and desperate system of being ordered about, interfered with and pestered by legions of policemen, tax-collectors, busy-bodies, censors, and other "caterpillars of the commonwealth." But these officials are employed in a vain attempt to manage a vast and complex civilization which refuses to look after itself because of the responsibility involved in so doing, and which is incapable of behaving honestly without being threatened with prisons, floggings, death-penalties and fines. Under such circumstances it is small wonder that our civilization has reached a critical condition which defeats the best statesmen and economists in the world. It should need no more statement than the fact that two and two make four, that the world's body cannot be healthy when its soul is sick; so vast and complicated has civilization become, and so negligible has its spiritual development been in proportion, that the task of government, even when aided by tremendous numbers of officials, verges on the impossible. Moreover, the power which science has given us over nature, the power which has given us fast travel, newspapers, telephones, hospitals and our high standard of living, is by no means equal to our fitness for using it, and where we have not abused this power by turning it to warfare and oppression, we have become so attached to it that its loss would seem a universal calamity. So dependent are we upon it for controlling the world and for ordering our own lives that we are slowly losing the ability to do these things for ourselves, and instead of mastering our creations we have become their slaves.

Buddhism is *par excellence* the religion of mastery, for in its teaching that man should not attach his mind to externals it demands a mental control undreamed of in these days of dependence upon machinery. It does not ask us to destroy our machines; it does not preach any "back-to-nature" fanaticism; it merely asks that we shall rise superior to all machinery—to the machinery of personality, politics, science and religion. Our minds and bodies are engines to be employed for a purpose; the idea of self—the combination of *skandhas*—is a useful tool; but they are not ends in themselves, any more than the pen in my hand is an end in itself, and we must not be carried away by them, or be victims of the egoism which arises through attachment to any means of creation and expression. Thus if Buddhism can only teach us to rise superior to mere organization and machinery, it will have done much to solve the political and economic problems of to-day. But have its principles any chance of acceptance? Professor Dicey writes in his *Law and Opinion in England*:

*Success in converting mankind to a new faith,
whether religious, or economical, or political,
depends but slightly on the strength of the
reasoning by which the faith can be defended,
or even on the enthusiasm of its adherents. A
change of belief arises, in the main, from the
occurrence of circumstances which induce the
majority of the world to hear with favour the-
ories which, at one time, men of common sense
derided as absurdities or distrusted as
paradoxes.*

We have seen that circumstances have now arisen
which make the cultivation of individual perfection more
necessary than ever, but Christianity does not emphasize the
need for producing more than one Christ, it does not attempt
to *train* men of high spirituality because it inherits the fatal
Western belief that greatness is born and not made. Beyond
an attempt to "imitate" Christ it does not go; to try to equal
Him would be irreverent and impossible. For it has an unfortunate doctrine that Jesus was the embodiment of an unat-
tainable perfection, and therefore the majority of Christians
will always be content to worship Him and be His slaves.
The Buddha did not lay himself open so much to deifica-
tion; he emphasized the fact that he was an ordinary human
being who had become Enlightened through his own efforts.
His precepts are not laws for his subjects, and he was not,
and has never been thought of, as a king jealous of rivalry.
For in reality these two sages invited men, not to bow down
and worship them, but to sit beside them, and to revere
them, if at all, not as gods but as elder brothers. If we can
train ourselves, not by slavish imitation, to acquire the
spiritual greatness of those who have led the way in showing us what *can* be done—if only a few can do this—then
we may look forward with hope.

Is there any need to quote the famous passage on Sovereignty in the *Chammapada*?—"Better than a sovereignty over the earth, better than the heaven-world, better than lordship over all the worlds, is the first step on the Path of Holiness." Or in the words of Jesus, "Seek ye first the Kingdom of God and His righteousness, and all these things shall be added unto you." Much is said and written about the control which man has gained over Nature, but Nature is only allowing us "a breath, a little scene, to monarchize," and the time draws on for the reaction. We have tried to gain mastery by violence, by trying to bend Nature to our uses with all the external machinery of civilization. It is the story of Frankenstein over again—we have created an unnatural monster which is slowly overpowering us—while there is yet another course to be taken, the Way of the Buddhas, of which it is said, "Help Nature and work on with her, and Nature will acknowledge thee as one of her creators and make obeisance."

# BUDDHISM
# IN THE MODERN WORLD

From *Buddhism in England*
*Jan.–Feb., 1934*

●

## III. Buddhism and Sex

It is difficult to find a cause for our modern obsession with Sex, unless it be a reaction from a period when the subject was held to be taboo. Yet although it is right to give this question a reasonable amount of study and investigation, it is given a prominence to-day which is out of all proportion to its importance. Almost every novel and film has a "sex-interest," a large number of books are published every year dealing exclusively with it, societies are formed to discuss it and even a school of psychology has been invented which finds in Sex the whole basis of our mental and physical life. But perhaps one of the most interesting features of the modern attitude to Sex is the tendency to regard the sexual act and the phenomena connected with it as ends in themselves distinct from the ultimate outcome of the act, which is Reproduction. The ancient Greeks adopted a similar attitude, but for the most part human society has seen in reproduction the only sanction for the existence of Sex, and has regarded sexual intercourse between man and woman as definitely immoral unless performed with a view to procreation. But so great an authority as Havelock Ellis finds in the actual sex-life of a man and his wife, and in the erotic phenomena which it involves, the basis of so much that is beautiful and noble in human life that this modern tendency would seem in some measure to be justified. But the question still remains as to what position Sex should hold in our lives, as to whether we should consider it more in its relation to Love than to procreation, whether it is fundamentally material or spiritual, and lastly whether the highest form of man should marry or be a celibate.

Probably the first question that will come to our minds is, "What is Sex?" To this Professor Crew replies in his *Introduction to the Study of Sex*: "The layman may perhaps find an answer, but no biologist has yet given a sufficiently comprehensive and satisfactory reply. We do not know what sex is. Biology has not yet reached that stage of its development when it can describe the objects of its searchings." It is not necessarily the union of two opposite forms of a similar species to produce offspring, because there are forms of life which combine the two sexes in one individual; it is not solely an appetite, because it is to a great extent creative; it is not the creative force of the Universe (although it may be a manifestation of it), because that force operates in many ways that have no connection with the phenomena we associate with Sex. But for practical purposes we may be content to define it as the relationship between man and woman which has two aspects—the erotic and the procreative—and taking thus a Buddhist middle path we may proceed to an examination of other aspects of the subject.

A far more important question for our consideration than the actual nature of Sex is the position which it should hold in our lives and the moral attitude which we should adopt towards it. It is generally agreed nowadays that to regard it as something definitely taboo and rather disgusting is a harmful attitude, because in repressing a normal manifestation of sex-energy it diverts it into undesirable channels often with disastrous results. Moreover there is no moral reason why we should be ashamed of a perfectly natural act which is in no way insanitary or aesthetically offensive, why we should show signs of undue nervousness when it is discussed or even why we should consider it as something too sacred to mention. And on the other hand it is highly undesirable to make an obsession of it, to think and talk of little else, to introduce it into all amusements and to take every opportunity of bringing it into prominence. This is equivalent to mere gluttony in eating, and signifies an utterly unbalanced mind when there are so many other things of interest in the world. For Buddhists there is again the middle path between prudery and obsession. Yet the idea of sexual taboo is certainly not a mere mental perversion which arises in an over-Puritanical age; it seems to be almost a fundamental instinct in human nature and is generally more developed in women than with men.[1] Perhaps if we turn to the Eastern Wisdom we may find the real cause of taboo, in a theory which is not accepted in the West, but which

[1]*See Havelock Ellis,* Man and Woman, *p. 234,* et seq.

may yet prove to be one of the most interesting facts of biology.[2]

Before going on to consider the Eastern teachings on the origin and eventual destiny of Sex as we understand it, it must be remembered that the Buddha quite definitely forbade all forms of sexual intercourse for those who took the bhikkhu's vows and decided to devote their whole lives to treading the Path. "If the woman be old, regard her as your mother, if young, as your sister, if very young, as your child. The *shramana* who looks at a woman as a woman, or touches her as a woman has broken his vow and is no longer a disciple of the Shakyamuni." The concentration required for treading the higher stages of the Path must not be divided; the whole mental force must be directed to the one end, and Sex is too strong a distraction to be allowed to exist alongside with the strenuous effort for self-purification which the attainment of Bodhisattvahood involves. So great is the purity required of the aspirant that at a certain stage he must not even touch other human beings and even certain plants and animals. A certain Thibetan book dealing with this highly advanced religious training says, "A disciple has to dread external living influence alone (magnetic emanations from living creatures). For this reason, while at one with all, in his *inner nature*, he must take care to separate his outer (external) body from every foreign influence; none must drink out of, or eat in his cup but himself. He must avoid bodily contact (i.e. being touched or touch) with human, as with animal being." Of course it will be raised in objection to this system that it destroys one of the most beautiful and vital aspects of human life—namely the love of man for woman—because in taking Sex out of the mental make-up of the perfect man one condemns it as a thing

[2]*See below on the division of the sexes. Several schools of Eastern philosophy hold that the earlier prototypes of man were dual-sexed, and it may be that the sense of shame is partly due to an instinctive attempt to cover up our present incompleteness. This, however, is only a tentative theory.*

of no ultimate value. But it is mistaken to think of this purification as a suppression of Sex, for it is really a sublimation of Sex, the transmutation of this powerful energy from the physical to the spiritual plane and of individual to universal love. Bodily contact with other beings gives way to spiritual union—the sage *seems* to hold aloof from others but is really in close harmony with all that lives, while the sensualist, though seeming to be in contact with others, is actually separated from them. It is a simple turning of the balance.

The same idea is to be found in Yoga. The vital force (*Kundalini*) is raised from the sacral plexus (*Muladhara*), which is the sexual nerve-centre, and passed up the spinal canal (*Sushumna*) into the brain where it manifests its activities on the highest plane of spirituality. Mahayana Buddhism hints at the same process—the sublimation of Sex from the physical to the spiritual—in its teachings on the Heavens of Desire.[3] The higher the plane of existence the more spiritualized does sexual activity become; in the first heaven (Shi-Tenno-Ten) marriage is similar to marriage on earth, while in the second (Sanjiu-san-Ten) procreation is effected by a simple embrace and in the third (Emma-Ten) by the gentlest touch. So sublimated does the process become that in the sixth (Take-jizai-Ten) a new being may be produced simply by the power of thought. And in the meantime the love of man for woman, which indeed is beautiful, has become transformed into something so much more beautiful that it defies all power of description.

But for ordinary beings such as ourselves, who have not yet attained such heights of perfection, some of the conceptions of Bhakti-Yoga will prove more interesting and useful. I refer to systems outside those outlined in the Pali Canon because most Buddhists will probably agree that the Buddha (from a modern point of view) did not deal adequately

[3]*See Lafcadio Hearn,* Gleanings in Buddha-Fields, *p. 208, 1927 edn.*

with the subject of Sex. Most primitive peoples give their children a far more thorough education in the subject than is given to-day, and it may be that for this reason the Buddha refrained from giving as detailed a treatment of the matter as we should like.[4] But in Mr. Claude Bragdon's recent book, *An Introduction to Yoga* (a book remarkable for its sanity and its avoidance of the dangerous aspects of the system), the reader will find much valuable information on the Yoga attitude to the relationship between man and woman. It is suggested that in every male there is a certain half-developed female element, and this incompleteness causes him to seek rectification by union with woman, and *vice versa*. This attainment of inner balance, this completion of the partly formed element, is held to be one of the stages on the Path, to be achieved by real and vital love for a member of the opposite sex. When the man has completed his feminine and the woman her masculine aspect the necessity for this type of love no longer exists and both are prepared for higher stages of the Path, and they will be born into conditions where the sublimation of Sex is comparatively easy and harmless, having learnt the lesson which terrestrial love has to teach them. This teaching is probably rooted in the belief common in many parts of the world that our distant ancestors were dual-sexed—an idea which may contain much esoteric truth[5]—and that at some far off date the sexes are destined to unite once again. In the words of Aristophanes, ''After the division the two parts of man, each desiring his other half, came together, and throwing their arms about one another, entwined in mutual embraces, longing to grow into one; they were on the point of dying from hunger and self-neglect, because they did not like to do anything apart . . . Human nature was originally one and we

---

[4]*See Ernest Crawley's* Mystic Rose, *and Seabrook's* Jungle Ways.
[5]*See Blavatsky's* Secret Doctrine.

were a whole, and *the desire and pursuit of the whole is called love.*"[6]

In the East there has never existed a "Sex Problem" on the scale in which it exists in the West, and it is mostly for this reason that it has not been dealt with as fully as we might wish by the Eastern philosophers. Our puritanism has made us look upon Sex as something infinitely more serious than our other natural functions; it has been regarded as something essentially ugly, as something pertaining exclusively to man's lower nature. But in the East, though there too there are prostitutes and sexual excesses, man's desire for a woman's embraces is not looked upon as an evil. Courtesans exist just as caterers exist, and the Eastern courtesan is infinitely superior to the Western harlot because she is not a despised outcast, not a dealer in sin associating with those who imagine that they are doing something evil, but a person with a certain artistic charm. We do not feel ashamed of ourselves when we delight our senses with a beautiful picture; why should we feel ashamed when we delight them with a beautiful woman? The only evil in Sex comes through excess (as in eating or listening to music), but in the West we make an additional evil by an irrational and inconsistent condemnation of its pleasures.

[6]*From Plato's* Symposium.

# BUDDHISM
# IN THE MODERN WORLD

From *Buddhism in England*
*March–April, 1934*

•

## IV. Buddhism and War

Looking through some back numbers of *Buddhism in England* I found on pp. 21, 44 and 67 of Vol. VI, some interesting correspondence on the subject of Buddhism and War aroused by a paragraph in Prof. Suzuki's *Outlines of Mahayana Buddhism* which reads: "The first Precept, for instance, forbids the killing of any living being, but the Bodhisattva will not hesitate to go to war if he considers the cause he espouses is right and will ultimately be beneficial to humanity at large." This masterpiece of casuistry was replied to in a letter from "G.H.Y.," provoking an answer from "Haereticus" who took up a position which seems to be popular among a large number of Buddhists—namely that in time of peace one should do all in one's power to promote peace-movements, but when faced with War it would be quite possible to fight in a just cause and still remain a Buddhist. Before I go any further with this interesting subject I must make it quite clear again as in the article on *Buddhism and Politics* that I do not write with the authority of Buddhism as a whole behind me. The fundamental ideas expressed may be absolutely Buddhist, but "the string that ties them," my own application of them to modern problems, my own reasoning, is not *necessarily* Buddhist, although I shall attempt to show that it is quite in accord with the spirit of the Dhamma. Buddhism does not, as

Haereticus points out, *compel* its adherents to accept any particular dogma.

I fully realize that it is almost impossible to deal adequately with so controversial a subject as this in one short article, but in the hope of provoking further thought and discussion I shall try to lay down a few reasons why no true Buddhist should adopt the casuistical course of going to war "for the good of humanity," but why everyone who has the interests of his fellow men at heart should refrain from fighting under all circumstances. The usual pacifist arguments will not be used; they are hardly Buddhist arguments since their aim is either to produce a violent anti-war fanaticism by filling men with terror at the prospect of warfare aided by the latest scientific discoveries—in other words by pandering to the instinct of fear—or else by attacking patriotism, which is a merely negative argument, having no weight beside the contention that a man should work and fight for his own family or friends—a contention which is at least positive and human. To aim at instilling mankind with a violent fear of war is to run a great risk of producing hysteria. If on the eve of a future war people were suddenly made to realize the horrors of a gas-attack from the air, there would be a panic resulting from hysterical terror; it is only one step from hysteria to violence and the old fallacy of "a war to end war" which contains about as much sense as a crime to end crime, a debauch to end debauchery or a hate to end hatred. Nor will the sentimental, "sob-stuff" pacifism so common to-day find much sympathy among Buddhists. The path to Peace is not a path of roses but a path of thorns which sentimentalists will find difficult to tread; it will be hard enough for those who are not sentimental, for true Pacifism is the path of realists, of men who understand how great is the price to be paid for Peace and who are prepared to pay it at all costs.

Taking Pacifism to mean the refusal to take part in any war whether fought in a just or unjust cause, we find that there are three main arguments against it. Firstly, that human nature being what it is, war is almost inevitable for the time being, and until such time as humanity is prepared for Peace a man must fight for his country in a just cause to preserve the *status quo*; secondly, that all those who wish for Peace should be ready to go to war with any nation which attempts to upset the peace by an act of aggression; and thirdly, that it is the duty of every man to protect, if necessary by slaughter, his family and his friends from the tyranny of an invader. This last argument is the only one that is really formidable, because it is based on what is to some extent a noble motive and because it is a human argument, while the other two are little more than bad reasoning. As a typical example of the first I shall take a passage from Haereticus' letter: "The true soldier is one who prepares for war only that he may be in a position to keep the peace. But until the world as a whole is ready for universal peace, it is only one out of touch with the realities of life who says 'there never is a righteous reason for war.'" If such a one is out of touch with the realities of life, Haereticus is out of touch with the faculty of foresight. He is one of that multitude of "idealists" who speak vaguely of the time when the world shall be ready for universal peace, of the time when human nature shall have made a decided change for the better, without realizing that these changes are not brought about merely by preaching love for humanity or by organizing "leagues of nations," but by setting an example by desisting from war and other evils *here and now* whatever the sacrifice required. For compromise in this matter is useless; we must not talk peace to the world and then go and fight someone who doesn't agree and who thinks it would be a good idea to upset our ideals by force. To give any strength to our arguments our conduct must be consistent with them. It is futile to say to the world, "We stand for universal peace, and anyone who doesn't agree with us will be punished by warfare," because war can never be a punishment and for two reasons: first, that history has shown that a defeated nation never considers its punishment just because it is always under the delusion that it went to war for a righteous cause; and second, that warfare can never be permanently checked by counter-warfare. And this brings us to the second argument against Pacifism, namely that Peace must be preserved by fighting those who attempt to disturb it.

If someone swears at you in the street, do you stop him by swearing back? If you have tried this way, you may have noticed that so far from stopping the swearing, the volley of abuse increases and that each side tried to get the mastery by making the language louder and coarser. It is almost exactly the same with war. One nation attacks and the other resists, perhaps checking it for the moment by inventing superior tactics or armaments. But the aggressor soon finds even better tactics and armaments, and so the competition continues until warfare becomes an orgy of destruction bringing ruin to both sides, and ceases to be in any way chivalrous or sportsman-like. Now let us suppose that one party refuses to fight, and not only refuses to fight but decides to meet the torrent of hatred with the only thing that can possibly overcome it—namely love. Supposing the aggressor is met with this challenge: "Come on, shoot me. It's quite easy, and there's nothing to be proud of because I'm not going to stop you. You won't be able to boast to the world that you fought valiantly in a just cause and the war will bring you no glory. You can do your worst—enslave my men, rape my women and massacre my children. But you will only make a fool of yourself, gain a bad reputation and behave like the coward that you are!" That nation would probably have to make terrible sacrifices, but its example would be a far greater victory for Peace than a humiliation of the enemy by armed resistance—that is, if humanity is susceptible to such an example. Yet even if this rebuke found no sympathetic response from the rest of the world it would not have been made in vain, for the slaughtered people would come back to earth in the cycle of rebirth to make that sacrifice again and again until humanity took their example to heart and followed it. But killing solves nothing. You may slay the bodies of evil men but their karma you cannot slay; you can only show them how to slay it for themselves. If you wipe out the offending nation with machine-guns and gas-bombs, that nation will return to earth with its karma unfulfilled and increased in intensity by resistance. It is like cutting back a hedge; the more you cut the harder it grows. And what a karma of war we have now inherited because we did not return love for hatred long ago! It is a law of mechanics that no force can be checked unless it comes into contact with another force acting in the opposite direction; armed opposition is not the opposite force to armed aggression—it is a kindred force—and the Buddha explained this over two thousand years ago when he said, "Hatred ceases not by hatred alone; hatred ceases but by love."

And so we come to the final argument against Pacifism—the defence of innocent women and children. To call them innocent is to beg the question. If a man slays someone who attacks his wife, she is not innocent of that deed if she willingly saw him killed and made no attempt to stay her husband's hand. And however much we may dislike to admit it, the children too share in that guilt through evil karma created in past lives, which caused them to be born into such circumstances. So are we all just to sit down and be killed? It is not a matter of "just sitting down and being killed"; it is not what we appear to do that counts, but what we *think*. If we "turn the other cheek" to the enemy with thoughts of hatred in our minds we are no further than before; but if it is with thoughts of love our action is given an entirely different value. The Westerner will ask, "And what good can mere thoughts do?" The Buddhist knows that thoughts are the most powerful forces in the world, and that they count for far more than deeds, for "all that we are is the result of what we have thought; it is founded on our thoughts; it is made up of our thoughts." But let us make our actions consistent with them, and above all let us not be led into the delusion that our actions do not matter at all.

Yet I do not imagine that these things can be brought about at once; a whole nation will not suddenly sacrifice itself in this manner, for such changes are only brought about by degrees and it remains for a few individuals to "set the ball rolling" not only by preaching against evil, by starting movements against it, or by setting up high ideals—all these things must be done and we must not forget them in our enthusiasm for another aspect of the struggle—but in addition we must deal with these evils here and now by dazzling them with good, by returning love for hatred and not be content to wait until this can be done with safety. Safety is not offered, nor even success for those who would start out upon this adventure, but only suffering, frustration, scorn and abuse. It is a burden to be borne without thanks or reward, and strange to say, no one in the world can explain to those who have not shouldered the burden for themselves why it is at all worth bearing. Let him take it up who dares.

However, Pacifism—in the sense of refusal to take part in warfare—is not by itself a solution to the problem. Indeed I may perhaps be guilty along with the vast majority of pacifists of giving it too much emphasis. For it must always be remembered that the principle which lies behind it— that of overcoming hatred with love—is of primary importance, and we must not lose sight of the fact that Pacifism is not only a course of action to be adopted at the outbreak of war, but a constructive movement to build up Peace and to see that Peace is not regarded as an end in itself, but as a means to a more fruitful life.

### In Conclusion

And so we come to the end of what has, of course,

been a totally inadequate survey of but four of the great problems which confront the world at the present day. But the articles were not intended as an exhaustive treatment of these vast subjects, nor even to provide solutions for the questions raised. As stated at the outset, their aim was to arouse further discussion and treatment of themes which modern Buddhists have been rather inclined to overlook in their zeal for studying Buddhist history and literature, and I trust they will move more capable writers with a wider experience of these matters than myself to make a special effort to show that Buddhism and the Wisdom of the East as a whole is not a dead system of doctrine or a philosophy for dreamers, but a living force which has a definite message for the modern world. Perhaps Buddhists who have expert knowledge in these various subjects will lend a helping hand, but at all costs we must prove the Dhamma to be a thing of the present and the future as well as of the past, by studying, discussing and writing on the problems of today from the Buddhist point of view. And finally (of course we have all heard this before) we must prove the value of Buddhism by living it. It is not sufficient to refrain from eating meat, killing animals and fighting in wars or to make much ado about all the external behaviour of the Buddhist. The Buddha did not point out a Way for cranks, for those who are obsessed with virtues of secondary importance; he emphasized the fact that our first concern must be with our thoughts, and that it is far more important to be virtuous in the mind than to be anxious to show off our virtues in action. As is said in the *Tao-teh-King*, "The highest Grace makes no pose of Grace, and for this reason really is Grace; whilst the lower quality of Grace may never divest itself of Grace, and yet never feels like true Grace."[1] It will be said that all this is so many platitudes, it is always being said and has been said much too often. I have often thought that

---

[1]Tao-teh-King. Trans. Prof. Parker, p. 24.

"platitude" is a name given to an inconvenient truth in order to make it appear futile. If these old sayings seem trite and uninteresting it is probably because we have only accepted them as catch-phrases and have never troubled to see how much they involve. One is bound to tire of the mere repetition of a truth simply because it is a string of words and little more; but only those who listen to these old sayings without thinking about them or putting them into practice will call them platitudes; they appear to be obvious and almost naive, but therein is their profundity, for the fool is too proud to examine simple things.

I can think of no better conclusion for this series of articles than to quote a passage from Professor Radhakrishnan's *Kalki* which seems to sum up all that I have tried to say. He writes:—

> *Man is neither the slave of circumstance nor the blind sport of the gods. The impulse to perfection working in the universe has become self-conscious in him. Progress happened in the sub-human world: it is willed in the human. Conscious purpose takes the place of unconscious variations. Man alone has the unrest consequent on the conflict between what he is and what he can be. He is distinguished from other creatures by his seeking after a rule of life, a principle of progress. It is by transforming ourselves that we shall be able to transform the world. The soul of all improvement, it has been rightly said, is the improvement of the soul.*

Yet while we strive in this present time to make of ourselves fit instruments for the service of Man, it will be well for us to "consider the Tao of Old in order to arrange the affairs of Now."

# IS BUDDHISM SERIOUS?

From *Buddhism in England*
Sept.–Oct., 1935

●

You may have noticed that those who talk most about their internal organisms are those who suffer from indigestion. In the best society this is "not done," not because they feel that it is an indignity to possess anything so degrading as a stomach, but because they have better things to talk about. A glance at the daily papers is sufficient to show that society is unusually pre-occupied with its internal organism, for the most important columns are concerned entirely with the troubles of its economic stomach and the palpitations of its political heart. In fact the papers read so much like a gastronomic journal that I look forward to the day when it will be just as "not done" to mention economics in polite society as it is to talk of one's digestive mechanism in a drawing-room. Yet the obvious indigestion of society is rooted in the deeper indigestion of the individuals who make up the body politic. It is revealed in the individual's obsession with his "ego." For the distinction between "I" and "Life" can only arise when there is disharmony between the two, for if the "I" were in harmony with life we should no more be conscious of its existence than we are conscious of our internal organs when they are functioning in order. In the same way, if you would listen to music or read a book you must not allow the concept of yourself listening or reading to occupy the mind while it should be engaged on the music and the book.

Now there is something comic about people who talk incessantly about their indigestion, for their disorder has produced the illusion that the stomach is the most important thing in life, and it is incongruities of this kind which lie at the root of the comic. Little things are funny when they pretend to be big, and *vice versa*, and nowhere is there a more important instance of this than in the behaviour of the ego, which puffs itself up with the conceit that it is eternal and that it is the centre of the whole universe. Investigation will show that all religions which are concerned with the eternal salvation of this ego are grave and serious, since they are unable to teach men how to make light of themselves, when it is believed that a man's ultimate safety is the most important thing in life.

Buddhism is *par excellence* the religion of seeing the joke about the ego, because it can see the comic side of this small illusion pretending to be a great reality. For Buddhism has a view of life which is based upon an acute sense of proportion, and to the extent that this is another name for a sense of humour Buddhism is by no means a serious religion. Right from the start it dethrones the ego from its dignity by saying that it does not exist. It views the world from the intuitive mind which blends "I" and "Life" into a single harmony, while the "discriminative" mind cuts it up into intricate discords. As is said in the *Lankavatara Sutra*, "The discriminating mind is a dancer and a magician with the objective world as his stage. Intuitive mind is the wise jester who travels with the magician and reflects upon his emptiness and transiency."

# THE GENIUS OF CHINA
## Notes on the International Exhibition of Chinese Art

From *Buddhism in England*
*Jan.–Feb., 1936*

●

At first you see only the top of its head, but as you go further up the steps into the exhibition galleries at Burlington House, the whole figure comes into view. It is a towering statue of the Buddha Maitreya (2360)* standing in the central gallery and looking down upon all who come into this treasure house of 3,000 years of Chinese Art. The head of this figure reaches almost to the roof and its weight must be immense because it is carved out of solid marble. But such was the genius of the sculptor that it appears to be light enough to stand on clouds, and the long slender body is so perfectly poised on its lotus pedestal that it looks as if it would rise at any moment into the "middle air." And from a height of nearly twenty feet one is gazed upon and refreshed by a face which tells of the peace past all understanding.

Is this just sentimental unreality? Certainly it is if one does not remember that this peace is only attained after tremendous struggle. Walk up to this figure and turn right into the Lecture Room where the Buddhist sculpture is displayed. Here is a coloured pottery image of a Lohan (2438), similar in style to the one in the British Museum. He is looking slightly to one side, and if you stand so that you can see

* *Catalogue numbers are given in brackets.*

straight into his eyes you will see not only peace and compassion but profound insight and a vast reserve of power. If the figure were not so large it might easily be mistaken for a living man in a dim light, so natural is the position and so exquisite the workmanship. Yet this exhibition does not contain only things that are peaceful and quiet. At the far end of this room is a cast-iron figure of a temple guardian (2394). It is so rough that the artist has not even troubled to remove the marks left by the mould in which it was cast, but this only adds to its elemental strength. The face is almost negroid, the muscles are over-developed and one fist, grasping a loop of rope, is clenched against its huge chest. It is the absolute personification of force.

Now pass into the next room and look to your right. High up in the near corner you will see a curious gilded image of the Buddha (640) with his chin resting on his hands, which are clasped over one knee. Nobody seems to pay very much attention to him, and while they are busy with all the other objects shown below him, he looks down on their heads with a huge grin. The person who arranged this exhibition (it was Mr. Leigh Ashton) must have a most pleasing sense of humour.

Passing out of this room to the left we come to the first gallery of the Sung Dynasty. There are four galleries devoted to this Dynasty, and to appreciate them properly would require several days in each. Therefore I can only mention three or four of the astonishing collection of paintings produced by the artists of this Golden Age of Chinese Culture when Zen Buddhism was at its zenith. Firstly (although this is of later date than the Sung period) there is Ku An's picture of "Bamboos and Rocks" (1130). This is so beautiful that I hesitate to say anything about it. Yet at the same time it has none of that cold beauty which is found in Western masterpieces. That is to say it is not so absolutely perfect and complete that there is no scope for the beholder's imagination, for the particular genius of the Chinese painters was their power of suggestion. With a religious background of Taoism and Zen they held that the absolutely perfect was the same as the absolutely dead, for it was no longer capable of growth and development. Therefore the function of the artist is not to create a picture which is complete and finished in itself, but to suggest something which will rouse the beholder's imagination and so initiate a living process. The picture does not end with the artist. With a few lightning strokes of his brush, without stopping to correct, delete or overpaint, and with a vital spontaneity he transfers the unceasing and elusive movement of Life, the Tao, to paper or silk. That movement goes on in the beholder's mind where it leaves off in the picture, and the result is that the picture invites you to come and take part in its own life. It does not exclude you, making you a mere admirer, by being so complete that there is nothing left for you to do but to whisper, "How marvelous!"

Thus, "Bamboos and Rocks" suggests a fierce blast of wind, sweeping through the leaves and scattering the mist. Then there is a long scroll by Ma Fên—"The Hundred Geese" (1387)—which is carried out in the same spirit of suggestiveness. I cannot imagine a more satisfying picture of geese, and yet each one is executed with the greatest economy of brush strokes; the pond over which they are flying is simply indicated by the presence of rushes and slight wavy lines where one or two geese swim and dive. Ma Yuan's "Boating by Moonlight" (1163) is again sublimely reticent, with the dim outline of a hill in the background and the frail boat resting on the mist-covered water. The moon is nowhere to be seen, yet it is undoubtedly there. You should also be careful to look out Mu Chi's "Two Sparrows on a Bamboo Branch" (1117), Hsia Ch'ang's "Bamboos Seen Through a Window" (1371), Ma Yuan's "Gazing at the Moon" (996), and Yen Hui's "Indifferent to Cold and Snow" (1223). By this time you will have seen far too much for one day,* although you must have a look at the ivory carving of the Taoist sage Hsu Yu (2943) in the Large South Room. He was so wise that the Emperor asked him to be Prime Minister, a request which he respectfully declined. When the imperial envoys had departed he was so afraid of the pollution that might result from hearing such a message that he was careful to wash both his own ears and those of the ox on which he was riding. From the look on his face I should say he invented that story himself. At any rate, he's certainly got some joke in his mind.

* *There are 3,080 exhibits.*

# PART THREE

*The Early Writings of Alan Watts*

# THE EDITOR
# WRITES . . .

# PART THREE

A wonderful year for the budding Alan Watts was 1936, and among the good things that fortune bestowed upon him then was the editorship of *Buddhism in England*. He was still only twenty-one but had a remarkable track record as a writer already, to cap which his first full-length book, *The Spirit of Zen*, had just been eagerly snapped up by John Murray, the publishers, for their Wisdom of the East series. As for editorial skills, he had been developing those working both on *Buddhism in England* and on Mitrinovic's *The Eleventh Hour*; in addition, he had also been studying the typographic techniques of the great Catholic artist-craftsman Eric Gill, whose enthusiasm for integrating sexuality and spirituality may also have influenced him.[1] In heralding Watts as the new Editor, Christmas Humphreys commented on his youth, but noted that, as he himself had only been twenty-three when he had founded the Buddhist Lodge, there was a precedent, "if not for like ability, at least for like enthusiasm." He went on:

> *As is to be expected, our new Editor is full of ideas for promoting the sales and importance of the Magazine, and we await with interest the opening number of volume eleven, which is timed for Wesak day. Valete, Mr. A. C. March. Salve, Mr. Watts.*

Among those whom Watts published in the journal during the next two years may be counted Dr. D. T. Suzuki, the man who arguably more than any other can be credited with first bringing knowledge of Zen Buddhism to the West; his American wife, Beatrice Lane Suzuki, whose special interest lay in Mahayana Buddhism in general; Christmas Humphreys; Sohaku Ogata, a Japanese who had been head monk of a Zen Buddhist monastery in Kyoto and who for many years helped Western students of Zen in Japan; Clare Cameron (née Burke), basically a Christian, who nevertheless worked and wrote enthusiastically for the journal and eventually took over the mantle of Editor when Watts finally departed for the United States; the great French mystic, Madame Alexandra David-Neel, who had travelled extensively in Tibet; Sir Francis Younghusband, in 1904 the leader of a British expeditionary force to Lhasa in Tibet, and later the founder of the World Congress of Faiths; G. Constant Lounsbery, an American lady Buddhist who founded *Les Amis du Bouddhisme* in Paris in 1929; Ronald Nicholson, one of Toby Humphreys's contemporaries at Cambridge, who became *sadhu* Krishna Prem; Mrs. Caroline Rhys Davids, a pioneer Pali scholar; and a German refugee orientalist and philosopher named Frederic Spiegelberg who in the 1950s was to invite Watts to join his American Academy of Asian Studies in San Francisco. Watts also published in part form a new translation of the *Tao Te Ching* by Ch'u Ta-kao, a Chinese who turned up at the Lodge. Nepotism crept in too: he published his own father, Laurence W. Watts, who had followed him into the Buddhist Lodge and who became its Hon. Treasurer. And of course he also published Alan Watts—and in quantity. The first issue that he edited, that for May/June 1936, in addition to an editorial, news and notes, carried a lengthy book review by Watts himself and two substantial articles.

The assumption of the editorship was an auspicious moment for Watts to inaugurate a new series of articles in *Buddhism in England*; accordingly his first issue contained Part One of "On the Meaning of Symbols," published under the pseudonym "Interpreter." In that and the subsequent three issues, he examined the symbols of the Lotus, Wind and Water, Fire, and Man, Woman and Child. When the series was later reissued as a pamphlet by the Buddhist Lodge, it was prefaced with the famous quotation from the second part of Goethe's *Faust*:

*Alles Vergängliche*
*Ist nur ein Gleichnis*[2]

The pamphlet was also dedicated to Richard Anthony
Weeks, an old schoolfriend of Watts who had followed him
into Buddhism. In his autobiography, Watts describes Weeks
as "a still river, running at great depth," and he recalls their
pleasant strolls together in the Kent countryside or in the
precincts of Canterbury Cathedral, when they discussed
poetry, religion, philosophy—and magic, to which Weeks
was particularly drawn. He later pursued this interest in earnest by joining a secret group in London, but got badly burnt
when he woke up one night to find himself under the evil
eye of a "Presence of unfathomable malice and horror." He
promptly joined the Catholic Church, but when Watts met
him many years later he had apparently got over the trauma
and had transferred his loyalties to Sufism.

"On the Meaning of Symbols" represents the first
major work by Watts that places primary focus on psychology, an area in which he was particularly interested from
a young age. Indeed, the two main pillars of his life and work
might be said to be Buddhism (especially Zen Buddhism)
and psychology, and he made efforts to build bridges
between the two, which he regarded as mutually complementary. By his own account, he had been reading the
works of the great Swiss psychoanalyst, Carl Gustav Jung,
while he was still at King's school, and when he became
a young brahmin-about-town in London, many of his mentors and friends were either involved or interested in psychology. Dmitrije Mitrinovic, for instance, besides his other
concerns, was studying the psychotherapeutic techniques
of Alfred Adler and Trigant Burrow, and had evolved a primitive form of the encounter group. Watts participated in the
sessions of one of these groups for some months, during

which "we resolutely destroyed and rebuilt each other's personalities." Watts was also friendly with a "more-or-less Jungian" Dutch psychiatrist named Philip Metman, and with Eric Graham Howe, another psychiatrist with consulting rooms in London's most prestigious medical enclave, Harley Street, and cosy living quarters in the mews behind.[3] Watts was not on his roster of patients; Howe was just a "genial, dignified and reassuring doctor who let me in on his mind." Howe wrote books: *I and Me* and *War Dance*. Watts reviewed the latter in *Buddhism in England*, and his review identifies certain themes that can also be traced in "On the Meaning of Symbols;"

> *The very existence of life depends on the existence of opposites—joy and pain, living and dying, good and evil. The first form of aggressiveness is to cling to one opposite and reject the other, to imagine that pain, death and evil are. . . "Bad Things" which must be crushed and eliminated with the greatest possible speed and thoroughness. . . .*
>
> *Dr. Howe's constructive theme is that we should learn, firstly, not to be so warlike towards the Devil—in other words to welcome and accept the dark side of life in the same way as the tree extends its roots into the dark earth. . . .*

There is also a "dark side" in every human being:

> *By ordinary moral standards this dark side includes much that is thought Bad, as for instance those uncontrollable impulses of fear, hatred and desire. Yet the author wisely points out that far worse than being afraid is the fear of being afraid, and the fear of the fear of being afraid. For this flight from fact involves us in what he terms "infinite regress," an*

*increasingly panic-stricken attempt to avoid
the karma of our folly, to save ourselves from
the salutary condition of accepting our guilt
and imperfection.*

Watts's essay on the meaning of the symbol of the
lotus immediately raises the matter of duality, for the pristine flower that the eye beholds has its roots sunk deeply
in the "primaeval slime." So, too, our conscious life has a
complementary unconscious that runs exceedingly deep. It
embraces personal contents, plus racial and even cosmic ones
as well. And just as the lotus needs its roots and draws
nourishment from them, so too we must accept the entirety
of the unconscious, including its apparently dark contents,
for it is the wellspring of all that gives us life. All of which
implies, of course, that it is foolish to strive after a kind of
perfect but essentially disembodied spirituality cut off from
the complementary earthly side of our natures. The truly
transformative path is the path of wholeness: the one that
integrates both the light and the dark sides, that puts each
in right relation to the other.

The essay on the meaning of the symbols of wind and
water, on the other hand, stresses that life is process: always
moving and essentially impermanent. The person who
wishes for permanence, who yearns to possess any of the
forms of life, will only succeed in killing the winged joy
as it flies. The true sage is he who contemplates the dance
of life and loves it for its ever-changing play of ephemeral
forms.

The third essay, on the symbol of fire, deals with passion and desire—things that both give life and destroy it.
Because of their destructive aspect, many fear them and seek
to cut them out of their lives. This is as negative a response
as it would be, say, to eschew the use of actual fire because
of the possibility of getting one's fingers burnt. Rather, the
challenge is to learn how to use fire—and hence passion and

desire—correctly: to be masters of them and so allow their creative potentialities to flower. The ascetic path is for those who have become masters of passion and desire in this way, not for those who would run away from them in fear . . . here again counsel for an integrated, holistic approach to life.

In his preamble to the fourth and final essay in the series on symbols, on man, woman and child, Watts deals at length with the warring pairs of opposites that apparently bedevil human life. The agony is all of the mind's making, he contends, for it is forever one-sidedly opting for one of any pair of opposites and striving to annihilate its complement, thereby hoping to place itself in a controlling position—a futile undertaking in any case. What needs to happen is for the opposites to be harmonized. This can be done by accepting them and understanding their mutual dependence and their mutual creativity, for out of each pair a "Higher Third" may arise. In the case of man and woman, this is the child that gives meaning to their union. On a higher level, there is also a Holy Child that may emerge from the union of life and death. Acceptance and understanding of the apparently warring dualities brings mastery—but here the great danger of inflation arises. In order to avoid this, the sage renounces his victory and surrenders himself in humble acceptance of the world as it is.

In reviewing the pamphlet version of the series, retitled *Seven Symbols of Life*, Christmas Humphreys commented perceptively on Watts's style and originality (or lack of it) when he wrote:

> *The writer, as readers of this Magazine know well, has an unusual style of his own combining an impetuous exuberance of diction with a stark clarity of thought, which causes one of two reactions. At times one is as suspicious of his whirlwind conclusions as of Shaw's famous*

*Prefaces; at other times he stumbles without warning on profound ideas which, if not new, at least are presented in a novel way, and therefore have the force of newness. The latter faculty is here exemplified. As studies of the inner meanings of universal symbols, only the first, the Lotus, is carefully worked out, and there is stuff in this which deserves a better resting-place than the usual limbo of old magazines[4]. . . .*

Also in the first issue of *Buddhism in England* that he edited (May/June 1936), Watts started a new regular feature, "Letters I Receive," which was intended as a vehicle for offering general replies to questions that had arisen in correspondence from readers. In those days the duties of the editor of the journal went beyond mere editorial matters. He had to be a kind of spiritual Agony Aunt and give advice to isolated Buddhists on their problems: what to read, how to understand particular Buddhist teachings, etc. The first of these features was subtitled *The "What" and the "How"* and dealt with a classic spiritual teaser: it is all very well to talk or write very plausibly about profound spiritual matters, but how is one to get beyond words and concepts and achieve genuine realisation in one's own life? Actually, Watts does not seem overburdened with ready answers. In fact, he even goes so far as to admit that he's still struggling himself. He does, however, hint that there's virtue in the quest itself, and also throws in the old adage that we all have a Buddha in us—if only we can find it.

In the "Letters I Receive" feature in the next issue of the journal, Watts applied the notion of the warring pairs of opposites to War itself, which he says was then the matter uppermost in people's minds. He dismisses the more obvious explanations of the causes of modern war—that it may result from economic motives, for instance—and instead declares that its principal cause is now psychological: the sudden explosion of collectively repressed irrational desires. In more primitive societies there were special rites that acted as safety valves for those desires, but they have been lost in modern society, which makes the impossible demand that its citizens be unremittingly civilized—with periodically disastrous results. Thus, people and societies swing back and forth between the poles of civility and barbarity, peace and war, etc. There might be a solution, however, Watts suggests, if instead of allowing themselves to be helpless victims of this pendulum situation, people were to withdraw to a "Higher Third": a centre of being detached from the opposites. This is the "place" (no-place?) where buddhas take their stand, and the idea is in fact quite central to Buddhism. It has also crept into Jungian and other psychoanalytic theory. Essential to it is the notion of being an observer—of being Buddha: "the one who knows." Thus when material rises from the subconscious, instead of identifying with it and being swept away reactively by it, one just allows it to rest in consciousness and it thereby loses its compulsive character. This is the proverbial "making the darkness conscious."

One of the especially exciting events that took place in 1936, that *annus mirabilis* for the young Watts, was the meeting of the World Congress of Faiths that was held at London University. The Congress was the brainchild of Sir Francis Younghusband, an old British Imperialist warhorse who in 1904 had won national glory as the conqueror of Lhasa. One might expect such a man to have been an insensitive and highly unspiritual jingoist, preoccupied mainly with swilling whiskey, abusing natives and slaughtering wild game. Actually, the opposite was the case. Younghusband was highly spiritual and sensitive; so much so, in fact, that he had a profound mystical experience while he was riding in the mountains just outside Lhasa, the Tibetan capital. He also had a deep respect for the spirituality of the peoples both of that country and of India, China, and Mongolia, among whom he had lived and worked. "Perhaps . . . I may have caught a little of the spirit of Buddhism," he wrote in "A Message to the Buddhist World[5]" published at this time, recalling in particular the intense enthusiasm he had experienced reading a book on Buddhism while exploring in the Himalayas in 1889. When he had met a Russian explorer a few weeks later, he had insisted he take the book (it was Monier-Williams's *Buddhism*) and have it translated when he got home. "What has struck me in travelling through Buddhist lands and conversing with Buddhist people is the atmosphere of serenity and calm which surrounds them." He had found this same gentleness and composure among the leading Buddhists of Lhasa. True, he admitted, he met three men who had been commissioned to curse him for a week; but when they found out that he had not come to destroy their religion their attitude completely changed:

> *They were most warm in their attitude to me. They showed me round the great monasteries. They invited me to attend a service in the Cathedral [the Jokhang]. And on my leaving Lhasa, the Regent [the Tri Rimpoche of Ganden monastery] presented me with a little figure of the Buddha and asked me to think kindly of Tibet.*

Watts loudly publicized the Congress in the columns of *Buddhism in England* and proclaimed the Lodge's wholehearted support for it:

> *. . . particularly because of the very realistic attitude of those who are responsible for it. For they declare that its main object is not an appraisement of the various religions, still less an attempt to merge them into one. It is a world fellowship in which each fellow will be allowed full play for his own distinctive*

*individuality, as only through recognizing differences can the closest unity be attained.*

Watts developed this theme in an address that he gave to that year's Wesak Meeting. It was reprinted in the journal as "The Truth that is More than Teaching," subtitled "An Appeal to Buddhists on the Occasion of the World Congress of Faiths." The Buddhists of the different schools and traditions should appreciate that they are ultimately united in something larger and greater than the sectarian differences that appear to divide them at the relative level. But this isn't to say that those differences should be swept away and that all Buddhists should merge in some standardized Buddhism. Watts sharply distinguishes here between *unity* and uniformity. Unity is not inimical to diversity; in fact it welcomes the flowering of individuated potential within a wider matrix which sees that "all forms have a common essence." Uniformity, on the other hand, is a manifestation of the totalitarian spirit[6] that would make everything boringly the same. That having been said, Watts goes on to counsel his readers not to place too much reliance upon the particular forms for which they have opted; also not to cling to beliefs. Buddhism is neither about belief nor does it encourage attachment to forms. It is ultimately about being liberated from all forms of clinging, including attachment to the *Buddhadharma* itself. Thus, "That road is the best upon which we feel we need depend least, for that road leads to nonattachment, to freedom from dependence."

Reporting in the "News and Notes" section of the next (September/October 1936) issue of *Buddhism in England*, Watts remarked that time alone would tell in what measure the recent session of the World Congress of Faiths, which had by then been and gone, had been successful in achieving the high ideals which it had set itself. In innumerable lesser ways, however, it had been a resounding success. Never, in fact, had "such a varied gathering of such highly intelligent and interesting people, people holding such diverse opinions and coming from so many different countries . . . managed to work together for a fortnight with so little animosity and so much friendliness." It had also afforded those who had attended it a unique opportunity for widening their personal contacts—and for Watts himself this meant one personal contact in particular. The World Congress had in fact allowed him at last to meet his primary literary mentor in Zen: Dr. D. T. Suzuki.

Daisetz Teitaro Suzuki (1870–1966) was a great *Dharma*-spreader and a great bridge-builder between East and West. Born into genteel poverty in Japan at a time when that country was undergoing great changes, various personal tragedies and difficulties had led him into Zen training at Engakuji, a temple in Kamakura, first under Kosen Roshi and then under his successor, Soyen Shaku. He had achieved deep insight into the meaning of the *koan Mu*[7] during the *Rohatsu Sesshin*[8] held at Engakuji in 1896. He had then departed for the United States, where he lived from 1897 to 1908, working for a religious publishing house. This gave him an opportunity for perfecting his English and studying Western religion, philosophy and culture, thus obtaining all the equipment necessary for introducing the West to the treasure-house of Mahayana Buddhism in general and Zen Buddhism in particular. He later returned to Japan but came back to the West many times during his long life—he lived to the age of ninety-five—and even when well advanced in years he undertook strenuous teaching programmes in the United States and Europe.

Suzuki was sent to London in 1936 by the Japanese Government as a kind of cultural ambassador. He was then sixty-six years old and fairly stole the show at the great public meeting held at the Queen's Hall on July 9, when the topic to which those invited to take the platform spoke was "The Supreme Spiritual Ideal:"

*As he sat on the platform listening to those
ahead of him speak, he seemed to be dozing.
When his turn came, the chairman had to
rouse him. This humorous distraction awoke
the whole audience to attention for his speech.
He started off by confessing that the phrase,
"Supreme Spiritual Ideal" meant nothing to
him. So instead of a lecture on Buddhism or
Zen, he started describing a typical Japanese
straw-thatched house. He spoke of how the
large windows opened into the garden, of how
the house and the garden are one; in fact, the
whole house and its occupant were one unit—
and "nature, you and I are one". . . . He told
about the trees, the fish, the water in the pool,
the straw mats on the floor, the flowers, the
hanging scroll on the wall. He implied that
through simple daily things one could find a
sense of oneness; for him the spiritual and the
material were one. He ended with the famous
story of "Joshu's Stone Bridge," which was but
a wooden plank over a stream. For those present at the meeting, Suzuki's talk was their first
experience of a living man of Zen. The impression he left behind was one of a small, frail,
elderly man with a memorable smile, infused
with a spiritual joy in life.[9]*

Suzuki was quite a hit with Watts too, who was
impressed with the readiness of this venerable Japanese sage
to listen to and learn from "those who know a mere fraction of what he knows," and with his very genuine
humility—a humility that "does not grovel." Suzuki also had
a simplicity that was blended with an engaging sense of
humour.

The other representative of Buddhism who spoke at
the World Congress was Dr. G. P. Malalasekera of Ceylon

[Sri Lanka]. Digests of the papers given by Malalasekera and by Suzuki appeared in Watts's review of the proceedings of the event, which were published under the title, "Faiths and Fellowship." We have reprinted this review in this section.

Watts turned to a perennial Buddhist enigma when he next composed a "Letters I Receive" feature for the journal. Subtitled "Is There a Self?," it deals with *anatta*, which is one of the Three Signs of Being (*alt.*: Three Marks of All Conditioned Things), a basic Buddhist doctrine. The two other Signs are: (1) *dukkha*, usually translated as suffering but meaning something wider than that—a general sense of unsatisfactoriness, of dis-ease, of things never being right; and (2) *anicca*—impermanence, the fact that everything is subject to change. *Anatta*, however, is rather more difficult for Westerners to grasp. It is usually translated as no soul or not self and in the case of human beings implies that there is no enduring personal essence, no substantial "I" underpinning the phenomenal person. What, then, is a person according to the Buddhist view? The answer is, just an aggregation of component parts—the physical vehicle, thoughts, emotions, etc.—all of them causally rather than self produced, and in themselves unstable, subject to continuous change both internally and in relation to each other. The root cause of suffering lies in that universal craving for personal existence that encourages the notion of an "I," with all its native desires and aversions and its various sectors of special interest designated "mine," to arise within these unstable aggregations. The cure that the Buddha prescribes is to disperse this spurious self identification by discouraging those habits ("selfish" habits) of body, speech, and mind that continually strive to substantiate the "I." But then the question arises: beyond "I"-what? Is there just nothing, in the sense of pure non-existence, perhaps? This would imply the Annihilationist view, which the Buddha consistently rejected. But to make things complicated he also rejected its opposite, the Eternalist view. In fact, the great teacher of men and gods tended to maintain the proverbial noble silence upon the matter of the ultimate transpersonal nature of the human being, which in Buddhism as elsewhere is regarded as identical with Ultimate Reality. He had perhaps seen how in the India of his own day ideas and opinions about this great mystery had tended to crystallise into rigid views that were all more or less mistaken, for Ultimate Reality can neither be grasped by conceptual thought nor accurately described in words. According to Buddhist doctrine it lies beyond all the conventional categories of the relative world—beyond all notion of "is" and "is not," of "existence" and "non-existence." It must be seen directly, realized by each person for themselves; then, we are assured, all the restless probings of the inquisitive mind will be put to rest once and for all.

One might suggest, therefore, that the *anatta* doctrine is essentially dialectical insofar as it functions to undermine the "I"-building disposition rather than to convey anything positively descriptive about the nature of Ultimate Reality. Put another way: instead of adding new concepts, *anatta* clears space in the mind and that potentially prepares the ground for direct insight into the ultimate enigma. And what a supremely elusive enigma it is, as Watts brings out so admirably towards the end of "Is There a Self?" To try to grasp it is like clutching at a slippery fish in dark waters: it shoots through one's fingers and vanishes back into the unknowable depths. And this is as it should be, for the greatest error is to think that one can catch it, i.e. grasp it conceptually. A good rule of thumb would seem to be: Whenever we think we know what it is, then . . . we've got it wrong . . . The only thing to do then, Watts argues, is to desist from chasing after it—and just *walk on!*[10]. This is a very Zen-like thing to say and may be appropriate in the right time and place. But even in the Zen school we find advice that, within the matrix of a system of practice, trainees should constantly conduct direct enquiry into their essential nature. This sort of enquiry (*enquiry*, note, as opposed to *speculation* or *discussion*) is not the same as mere self-preoccupation, for it leads beyond the personal, and, hence, if carried through to its conclusion, breaks rather than perpetuates the circles of *samsara*. In short, in the last paragraph of this piece Watts seems to be confusing discussion of the nature of and belief in a limited personal self (*atta*) with authentic spiritual enquiry, which is surely not something that the Buddha ever "advised us not to trouble about. . . ."

When Watts next composed a "Letters I Receive" feature, he elected to deal with the subject of *karma* and subtitled his piece, "Karma, or 'You Have What You Want'". *Karma* is a fundamental notion in the Buddhist-Vedantist religious continuum, and the word has even in recent years entered English parlance. Buddhism specifically denies any Prime Mover or external causative agency, but sees everything that happens in the universe as being the effect of preceding causes. *Karma* is the neutral law that governs the workings of cause and effect, but it is often popularly misconstrued as being quasi-judicial: a man "reaps what he sows." Watts rightly criticises this simplistic view, and points out its affinities with the concept of a "schoolmaster-God" that crops up in certain primitive forms of Christianity. He also criticises the view that *karma* implies a rigid determinism—which is natural enough, for, being a free spirit, he is dispositionally inclined to believe in free will. However, he finds it hard to establish a convincing case for free will and concedes that, in terms of hard logic, the determinists seem to have it much their own way. Actually, however, although he doesn't seem aware of it, Buddhism is on his side here. It does not deny free will or volition (*Pali: Cetana*). It is one of the seven mental factors inseparably bound up with all consciousness. Once an action has been freely performed, however, then the law of *karma* comes into force and the results are strictly *vipaka*: causally determined. If an action is not freely performed, on the other hand, then there are no karmic consequences. In a sense, therefore, *karma* could be said to *be* free will.

In the same item, Watts explores the derivation of the word *"karma"* and again rightly relates it to the root *kri* in the Sanskrit, which is often translated as "to do" or "to make." Finally, he goes on to appeal to depth psychology to reinforce an argument that *karma* is really getting what we secretly desire; and, if we get suffering, it is because at some deep, subconscious level, for veiled sado-masochistic reasons, we actually want to suffer. This inevitably begs certain questions. Do these subconscious desires really originate in "me?" If they are not fully conscious, how can "I" be said to choose them? How can we be sure that they don't originate *beyond* the personal strata of the subconscious psyche? In fact, there are strong grounds for arguing that I don't have these secret desires but that they have me! . . . The concept of *karma* is complex and deep, and although he raises some valid points about it and seems generally pointed in a constructive direction, Watts fails in this article to develop a thesis of any real depth or to arrive at any really convincing conclusions.

And so into 1937, the year in which Watts's second full-length book, *The Legacy of Asia and Western Man*, was published by John Murray. This was an altogether more ambitious work than *The Spirit of Zen* and sought to relate Eastern thought and mysticism to Christianity and "that young but swiftly growing science—Psychology." In reviewing the book in the November/December issue of *Buddhism in England*, Christmas Humphreys hailed it as superior to anything the Watts had yet written and suggested that at some future date it might be recognised as a transitional work between "the awkwardness of inexperience and the full maturity of style which is to come." He went on:

*The whole book is full—some might say a cosmos, some a chaos—of ideas, all of which are challenging, stimulating and provocative of deeper thought. . . . The author is here revealed as a modern to his intellectual finger tips, a mental child of to-day, impatient of the past, omnivorous of all experience and forgivably delighted in his own brilliance. . . .*

Humphreys was worried, however; the brilliance seemed "born of the metallic qualities of an intellect as yet but little warmed by the flame of compassion." Watts in fact spoke from the head, whereas the East spoke from the heart and its "greater depth of understanding is immeasurable." Still, with his usual generosity of spirit, Humphreys concluded: "A fine symphony, Mr. Editor; may its music echo far and wide."

A topic of general contemporary interest formed the subject of the "Letters I Receive" feature, "Education for Progress, with a Capital 'P'," that was published in the January/February 1937 issue of the journal. This was the materialistic bias that was becoming dominant in education—as indeed in most other departments of life. Watts argued that it was no good solely teaching the young utilitarian skills and inculcating desire for ever-increasing quantities of "things" in them; due concern should be given to quality, to the training of character, and the development of wisdom. The challenge was in fact not to produce successful business-men but successful human beings . . . . These arguments still carry force today, when we have gone even further down the materialist road and our less enlightened politicians and pundits openly call for institutions of education to teach only "useful" subjects—i.e., ones that are of merely economic use—and to abandon the old humanities. The latter, while not directly generating wealth, certainly generate profoundly useful social effects by producing numbers of citizens endowed with humane, enlightened and generally civilized qualities. The materialistic and utilitarian bias can only have a retrogressive effect on the actual quality of our societies in the long run.

We have included next an article that appeared in the March/April 1937 issue of *Buddhism in England* entitled "Not Only But Also." Here Watts begins by emphasising the profundity of the Buddha's teachings. One may think that one has intellectually grasped the meaning of the basic doctrines, but after a while one is amazed to find whole new dimensions of meaning emerging—and one then beholds the depths of one's ignorance. He then goes on to enumerate certain misunderstandings prevalent in the popular Western Buddhist mind and tries to account for these. Some are due to difficulties of language, he suggests, but more precisely he identifies a "Not Only" or exclusive disposition that, in terms of any pair of opposites, will tend to opt for one and discount the other: if this, then not that. Against this Watts proposes a "Not Only But Also" approach, which affirms that either party in a pair of opposites cannot exist without the other, and which keeps both and the relation between them in view. From this relation meaning arises. Thus while there is infinity, there are also finite things— which in fact is precisely what Dr. D. T. Suzuki had told the Buddhist Lodge when he had paid a visit there on July 20, 1936: ". . . in oneness there is manyness, and in manyness there is oneness. The transcendent and the immanent God exist at the same time"[11]. Suzuki also wrote in *Buddhism in England*: ". . . our logic has never taught us to rise above dualism, and we have always interpreted all our experiences on the basis of a bifurcation or dichotomy"[12] . . . . Watts concludes that delusion arises from such one-sidedness; and from delusion arises *dukkha*, which he suggests should be translated as "discord" or "lack of harmony."

In "Simple Language," another "Letters I Receive" feature, Watts takes as his gambit the fact that many of those attending Buddhist Lodge meetings and correspondents to the journal were complaining of finding Buddhism complicated and fraught with abstruse technical terminology. This raises the whole question of the communication of spiritual ideas. How is it to be successfully done? Should Buddhism be explained in "simple language"? Well, there are many difficulties with "simple language," as Watts amply demonstrates. Then he comes to the heart of the matter: "The paradox is that profound Truth is complicated because it is simple." Yet complicated Westerners tend to believe that "profound Truth" must be difficult and somehow distant. They therefore look for the wrong thing in the wrong place and thereby miss the genuine article, which is right under their noses all the time.

This is a very important point and one that needs emphasising as much today as when Watts wrote the item fifty years ago. For our disposition is still to imagine that spiritual enlightenment consists of some "peak experience," highly aesthetic and uplifting: the clouds open and pillars of light appear. One of Dr. Suzuki's great contributions was to emphasise the *ordinariness* of profound spiritual insight: "the most ordinary things in our daily lives hide some deep meaning that is yet most plain and explicit, only our eyes need to see where there is a meaning. . ."[13] That unique and original contributor to the understanding of Zen in the West, Douglas Harding (author of *On Having No Head*) talks about one's ultimate or supreme identity being supremely obvious and always perfectly available. People in fact reject it precisely because it doesn't match up to their inflated expectations: they find it prosaic, boring, unimpressive—a let-down! Watts winds up the article by concluding that what people really want is to have Buddhism explained in their *own* language, and that it is the special skill of great spiritual teachers that they are able to see how to communicate with each individual at that person's level. It may even be that, in certain cases, a single word or a gesture may be enlightening. . . .

Watts returned to the theme that everyday life is the true arena of spiritual practice in "The Experience of Mystery," his next "Letters I Receive" feature. Again he pointed out that all too many seekers are frankly unwilling to keep their feet on the ground and their noses to the mundane grindstone. Rather, they go shooting for the stars: they pursue all kinds of marvellous transcendental states or seek to acquire occult powers. These aspects of the spiritual hinterland are always with us. There are indeed "higher states of consciousness" beyond the ordinary: refined states of consciousness which are often states of great bliss. They are called the *jhanas* in Buddhism, and there is a whole hierarchy of them. They are definitely not, however, to be confused with the central matter of Buddhism: the Enlightenment that the Buddha achieved beneath the Bodhi tree at Bodh Gaya. That led to the Deathless, a state of being that was not subject to old age, sickness and death, not subject to *dukkha, anicca* and *anatta.*

In Buddhist cosmology the *jhanas* are identified with the abodes of the the various orders of gods or *devas*, who live for enormous spans of time in delightful environments, enjoying all manner of pleasure and luxury. But because the *devas* are still subject to the law of impermanence (*anicca*), the bitter day will eventually dawn when the beautiful flowers in their hands begin to wither and their bodies give off an unsavoury odour that makes them uncongenial to their godlike companions and consorts. They then know that the bliss of heaven is to be taken from them and that once again they are about to be recycled through the lower worlds. This poetically illustrates the drawbacks of these "higher"states.

Occult powers, on the other hand, are called *siddhi* in Sanskrit, and consist of healing powers, the ability to materialize objects, to travel on the Astral Plane, to levitate, conjure spirits and occult beings, to foretell the future, and so forth. Such powers may well come to seekers as a by-product of spiritual practice, but all the great traditions warn against being seduced by them, for once a person has been entrapped by power of any sort it is difficult to break free. Furthermore, the possession of "powers" is definitely not a sign of true wisdom, which in Buddhism is always linked with humility and compassion. Many great wonder-workers have in fact been inspired by very venal motivations. Best then, as Watts emphasises, to stick to the ordinary, the everyday, for here resides all we need for our practice—and, indeed, what could be more wonderful than that we actually exist, that we are here at all. It is indeed a great mystery, the greatest mystery. The eminent modern Western philosopher Ludwig Wittgenstein clearly had much the same view in mind when he wrote: "It is not *how* things are in the world that is mystical, *but that* it exists"[14]. Or in the words of the "Chinese poet"—specifically Layman P'ang, a Chinese Ch'an (Zen) Master—that Watts quotes:

> *How wondrous, how miraculous, this—*
> *I draw water and I carry fuel.*

If we scan through the "News and Notes" sections in the issues of *Buddhism in England* that appeared in 1937, we can trace various developments that had a bearing upon Watts's own personal life. The September/October issue reported the staging of a Second World Congress of Faiths in Oxford. Dr. Suzuki was not there this time, so Buddhism was represented by a Burmese, Maung Aye Maung—and of course Alan Watts went along, too. The Congress had again the important effect of facilitating "the making of new friends and coming into personal contact with the great minds of other faiths . . . also, living together for a long week-end afforded many opportunities for personal conversations, and some of us stayed up until the early hours of the morning enjoying the company of new-found and fascinating friends." We know from his autobiography that Watts shared a room with Baron Hans Hasso von Veltheim, a "big, boisterous and warm-hearted" ex-Zeppelin commander with a deep contempt for the Nazis—a contempt for which he later paid with his life. One lecture given at the Congress particularly impressed Watts. It was by a lay theologian from Rome named Ernesto Buonaiuti, who was apparently "a disowned member of the Catholic Church." He picked Watts's brain about Buddhism as they strolled together around the quadrangle at Balliol, where that session of the Congress was held that year, talking in bad French, their only common language. Watts in his turn was amazed by Buonaiuti's profound understanding of Catholicism.

At the Buddhist Lodge, meanwhile, a special study was being made of Zen Buddhism using Dr. Suzuki's *Introduction to Zen Buddhism* as text-book. Fortuitously, on June 14, a wealthy American lady hailing from Hinsdale, near Chicago turned up at a Lodge meeting—a lady who had actually been in Japan and studied Zen under a real Zen Master! She even had a Zen name: Sui Getsu Kuge. Naturally the Zen Class enthusiastically picked her brain about the "purpose, technique and results of Zen meditation." The lady had a curious way of looking up at the ceiling as she spoke, Watts recalled. So many questions were posed that the meeting had to be adjourned and continued on another evening.

This lady was Ruth Fuller Everett, and she is now regarded as one of the pioneers of Zen Buddhism in the United States. She eventually married Sokei-an Sasaki (Sokei-an Shigetsu Osho; 1882-1945), a fellow pioneer who founded the First Zen Institute of America. At the time of her first visit to the Buddhist Lodge, however, she was unhappily married to Edward Warren Everett, a "genial but fearsome red-haired Chicago attorney,"[15] who according to Watts had developed a formidable will and a fair measure of misanthropy in his fight against the after-effects of polio. To live with such a man, Ruth had had to develop an iron will of her own; she was also highly cultured and something of a social climber. At one stage she came under the influence of a rascal-guru named Pierre Bernard who kept an "ashram-cum-zoo" at Nyack-on-the-Hudson, where he taught various forms of yoga to a following that included a number of New York socialites. It may have been at Nyack that Ruth heard about Zen. Later she went on a world cruise with her husband and, while in Japan, they were introduced to Dr. Suzuki. The kindly doctor gave Ruth one of his books and also some rudimentary instruction in *zazen* (sitting meditation). When she returned to Japan subsequently with her fifteen-year-old daughter, Eleanor, Suzuki introduced her to Nanshinken, the revered *roshi* (lit.: "old master") of Nanzenji, the famous Zen monastery founded in Kyoto in 1293. Nanshinken took a liking to Ruth and allowed her to join the monks in their morning *zazen*. The spiritual instruction that he gave to Eleanor, on the other hand, consisted mainly of sitting out on veranda with her, leafing through picture magazines in search of a suitable husband among the super-portly *sumo* wrestlers on offer. Mother and daughter stayed in Kyoto on that occasion for about three and a half months.[16]

Eleanor visited the Lodge on 12 July and it took the lusty Alan about a week to fall hopelessly in love with her. She was buxom, talented, and vivacious, if not stunningly beautiful. Another recommendation was that she was as eager for erotic experiment as he was. When Ruth left to return to the States after a short while, she obligingly left Eleanor to Alan's tender mercies, though with the parting comment (something of a put-down, really): "He's all right, but he'll never set the Thames on fire." Now Alan no longer had to race for the last train for Chislehurst every night; he often stayed up in Eleanor's London flat, something that probably caused a certain amount of disapproval back at home.

Alan and Eleanor now regularly attended meditation sessions at the Buddhist Lodge together and one night as they were walking home she helped him to an insight that he rated as a premature *satori*.[17] He was experiencing some frustration in his attempts to remain choicelessly aware of the present moment in the manner of Krishnamurti's teaching. Eleanor pointed out that whether one was ruminating about the past or fantasising about the future, those thoughts were precisely the present contents of the mind.

"The present is just a constant flow, like the Tao, and there's simply no way of getting out of it," she told him—and for a whole week afterwards he simply floated.

Watts also credits Eleanor with loosening him up considerably. Inroads began to be made into the stiff Anthony Eden style of dressing that he had hitherto affected. He now sported colourful ties, more casual clothes and even bought a tweed jacket and matching felt hat with a jaunty feather in the band. She was also well-placed to educate Alan musically, having come to London to study piano with a teacher named George Woodhouse, who had a theory that the mind should slow effortlessly along with the melody. They therefore went to concerts, the opera and the ballet together. And another of her accomplishments was that she had studied the *hula* in Hawaii, so she "showed me that there was much more to dancing than formal stepping, prancing and turning. . . ."[18]

Alan of course kept up his duties as Editor of *Buddhism in England* during this exciting period, and in the November/December 1938 issue we find him printing a short *haiku*-like poem by Eleanor. It is called *Steps to the Gate*.

> *Laden with snow*
> *The bamboo bends,*
> *But does not break.*
> *   *   *

Zen
*The man who asks*
*No help*
*From the saints*

       *     *     *

*The heart of gold is within thee,*
*The heavens be empty and below the earth—*
*There is naught.*

The burgeoning affair with Eleanor does not seem to have impeded Watts's literary output in any way, for articles continued to appear in *Buddhism in England* under his name. In "The Man and the Means," for instance, he raised a classic teaser about motivation on the spiritual path, specifically citing a reader's problem with the dictum in the Richard Wilhelm translation of the Chinese Taoist classic, *The Secret of the Golden Flower,* to the effect that if the wrong man uses the right means then the right means work in the wrong way. How then can any of us do anything at all about ourselves spiritually for we all start off wrong— i.e., deluded, full of egoism and desire—a million miles from being pure and clear? Some of us undertake the spiritual path because we want to escape from life and its attendant problems, but how do we escape from trying to escape? The seeker seems inexorably caught in a circular dilemma—and this is a theme to which Watts was to return many times. Basically, it boils down to the absurdity of the ego trying to become egoless, which is like asking a man to pull himself up by his own bootstraps. Later he was to propose "solutions," but here he really does little more than identify the basic problem. A correspondent to the following issue of the journal upbraided Watts for this. He had only succeeded in making the problem seem more acute by "adding to the original proposition the weight of irrefutable logic." It was a fact, the correspondent went on, that over the millennia a few *had* managed to tread the spiritual path successfully and had left instructions that those coming in their footsteps might follow.

In the first issue of 1938, Christmas Humphreys announced "Our Editor's Engagement" to Miss Eleanor Everett, who "has already acquired, when visiting Japan with her mother, a practical knowledge of Japanese Buddhism." She was proving to be most capable in the new executive post of Assistant Editor to which she had lately been appointed. Toby Humphreys also reported that the young couple, who were then spending Christmas in Chicago, had fixed the date of their wedding for May.

Alan and Eleanor had in fact sailed for New York on the *Bremen* on December 17, 1937, having celebrated their engagement at Rowan Tree Cottage the previous day. The Watts family and the Buchans had been duly impressed with Alan's "American fiancée," but once on board the Transatlantic liner Alan found himself in another world entirely. He and Eleanor gorged themselves on the exquisite cuisine and the savour of one particularly choice wine—an Osterreicher Holle Riesling Spatlese, 1927 vintage—lodged in his memory for the remainder of his days. Then, on landing, he found himself zooming through the canyons of New York and on to Chicago aboard the overnight Commodore Vanderbilt train. On arrival at La Salle Station, he and Eleanor were met by the Everetts and their Philippino chauffeur, Ishmael. Alan found to his delight that he got on well with Warren Everett, despite the man's irascibility: they shared certain minor vices in common and Alan could effectively use his English charm and manners to draw the lawyer out about his career. With a few notable exceptions, however, he found the remainder of the Warren family "pompous and vapid," but Eleanor's youthful friends were another matter altogether and he kept in touch with some of them for long afterwards. The food in the Everett household was again exquisite and every item on the Christmas Day menu impressed itself indelibly upon the impressionable Alan's memory. Then it was back to England on the *Bremen* again, waltzing crazily to a Bavarian band on a rolling dance floor in rough seas and playing chess with a young German professor who plied him with so much Benedictine (an unsubtle gambit?) that on one occasion he was well and truly sozzled. It had all been a magnificent whirl through a magical new world and one can vividly appreciate Alan's delighted intoxication with it all.

The next issue of *Buddhism in England*, however, announced that the date of the editor's forthcoming marriage had been changed. It was now scheduled to take place privately in London on April 2. The venue for the ceremony was the parish church of the Earl's Court district of west London—and a somewhat puzzling one in view of the young couple's Buddhist inclinations, in which, moreover, they were joined by *her* mother and *his* father. Evidently, however, a conventional church wedding was necessary for social reasons. The Humphreys's wedding present was to be a silver sugar salver that Puck, an accomplished silversmith, had made personally for them. However, Eleanor rejected the item when she noticed that the she-goat on the lid was pregnant: a detail that was a little too close to home.

After their marriage, Alan and Eleanor moved into an "almost palatial duplex" at 28 Courtfield Gardens in Kensington. Alan must have been well-pleased. He at last had the consort for which he had so long been wishing; and he had also moved out of his parents' tiny cottage in Holbrook Lane, Chislehurst and was living in the style to which he ardently wished to be accustomed. His cousin, Joy Buchan, used to go up to give him secretarial help with the book reviewing work on which he was engaged at the time, having given up his previous job. Joy thought that Alan and Eleanor seemed very happy together then.

At this time, Watts contributed a major article to *Buddhism in England* entitled "The Monkey Mind in Religion." Here he defined a sort of spiritual materialism that predates the Chögyam Trungpa Rinpoche book, *Cutting through Spiritual Materialism* (1973), by thirty-five years. People in fact try to get something for themselves out of spirituality (it may be just self-aggrandizement or something more sinister—like the acquisition of *siddhis*, occult powers) and many—here there are clear resonances of Krishnamurti's teaching[3] and also of the early Chinese Zen Masters—become mere copyists, clinging to outward forms or aping the superficial behaviour of adepts. This will not do, Watts contends; one must not cling on to props and supports; one must be free and original and creative. He also emphasises that spirituality isn't a kind of special sphere of activity separate from the main flow of life—'spirituality is precisely creative and spontaneous *living. . . .*"

It is all good stuff, bold and fresh and straight from the shoulder; but one feels there is something slightly amiss too. It moves a little too fast, goes a little too far. Certainly there can be blind clinging to forms and techniques—and that is certainly negative. The Buddha pointed this out himself in his analogy of the *Dharma* being like a raft that one uses to cross a mighty river. It is useful to get us from the unenlightened state to the enlightened one; but just as it would be absurd to go on carrying the raft on one's back after one has reached the further shore of the river, so it would be equally absurd to cling to the forms and techniques of the *Dharma* once they had served the practical purpose of leading one out of the deluded state. However, it is important to realise that one doesn't drop the *Dharma* until one has reached the other state. Thus forms and techniques (or disciplines) are vitally necessary in the early stages of any sort of training.

In the training of a Japanese swordsman, for instance, certain basic movements of the sword are practised with monotonous repetition—but finally, in the actual cut and thrust of an engagement, the swordsman is expected to throw technique away and make his manoeuvres freely. By then, however, his whole being will have been transformed by that monotonous initial training so that creative energy can flow through him in an informed—as opposed to an anarchic—way. To move into another sphere, we have all seen those awful attempts at poetry written by people who are contemptuous of the laws of prosody and believe that no initial practice of basic disciplines is necessary. It is simply a matter of opening the floodgates and letting it all come out—and it is bound to be pure gold. Almost invariably it is pure rubbish. . . . Freedom and spontaneity are only rightfully the prerogatives of those who have served long apprenticeship to discipline and technique.

Up to a certain point in the article one fears that Watts is going to overlook this point completely. But then one is proved wrong: he *does* mention it—but only fleetingly and without proper emphasis. The article thus ends up covering the basic ground of its theme well, but the overall balance is not quite right. This in a way throws light upon the workings of Watts's mind at this period in his life: it is sharp, mercurial, logical; as Christmas Humphreys said in his review of *The Legacy of Asia*, it is undoubtedly brilliant. Yet something is lacking: a deeper wisdom of the heart, perhaps.

By the middle of 1938, as Europe moved like a blind man on a sightless horse (to paraphrase Arthur Waley) towards an immolation that no-one seemed able to avert, the general climate in Britain was one of profound apprehension. At this dark hour Watts again took up his pen and composed an article on the subject of war, taking as his title "The Unimportance of War." This appeared in the May/June issue of *Buddhism in England*, and in it Watts uncompromisingly rejects the notion that there is anything basically noble or heroic about war. It is really a form of cowardice; therefore, if the anticipated war did break out in Europe, it would not be at all cowardly to betake oneself to a private sanctuary well removed from the cockpit of hostilities. It would, indeed, be good sense to do so; and

those who pursued this course could return after the conflagration was over and begin to pick up the pieces. They
would be the custodians of the future and of civilized values,
having refused to be dragooned into the recent collective
madness. In any case, the only other option would be to
stay behind and be killed, modern warfare having virtually
ruled out the possibility of defence. . . .

But this is not all that the article has to say. Why are
people making so much fuss about war? Watts wants to
know. People get killed, civilizations are destroyed—but so
what? We've all got to die some day. Civilizations also come
and go—and is the present civilization all that worthy of
preservation if it hasn't even the moral power to prevent
itself being blown up? In the vast perspectives of cosmic
space and time, all these things fade to insignificance anyway. We should console ourselves by reflecting upon such
eternal verities and attempt to abide in the eternal Now;
therein lies "unbelievable freedom of spirit . . . ."

All of which may be quite correct, but is it true?
Charles E. Ball of Chiswick, London, did not think so. He
wrote a Letter to the Editor which appeared in the next issue
of *Buddhism in England*.

> *Sir,* [he wrote]—*I think your article is not only
> too academic but harmful. Its airiness is too
> suggestive of the Japanese treatment of their
> devilish wholesale massacres of Chinese [in
> Manchuria] as an "Incident" and which must
> do much to prove to the world the apparent
> unimportance of Buddhism in Japan.*

Ball went on:

> *To say that wholesale death by every method
> of horror doesn't matter will convince ordi-
> nary rational people of the unimportance of
> the Buddhist outlook on matters of importance
> to everyone. If, as Dr. D. T. Suzuki tells us, Sam-*

*sara is Nirvana and Nirvana is Samsara,*
*earthly life is then not something that doesn't*
*matter, but rather what matters a great deal,*
*apart from the* first duty *of all to protect the*
*weak and unenlightened people of the world*
*from hopeless despair and atheism as they find*
*themselves again involved in one of these fren-*
*zied outbursts of demonaic destruction guided*
*by Rakshasas* [a class of demons in Buddhist
and Hindu mythology] *and elementals.*

W. J. Gabb, author of *The Goose is Out*, contributed
another Letter in which he appealed to the *Lankavatara
Sutra* (which Suzuki had rendered into English) to support
the argument that war was both important *and* unimportant. The wise man acted as *if* it were important, while the
Watcher within remained detached and aware that in ultimate terms there is no annihilation.

It is hard not to feel from this perspective in time that
in "The Unimportance of War," Watts was really publicly
rehearsing his personal rationalizations for what was to be
his own course of action in the face of the impending European conflagration. Now that he was married to Eleanor
Everett, an American citizen (and one with wealthy family
connections), he had, as he himself admits in his autobiography, the necessary "wings" to betake himself to the relative safety of the United States.

We have also included in this section a piece entitled
"The Original Face," attributed to one Wu Tao-kung, a fic-
titious Zen Master. It carries no other credits but we believe
it to have been written by Watts for he preserved it among
the cuttings of his published articles. It is an exuberant piece
of chinoiserie, or perhaps better, chanoiserie, *Ch'an* being
the Chinese form of the Japanese *Zen* and the Sanskrit
*Dhyana*, broadly meaning "meditation." The "original face"
of the title is our own true nature, which is the Buddha

Nature. We look out of it all the time and it is boundless and perfectly clear.

The last article that we have included in this anthology is the transcript of a lecture entitled "Can We Help Ourselves?" Basically it recapitulates many of the themes that we have already encountered, particularly one that cropped up in "The Man and the Means:" the circular dilemma of our trying to do anything to help ourselves spiritually. The spiritual is, in fact, a great mystery that Watts chose to call the *Tao*,[19] and its ambit is everyday life. It is always right here in front of us, supremely obvious, and there is nothing that we can do to put ourselves in touch with it, for we always *are* in touch with it. Once we realise this there is nothing more to be done except to get on with our lives.

The lecture was in its way no doubt brilliant. It contained witty and apposite stories, clever arguments, edifying remarks, and it built up a wonderful sense of deeply penetrative enquiry—that a great secret was going to be revealed at the end. It was no doubt delivered, too, with Watts's usual oratorical vigour and panache. But when all was said and done, did the audience perhaps not feel left in the air a little? For, despite all its emphases upon the impossibility of expressing the inexpressible, it is still a very wordy and highly conceptual piece.

The November/December 1938 issue of the journal informs us that the editor is "at present making another visit to America, and in the course of his visit is hoping to make many contacts with American Buddhists." This suggests that Watts had really not evolved final plans for emigration to the United States when he left England in 1938. He may have had it in the back of his mind to return home if the political climate in Europe mellowed, or if things did not turn out too well for him on the other side of the Atlantic. He, therefore, retained the editorship of *Buddhism in England*, with Clare Cameron holding the fort for him in his absence.

But events now began to move decisively. On November 14, Eleanor gave birth to a baby daughter, Joan, in New York. Then, in London, on November 28, at a meeting of the Buddhist Lodge, it was decided that Clare Cameron should replace Watts as Editor but that he should retain a link with the journal as Associate Editor. Finally, less than a year later, the urbane atmosphere of the capital of the British Empire was shattered by the wail of air-raid sirens. The long-anticipated European hostilities had broken out, and they were to rage with all the destructive fury of vast collective madness for more than five years. At the start of it all, another English expatriate was breathing the same "neutral air" of New York as Watts was then breathing. Sitting in one of the dives on Fifty-second Street, W. H. Auden wrote:

> *Waves of anger and fear*
> *Circulate over the bright*
> *And darkened lands of the earth,*
> *Obsessing our private lives;*
> *The unmentionable odour of death*
> *Offends the September night.*
> —September 1, 1939

Alan Watts never returned to live permanently in his native land. His British phase was over.

## NOTES

1. *A. E. R. (Eric) Gill, (1882–1940) designed typefaces for the Monotype Corporation and was an accomplished letterer and stone-carver; but he also produced sculpture, drawings and innumerable wood-engravings, many of which were highly erotic and portrayed 'loving couples' and suchlike subjects, Gill's philosophy might be summed up in his dictum, "Man is matter and Spirit, both real and both good."*

2. *Literally, "Everything transient is only a symbol [or parable]."*

3. *Eric Graham Howe introduced Watts to J. Krishnamurti in 1936.*

4. *Buddhism in England, volume 11, p. 151.*

5. *ibid. volume 11, p. 36.*

6. *This suggests that Watts may have by this time become a little more conscious of the true nature of totalitarian ideologies than when he wrote the* Buddhism and War *item in* Buddhism and the Modern World.

7. Koan: *this has connotations of a "case" in Law. It is an enigmatic question used in Rinzai Zen as a skilful means; it cannot be "solved" by the rational intellect, but requires a leap to the deeper wisdom that lies beyond.*
Mu: *"Not, or No, the Negative which is beyond mere positive and negative"*— Christmas Humphreys, A Popular Dictionary of Buddhism, *Volumes have been written about Mu but it ultimately defies conceptual description.*

8. Rohatsu Sesshin: *A sesshin, literally a "collecting of the heart" is a kind of Zen Buddhist retreat.* Rohatsu *signifies December 8, the date upon which the Buddha's Enlightenment is traditionally celebrated by Zen Buddhists. The* Rohatsu Sesshin *usually takes place in Zen monasteries during the week preceding the 8th, and everyone then strives to match the enormous effort made by the Buddha to resolve the central problem of his spiritual quest. It is considered a gruelling spell of practice, made all the harder by the rigours of the Japanese winter.*

9. D. T. Suzuki: A Biography, *by A. Irwin Switzer III, edited and enlarged by John Snelling. London, The Buddhist Society, 1985; pp. 32–33.*

10. Walk On! *was the title of a book by Christmas Humphreys.*

11. *"Dr. D. T. Suzuki on Zen, A Visit to the Buddhist Lodge."* Buddhism in England, *volume 11, p. 69.*

12. *D. T. Suzuki,* "Buddhism in the Life and Thought of Japan," Buddhism in England, *volume 11, p. 104.*

13. *"Dr. D. T. Suzuki on Zen, A Visit to the Buddhist Lodge."* Buddhism in England, *volume 11, p. 68.*

14. Tractatus Logico-Philosophicus, *by Ludwig Wittgenstein. London, Routledge and Kegan Paul, 1961; p. 149.*

15. In My Own Way *by Alan Watts, New York, Vintage paperback edition, 1973; p. 145.*

16. How the Swans Came to the Lake, *by Rick Fields. Boulder, Shambhala Publications, 1981; p. 188.*

17. Satori *is a technical term in Zen signifying an insight into the nature of one's true nature of varying degrees of depth and duration.*

18. In My Own Way, *(edition cited above), p. 144.*

19. Tao: *a Chinese term with similar connotations to the Sanskrit Dharma. It could be said to signify universal law or the way things are: a subtle and elusive essence fully penetrating and vitalizing all that exists. In Taoist terms, the art of life is the art of harmonising with Tao. See* The Way and Its Power, *by Arthur Waley; London, George Allen & Unwin, 1934.*

# SEVEN SYMBOLS OF LIFE

*Being an essay on eternal verities as expressed in the images of the lotus, of water, wind, fire, man, woman and child.*

*Published by The Buddhist Lodge, London, 1936*

●

## THE LOTUS.

*Alles Vergängliche*
*Ist nur ein Gleichnis.*
—Goethe

Of all symbolic flowers man has chosen the lotus as the one of most meaning. It figures in the art of every great civilization of Asia, and in the course of thousands of years has gathered to itself associations which, to the Western mind, are bound up with all that seems exotic in the life of the East. For the lotus is a mystery—a perfected glory appearing out of the unknown, a flower in whose circular spread of petals has been seen a symbol of the Wheel of Life and the rays of the sun. Yet while there is mystery in the perfection of its form, the greatest mystery is that such a form should appear out of the slime—the formless primaeval morass, where, in the earliest ages, stirred the first living creatures—the home of blind worms and slithering reptiles, feeding upon one another and begetting their kind in innumerable masses.

This underworld of the morass has been sufficiently described in Keyserling's masterpiece the *South American Meditations*, and there is no need to describe it further. But what must never be forgotten is that this underworld still exists in the soul of man; that while his spirit, like the lotus, struggles towards the light, so beneath him and surrounding and nourishing his roots is the primaeval slime. And further, below this slime is the world of minerals, the rocks and ores descending deeper and deeper into the earth right down to that flaming darkness which men have imagined as Hell. From all this the flower gathers its nourishment, while from above the sun and the rain bring to it the gifts of Heaven. *Both* are essential to the life of the flower.

It might seem to the eyes of man that the lotus is no more than a flower, that this resplendent creation exists of itself, floating detached and spotless above the water. But this is illusion. For just as the sage may appear spotless and detached from the world, he is like the lotus in that he has his roots in the primaeval slime—and knows it. Foolishly it is thought that the highest achievement of the human spirit is a heavenly purity detached from earth—a rootless flower suspended in the air and nourished wholly from above. Yet in the symbol of the lotus we see that there is no conflict between heaven and earth; above, the flower develops into the fullness of its glory, expanding joyously, opening its petals in welcome to sun and rain, while below, its roots stretch out into the morass, welcoming darkness and slime as the petals welcome light and air. For the life of the lotus is not in the flower alone; if it were, the roots would shrivel and die and the flower too would sink back into the mud. Nor is its life in the roots alone, for if this were so the flower would never raise its head above the water.

The realization of the truth contained in this symbol is the central problem of human life—the equal acceptance of both earth and heaven. Yet remember, it is the roots which accept the slime—not the flower, and the flower which opens itself to the sun—not the roots. The reverse of this would indeed be abomination and evil. But nothing can be evil so long as it is in its right place, for the conflict between good and evil is not a conflict between heaven and earth, but between a right and a wrong orientation of man between the two. For evil is when the flower turns and plunges into the slime, twisting up its roots to gesticulate meaninglessly in the light of day. Or again, evil is to withdraw from either the root or the flower, to try to deny either of the two by refusing it its right to reach out into its appropriate world. Thus the particular problem of modern man of the West is to recognize his roots. For hundreds of years his peculiar interpretation of the teaching of the Christ, his cult of consciousness, his moralism, his belief in progress towards the hygienic, the individuated and the independent has made him forget his roots in the primaeval slime. But he must remember that the roots are not to be recognized once more by searching them out with the flower; to attempt this would be to lose all that he has gained by his development, onesided though it be. It is this folly which we see at work in the West to-day, in the growing obsession with the irrational force of sex, of the herd, of blood and violence. Yet these forces are, in themselves, as pure as any of the virtues, and as full of life-giving nourishment as Reason and the cool thought of great philosophy. For this obsession is not recognition. It is feeding the mouth with the contents of the bowels, or, conversely, filling the bowels with undigested food.

What must be done, therefore, if man is to attain a right orientation between heaven and earth, and a full development of both root and flower? How can he fulfil the Eastern precept, "Grow as the flower grows, at peace"? How can he give full recognition to the slime, and at the same time rise upwards to the sun?

In the darkness below the surface of the water lies what modern psychology has termed the Unconscious. A little way down it remains individuated, but the further it descends, the more individuals are lost in the mass. Thus in the slime is the world of reptiles, an ever coiling and uncoiling world of flux, where the individual is subordinated to the one aim of reproducing the species—a world of extreme fertility and ruthless destruction—symbolized by the circle snake which swallows its own tail. In the depths of the slime below the reptiles are even more primitive and unindividuated forms of life—plasmic formations wherein even the distinction between the sexes has not developed, formations which reproduce their kind simply by dividing into two. And further down, beneath the bed of decaying vegetable and animal matter (the death from which life arises again and again), is the formless substratum of the mineral world. These depths have their counterpart in the soul of man, for his Unconscious sinks beyond the personal and the chain of his past lives and the lives of his forefathers, to the race, to the animal, vegetable and mineral worlds. Here lies hidden the memory of the whole Universe, and in these unconscious depths every man has his roots. From them he derives his life just as much as from the conscious world above the water. And by accepting them he transmutes the life of the slime into the glory of the flower. Therefore man must learn to recognize his foundation, to accept the primaeval slime as part of his nature—nay more, to affirm and welcome it with his roots, stretching them down deeper and deeper into the earth. For as men we cannot deny that we came into the world with blood and pain, that the powerful reproductive urge symbolized by the reptile stirs within us, that we have bowels as well as brains, that our life depends alike on growth and decay, and that what we have been accustomed to regard as dirt, violence and pain is an essential part of our nature. This is the meaning of the Resurrection, that life comes forth out of death and decay, just as the fruit must rot for the seed to grow into the tree.

Therefore nothing is to be gained by trying to escape from the primaeval slime; without it we should die, while in truth it is no evil. Indeed, the humility of the sage is his capacity to accept the lowliest of things, to find goodness in slime. Yet it is strange that this should have been perverted into the false humility of the ascetic who rejoices in the dirt on the outside of his body, for this again is obsession, it is making the flower descend to the root.

Some will ask if this is not a ghastly life where the most gorgeous of flowers depends on slime, where growth can only be had at the expense of decay, where great achievements of the human spirit have their roots in the darkness and "depraved" irrationality of the Unconscious. Indeed, there are those who are so revolted by this life that they deny both flower and root, growth and decay, light and darkness, conscious and unconscious—hating both. But their attitude is false, for they do not really hate both; they hate the dark side and would like to have the light, could it be had without darkness. When they speak of the vanity of life we must remind ourselves of the story of the sour grapes; they would not call it vain if it could be had without death. Yet nothing is to be achieved by revulsion and denial, not only because the attitude is fundamentally false, but because the denial of a thing does not make one free of it. Paradoxically, hatred binds one to the thing one hates, for if anything has enough power over a man to make him hate it, to that extent he is bound and conditioned by it. But while hatred is extracted, love is given. Therefore freedom comes not through hatred and denial, but through love and affirmation. "Love" is not meant in the sense of "like" as opposed to "dislike," for one may love without liking; the two are on different planes. To love both the root and the flower, earth and heaven, slime and air, death and life is not merely to like decay *because* it makes possible growth; it is to bring the two together into an inseparable unity and to become one with it by a complete acceptance, until, beholding it, man can make to himself that tremendous affirmation—*Tat tvam asi—That* art thou!

## WATER AND THE WIND.

In the Book of Genesis it is said that before the world was

made "the spirit of God moved upon the face of the waters." In all the cosmogonies of the ancient world, Water was made the symbol of the Mother of the Universe—the passive and yielding substance from which all things proceeded. Whether or no this myth will bear the test of scientific examination, its value does not consist in its being an historical truth. For the creation of the world from the union of Water and the Spirit is an allegory wherein we may read not so much a truth of the past as a truth which may give us light in the present. Spirit means breath, wind, life, movement, and Water means the substance which is moved. Spirit is light and Water is heavy; one is positive and the other negative, one male and the other female, and while both are in themselves "without form and void," their union is the birth of form. For the wind, entering into the water, rears up waves, and the whole surface of the ocean of life is stirred into an ever-moving vastness of dancing shapes.

In all the world there are no two things more elusive than water and the wind. Water may be grasped in the hands, yet it is never held, for the harder the grasp, the faster it slips through the fingers. A man may try to catch the wind, and though he feels it all around him there is nothing for him to seize. If it blows into a room, it cannot be caught by closing the door, for the air which is trapped is no longer wind. Whatever is separated, cut off from the living Whole, and shut away, loses its life.

Yet in a universe born of Water and the Spirit man cherishes the illusion that there is a permanence and a rigidity in things. But wherever there is life and form, the more there is of life, the more does the form change. Where is there more life than in the ceaseless play of waves on the shore of the sea? And where is there more subtlety and impermanence of form? The strange patterns of form on the shifting water,the leaping clouds of spray and the tumbling curves of the waves—all is unceasing movement and unceasing change, which nothing can stay or hold. Try to catch the spray, and it has vanished; pick up the water in your hands, and its life and movement have gone. So is it with all things in the universe.

Thus all forms are vain if impermanence is to be accounted vanity. Certainly forms are vain to him who seeks permanence. But the secret of life is to abandon the desire for the eternity of forms. Those who have surrendered this desire find in the endless play of Water and Spirit, form and life, the joy which is wisdom. For them, forms are no longer vain; they know that their evanescence is their glory. The cause of immeasurable vanity, abomination and folly is the longing to grasp and keep things which exist through movement and change. To try to fasten the universe into a set of ideas, to hold on to a feeling of happiness, to possess those whom one loves, to perpetuate the circumstances that bring joy—these indeed are vanities. The beauty of music would not exist if every note and phrase did not sound for just its appointed time and then give place to another; but hold a note for longer than its time and the melody is broken, the life and movement have gone.

Therefore wisdom is the love of change, of the movement, the dance of life, without which the universe would vanish into nothing. The fool strives to keep still and possess the forms of life that he may enjoy their loveliness for ever. Yet as the plucked flower dies, every form clutched in the fingers of his desire withers away and he declares that the form is vain. He is deceived. For he who has wisdom, knowing that things exist only through their impermanence, perceives their true loveliness. In affirming change he is born anew "of Water and the Spirit" for he enters into their play, he joins in their dance, seeing that he, too, is also a form and only has life because he must vanish away. This, then, is the music of life and the dance of the universe, the play of Water and the Spirit. To move with it is joy and life, but he who would not change, who would not die, is already dead.

# FIRE.

Out of fire came this earth, and all that live upon it has its life from fire. No one can compute the benefits which we receive from the sun: it lifts the moisture from the seas and scatters it over the land as refreshing rain; its rays give energy to all that grows; its heat protects us from ice and snow. Yet that same sun scorches our crops and dries up the rivers, bringing disease and famine, for of all the elements none is more useful and none more dangerous than fire. And just as there is a fire which gives life to this macrocosm of planets, so there is a fire which gives life to the microcosm of man. And as both give life, so also both give death. If we believe the ancient teachings, we shall conceive the visible sun as the symbol of a spiritual sun, of the Spirit whose rays are the spirits of all living things. So we may conceive that the visible fire in man is the lesser form of one of those rays which proceed from the greater sun. But this does not concern us here; we would speak of the fire in man which is visible, the fire which drives him, which is desire, emotion, passion, love. These things incite man to an abundant life and fill him with activity; at the same time they burn him just as flames eat away the logs and die out amid the ashes of forms that were not strong enough to hold them and survive. The more there is of activity and life, the more there is of decay and death. For Life is like the fair flower which feeds upon the filth of manure.

The precepts of wise men and teachers of religion contain many warnings as to the dangers of the passions and desires, but in all things there is a Middle Way and it seems that in such precepts too little is said of their uses. For desire and passion is no more an evil in itself than the sun or a flame; only the method in which we employ it may be judged good or evil. Much ill may be wrought when passion, when emotion is uncontrolled, and in the same way much destruction is occasioned when fire is not made to keep to its proper place. But only a fool would advise us to dispense with fire because, if we are careless with it in preparing our food, we burn our fingers. When primaeval man first discovered that flames might be produced by the rubbing together of sticks, he must often have hurt himself through unguarded use of his new power. If such hurt had persuaded him to abandon the use of fire, the human race would to this day be living in trees and caves, wearing garments of rough skins and furs. But, through courage, man learnt how flame might be controlled until it became the foundation of many arts and sciences.

Therefore those who have come to harm through ill use of the passions and desires, and those who have witnessed such harm in others, should not give too much heed to the fear which would have them abandon such things altogether. Many are those who have changed suddenly from the life of extreme sensuality to the life of extreme asceticism, but in this there is no wisdom. For before man can afford to ignore and to forget the fire of passion he must first become a master in its use. And this is true also of all the faculties and senses of body and mind. Being endowed with such faculties, man is responsible for their right use. It is ill to squander them, and it is also ill to deny them, to believe that wisdom can only be found through the complete abandonment of all desire and feeling like the man in the parable of Jesus who went and hid his talent in the earth.

Reading the teachings of the ancient sages of the East, there are some in the West who seek to strangle their emotions and root out their desires. But in so doing they misunderstand those teachings, forgetting that they are directed only to those who have first learnt the right use of their faculties. In any art the rules and responsibilities can only be set aside in favour of a greater freedom when those rules have been mastered. So in the art of life, there can only be freedom from passion and desire when that has been mastered until the possibility of its being squandered can no longer trouble the mind. The novice in the art of riding a horse must attend closely to the manner of holding the reins, of sitting upon the saddle and directing its footsteps. The unbroken horse must be carefully watched. But when the novice has learnt proficiency or when the horse is broken, then the rider can let his mind pass to other things and ride on his way undisturbed. The abolition of the horse, however, would not solve his problems. The Buddha is often recorded to have likened the mind and the desires to unbroken steeds, but it is necessary that they should be correctly used, not disused, before there can be any Nirvana. Disuse is mere regression; the log remains a log, for having no flame it gives no warmth; the muscles of the horse grow weak, for it is not exercised; man becomes again a helpless infant, for he refuses to develop his powers.

Therefore it is unwise to speak overmuch of the forgetting of all desire and of freedom from passion, for they are few who have any need for such freedom. Desire and passion do not exist simply in order that we may become free from them. Rightly used they can construct things of beauty and delight which none can claim to despise unless he can himself construct such things with so great a proficiency that they entertain him no longer. We cannot despise the things of the senses unless we are first masters of all the arts which pertain to them; otherwise we do not know what is best in the world of sense, and so cannot judge that world. Few indeed are those who are artists in the use of their faculties of body and mind. Every faculty has its art, which, when developed is a thing of delight and a legitimate joy. Therefore we have enough to occupy us in learning the arts of the faculties which are ours already, before we begin to think of new faculties which shall displace the old. But some, looking ahead, feel that there can be no satisfaction and no joy in these arts. They meditate on the vanity of all that can be achieved through artistry with sight and sound and touch, with feeling and emotion, with intellect and muscle. Most frequently, these are they who have never achieved anything in such artistry; for them the wine of life is sour, and in beauty of form and movement, in the fleeting joys of love, of friendship and of pleasure they see only emptiness and dust. But the sourness is not in the wine; it is in an ill digestion arising from an immoderate and unskilful drinking. If forms were not vain and transient, if desires and feelings and thoughts were not changing and perishable, if they were external, fixed and rigid, they would lose all beauty. For there is no greater ugliness than a monotony, even of perfection; perfection is death in that it permits of no further growth. He who desires it is welcome to it, but *we* shall give a new meaning to the enjoyment of vanity.

## MAN, WOMAN AND CHILD.

Like a pendulum man is swung between the pairs of opposites, hurled unwillingly from one to the other, involved in a war between them in which he, through ignorance, takes a part. For he imagines that one can be held and the other cast away, that in the end good can conquer evil, beauty ugliness, joy pain, and life death. His struggle is great, for he longs above all things to be free from the bondage which taints all joy with the certainty of pain, all life with the inevitability of death. Yet one is only known through the existence of the other. As is said by Lao Tzu:

> *When the world speaks of beauty as being*
> *beautiful, ugliness is at once defined.*
> *When goodness is seen to be good, evil is at*
> *once apparent.*
> *So do existence and non-existence mutually*
> *give rise to one another, as that which is*
> *difficult and that which is easy, distant*
> *and near, high and low. . . .*

Likewise, if the pendulum swings to one side, it must of necessity swing to the other, for the right implies the left and the front the back.

Yet conflict between the opposites exists only in the mind of man. In his striving for mastery the conflict is increased, for to set up one against the other is to disregard the law of his own kind whereby man and woman are not set at enmity, but wedded to one another. More than this, the harmony is achieved not simply by the bringing together of the two, but by what is born of their union. For the meaning of man and woman is the child. So also to the sage all opposites are given a meaning by that which is seen when they are known as mutually dependent. Just as there is a child of man and woman, there is a child of life and death, good and evil, joy and pain, liberty and law.

Now in a certain city there were two philosophers whose custom it was to hold debate in a public place. It happened one day that a sage of great repute came to that city, and as he walked in the streets he chanced upon the two philosophers in heated argument before an assembly of their disciples. And one of them said, "I tell you that in all life there is only law. Whatever comes into being proceeds from a cause, and every cause is the effect of a previous cause. Thus all things are predetermined by what has been, and each thought and deed is but the inevitable result of thoughts and deeds in the past. As each thing is born so must it die; all must pass through the cycle of being, and in passing must submit in every detail to the decrees of fate. From law there is no escape, and in the whole universe nothing happens which is not in obedience to law." But the other laughed at him, and turning to the assembly said, "Hear what this man saith. All, he says, is of law and moves on its way like the several parts of a machine. He would have you believe that life is dead, that all things are fixed to eternity by Fate. So he says because he cannot escape from the machine-like reasonings of his own mind. All that he touches he kills, for he cannot see it otherwise than as a machine. Certainly his logic is right, but logic is of law, and in life is no logic. Logic is only of man's mind which would fasten its own likeness upon the universe. But I tell you that in life is only liberty, and that which lives can in no way be defined by law. For that which lives unceasingly changes and moves, while definition remains fixed. Life is a machine! Aye, and if you truly believed that you would make an end of yourselves, for in living further in such bondage there would be no joy." In this strain they continued to debate, and no agreement was reached. But one who stood in the assembly grew weary of such talk, and interrupted them, saying, "Here amongst us is a sage of great repute. Let him decide the issue between these two." Whereat they consented, and turning to the sage were about to explain themselves to him, but he smiled and said, "Shall the night contest the existence of the day? Shall the right maintain that there is no left? You are both right, and also you are both wrong, for you are wrong in saying that the other is not right. If all were law then all would be strangled to the death. If all were liberty then all would perish in confusion. But if liberty is to live, its bounds must be set by law, and if law indeed exists it implies something free which is to be ruled. Liberty is of life and law of death, and law sets bounds to liberty as death sets bounds to life. Without death life would stand still and cease to live, for all things would remain just as they are for ever, and never grow old. Through death there is life, and through life, death."

Thus out of life and death there is born a child for which there is no name in our tongue. In Sanskrit it is called *Tathata*—"Suchness"—the condition of living and dying which is the greater Life. This is the Higher Third which is born of two opposites. But is such a Higher Third truly outside the opposites? Is there not yet another pair, comprising the Higher Third and the Lower Fourth? If the two opposites of man and woman produce the child, has not the child an opposite? Cannot the child be opposed to the adult? There is a saying *Divide et impera*, divide and rule, and if there is a Lower Fourth it is ruled and mastered by the Higher Third, because whereas the Third is one, the Fourth is divided. For the adult is either man or woman, whereby the Fourth ceases to exist and becomes the First and the Second which originally produced the Third. Truly, man and woman are ruled by the child, for in any household there is nothing more powerful than an infant. By his weakness and helplessness he commands all attention. Thus it is often that an adult, wishing to have power over others, becomes an invalid so that he may be treated once more as a child.

But the child-state of the invalid must be distinguished from the child-state of the sage who rules over the pairs of opposites. "Ye must become again as little children" is a precept which may be interpreted in two ways—as a means of escaping adult responsibilities, or as a means of entering that new life of which it is said that "except a man be born again, he cannot see the kingdom of God." So also, the quest for Nirvana may be an attempt to flee from the world or to accept it to the uttermost, so much so that the sage can have no peace until all things have entered into Buddhahood. Thus there are two kinds of children which may proceed from the pairs of opposites, the living and the still-born. Those who accept life and death are the living, and those who would escape them are the stillborn, for Enlightenment is not found outside the universe, but within it. In the words of Monoimus the Arabian: "Cease to seek after God (as without thee), and the universe, and things similar to these; seek Him from out of thyself. . . . And learn whence is sorrow and joy, and love and hate, and waking though one would not, and sleeping though one would not, and getting angry though one would not, and falling in love though one would not. And if thou shouldst closely investigate these things, thou wilt find Him in thyself, one and many, just as the atom: thus finding from thyself a way out of thyself."

In this way the sage awakes in himself the Holy Child, the Christ Principle, ascending from the state of conflict between life and death to the stage where both are seen as aspects of the greater Life. For the greater Life is in the ordered music of change, in the synthesis of law and liberty, birth and death, force and inertia, which in union make possible the movement of the Ever Living. Therefore, in accepting both pairs of opposites as essential not only to one another but also to the very existence of the universe, he becomes no longer the slave who is torn helplessly between them but the master whom they serve. He is born again of Water and the Spirit. Even so, his task is not yet finished. Indeed, the task of evolving life is never done, but beyond the mastery of the pairs of opposites there is yet another task for man.

There is a danger that, full of the pride of mastery, man may set himself in opposition to the pairs of opposites, and thus begin over again the struggle which he has resolved into harmony. To claim victory over the world of opposites, to take pride therein, to set oneself up as God as distinct from the world, this is once more to fall into illusion. He who glories in his conquest of the world has not conquered himself; he has become the victim of another opposite; he has created the opposition of a Higher Third and a Lower Fourth. For he does not perceive that the Lower Fourth is illusion, that there is no opposition between the man and woman and the child, between life-and-death and the greater Life. In the highest sense life-and-death *is* the greater Life, Samsara *is* Nirvana, the Son of Man *is* the Son of God. The Higher Third is in no way apart from the pairs of opposites; it is produced by them; it exists in them, and they in it. For the Higher Third is just the harmony of opposites wherein the opposites become, not blended into one another, but understood as mutually dependent and mutually productive. Hence the sage, attaining mastery, renounces all claim to victory. For to claim lordship over the world is to be a slave to the world, to be possessed by an illusion of the world, the illusion that one opposite can triumph over another. Truly to accept the opposites is not only to receive but also to give; victory comes through acceptance, but when acceptance is real there can be no thought of victory. Thus the sage receives the world into himself, and gives himself to the world. In giving himself he yields his claim to victory, for in truth there is no victory over the world; he has only seen the world as it is.

# CONCLUSION.

We have now enquired into the meaning of seven symbols, but as there is nothing in the world which is not an image of eternal verities, we might probe forever into hidden meanings. For in taking these symbols we have chosen those things which are alive and of the world of experience as distinct from such abstract symbols as the circle, the swastika and the cross. But of living symbols let this be said: the symbol is not less than its meaning. It is not enough to search for philosophy in the lotus, in water, wind, fire, man, woman and child, for through this we might think that the world of forms is no more than the outward representation of abstract principles. Certainly the world is such a representation, but it is more than this. The knowledge of meanings is of little avail unless it can teach us to know more truly the beauty and ugliness of the lotus, the wetness of water, the motion of wind, the heat of fire, the love between man and woman, and the birth of the child. Through philosophy we may learn that what we once considered ordinary objects and events are in truth mere symbols of an eternal world more real than the temporal. But this is not all, for we must see once again that the lotus is a lotus, that water is water, and fire is fire—with this difference: that such things will appear no longer ordinary, but miraculous and full of wonder.

# LETTERS I RECEIVE
## THE "WHAT" AND THE "HOW"
### By the Editor

From *Buddhism in England*
*May–June, 1936*

•

It is often said that letter-writing is a lost art and that nowadays no one bothers to write more than a sort of enlarged telegram. Don't you believe it. The people who used to write long and beautiful letters in the leisurely days that are past have their modern counterparts; their style is, of course, different, but I have no doubt they take as much trouble. The difference between now and then is that now more people write letters, and those who are responsible for these enlarged telegrams would not have been able to write at all if they had lived two hundred years ago. If you are a writer, and especially if you are an editor, and especially if your writing and editing is concerned with philosophical and religious subjects, you are bound to receive a large number of letters. Some of these raise such important and interesting problems that I have thought it worth while to devote some space in each number of this magazine to a discussion of questions of general interest, suggested by letters which I receive in the past two months.

"I know what you say is true. But when I read your article it seems so easy—whereas no one wants to know *what* must be done, but *how?* and *where?* and even more so, wherein don't we do it now? I am fogged by your stating a problem (my problem, and everybody's) in terms which do not help me to define it any more than giving it a poetic symbol and so perhaps sending it further from fitting an actual form."

It does not matter what the article in question was, except that it illustrated an ancient truth by means of a symbol. The writer of this letter had no difficulty in understanding that truth and its relation to the symbol; she even agreed that what was said was right, but thereafter she was at a loss, for although she knew *what* to do she could not see *how* to do it. That may seem a very simple matter to remedy. If I say, "We should build a bridge across this river," and my friend says, "Yes, I agree, but how?" then it should not be difficult to explain, "Well, we must cut some trees, saw them into planks and then lay them across from one bank to the other." Many more difficult problems could be explained with an equal simplicity, except that the explanations would be longer, but that is all very well when we are explaining things which it takes no more than the intellect to understand. Thus it is a simple matter to show how to add ten to eight, because both the explanation and the addition are performed by the intellect, but it is a very different matter to explain how to love, how to appreciate music or how to acquire wisdom. The trouble is that almost any explanation must be made in terms of intellect, that is, the reasoning faculty of the mind, which measures, calculates, makes deductions, discriminates, analyses and in short "puts two and two together." But such things as love, beauty and wisdom cannot be measured for they are qualities and not quantities. Thus we cannot devise a formula for a beautiful piece of music, such as: five hundred quavers, forty semi-quavers, a thousand crotchets, two hundred minims and eight semibreves arranged in bars, each bar being of the value of four crotchets, equals one Overture. Unfortunately, not all intellectual explanations of abstract qualities are as absurd as this—at least, not apparently so, or we might be more often on our guard against them. But leaving aside questions of how to write beautiful music or build bridges, let us consider the problem for which so many of us are seeking an answer and which, after all, is the greatest of all problems. How can I find happiness? How can I find Enlightenment? How can I find help from this Buddhism?

Well, we are always trying to give answers in this magazine. We say, "Give up selfish craving—the desire to make yourself God." Or "Study the Four Noble Truths. Keep the Precepts. Follow the Eightfold Path," and if more detailed instructions are wanted we write a long text-book on Concentration and Meditation giving numerous exercises in mind-control. We publish articles intended to be of help in the ordinary affairs of life, explanations of the workings of the mind and the emotions, and while some of these are advanced and difficult, others are so simple that one would think a child could understand them. But were we to enlist the services of sages to write for us, if we could have a Buddha to write a leading article in every number, we should not necessarily be of any more help to our readers than we are already. After all, do not most of us make a fairly regular practice of reading the words of the Buddha or the other great teachers of men? And yet, with all these great teachings at our finger tips, most of us still go on seeking, trying to find some interpretation of these teachings or some new teaching which will give us just that something that we lack. But what can we say that is new, and what can we write that has not been written already in another form? Even the Buddha said nothing new, for there were Buddhas before him, and their teachings were forgotten just as this may some day be forgotten.

So we might write and teach and preach for ever, but still people would fail to practise Buddhism; they would still go on reading and reading with an ever-growing hunger for words; they would still be unable to understand what we said or else come to us with the eternal complaint, "Yes, I understand what you say perfectly and agree with it entirely. You have explained what I should do in every detail, *but how am I to do it?"* I ask the same question myself, and I confess it worries me a lot, but I think I have found some sort of an answer. Let me return to the analogy of music. No one on earth could write a book giving a complete explanation of how to write *beautiful* music, although thousands of people have written books on the mere technique of music. Though there are works on Harmony, Orchestration, Counterpoint, Tempo and the rest, there is no work on how to become a Mozart. In just the same way all that appears in this magazine and even all that has been said by Buddhas and sages is no more than a collection of instructions on the technique of Buddhism. These instructions are very useful in their way, but by themselves are so much waste paper. They can be of use to you if you can use them, just as the technique of music is useful to one who has a beauty in his soul which he wishes to express. But it cannot give him that beauty. Similarly, if you already have a conscious spark of Enlightenment within you, you will be able to use the teachings of Buddhism to increase it and express it. But if you have not, no amount of words will create it and though you study till your hair turns grey you will find nothing because, in themselves, words are mere lifeless forms. Yet you are by no means a "lost soul."

The spark of Enlightenment is in everyone simply because everyone has life. But not everyone is conscious of the spark; in fact, this consciousness is an unusual achievement and there is no need to feel that you are an outcast or that you are subnormal because you haven't got it. (In strict confidence, I don't think I've got it myself.) But I believe that we can find this spark if we look, in the first place, not to words and teachings and technical principles but to living things. If this spark exists anywhere, where would one expect to find it? Surely the answer is—in the people who have it. Not in what they write, or say or do, but in what they *are*. To find someone like this, it is not necessary to go to Tibet or start hunting for a *guru*, for you have it yourself, only you don't know it. *You* are one of those people, so is your next-door neighbour. And once again you ask, *"How* am I to know that?" The answer to that is a question. Does the great music of the world seem lovely to you? If so, you have within you a little Mozart. Have you any regard at all for your fellow men? Do their interests or troubles seem of any importance, even if they have nothing to do with you? If so, you have a little Bodhisattva. Do you reverence wisdom when you meet with it, not in wise sayings or learned books, but in life, in people? If so, you have a little Buddha, a little spark of Enlightenment.

Wisdom can no more be found in books on Buddhism or any other philosophy than you can find out how to love your wife or husband in a text-book on Matrimony. If you cannot find it in living beings, in yourself and in others, all the scriptures in the world are worthless, for they are *about* wisdom; wisdom itself is alive and can no more be set down than sunlight can be caught in a box. But you may ask again, *"How* shall I recognize it when I meet it? You say that if I reverence wisdom, then I have a little Buddha, but I do not know that what I reverence *is* wisdom and I can't recognize my Buddha." It is like asking, "How do you love? And how can you know that your love really is love?" That is the most terrible question that can be asked; more than any other it presses for an answer, but it cannot be answered— at least, not in the same terms in which it is asked, in words or ideas. Some things can only be communicated from man to man by means of what is known in Zen Buddhism as "direct transmission"; that is, enabling someone to understand and develop a certain quality by showing it to him in yourself. Well, sometimes we are fortunate enough to meet someone who can help us in that way; yet if we believe in Karma, we may be sure that that is an opportunity which we have earned. It comes to all who are ready for it.

What more can be said? We have reached the point where words can go no further, but perhaps just a hint can be given to the answer of that most unanswerable of questions. It has been said; "You ask me how you shall find Truth. Would you ask me also how you should love? But I say it is by trying that you fail, for your strivings divide you from what you seek. Be not as one who tries to kiss his own lips."

---

# LETTERS I RECEIVE
## TALKING OF WAR
*By the Editor*

From *Buddhism in England*
*July–August, 1936*

•

It is with the greatest hesitation that I mention this subject at all. Nowadays everyone is talking about War, so much so that it seems to have attained the position of principal bee in the public bonnet. What with innumerable films, articles in the Press, speeches and movements, one feels that one owes one's readers a profound apology for adding yet another few columns of print to this interminable discussion. The danger is that what we think about, whether with pleasure or with pain, is inclined to happen. Thoughts create things, no matter whether they are thoughts of attraction or repulsion, and a widespread fear of War is just as dangerous as the popular militarism of certain nations which are described as "war-mongering." Yet several readers of *Buddhism in England* have written in the past two months asking for more prominence to be given to the problem of War and Peace, and it occurred to me that this would be a good opportunity of presenting the question in a way in which it has never been presented before in this magazine.

Going through back numbers, I find that all discussion of the evils of War has been based on the idea of War as a denial of brotherly love, of the fundamental Unity of Life which is the *raison d'être* of the Buddhist attitude to one's fellow beings.

No one can dispute that War is such a denial, but it does not necessarily follow that the chief cause of War is hatred of other people, especially in modern civilization. For instance, it would be absurd to argue that the entry of England into the last war was the result of age-old hatred between the English and German peoples. What hatred there was was stirred up at the last moment by Government propaganda, and of course it can be argued that the individual Englishman was in no way responsible for the conflict, that he was the mere pawn of a capitalist oligarchy. I do not want to enter into a discussion of economic determinism, but even if this theory is true, it in no way conflicts with the principle that a nation gets what government it deserves, and that if War comes upon it, from whatever immediate cause, it is the nation's Karma both collectively and individually.

At one time, warfare concerned, in the main, only a small section of society—the professional soldiers. Certainly cities and villages were attacked and their populations were massacred, but only in comparatively recent times has mass warfare become a phenomenon of European civilization. At the same time, the old motive for warfare, territorial expansion, has become obsolete, for under present economic conditions it is impossible for any nation to become more prosperous by conquering another. The expense involved cripples both victor and vanquished, and no amount of conquest will solve the fundamental economic difficulty of this age—the problem of scarcity amid plenty. No one in his right mind could pretend that Italy went to war with Abyssinia out of greed for wealth. The Italian Government must have known from the beginning that the war would ruin the already unstable financial position of the nation, and the only possible political motive was the glorification of Fascism by means of a victorious war. But underlying this was a psychological motive—a motive which is intensified by Fascism but not caused by it, a motive which exists to-day in almost every European country.

With the progress of what we are pleased to call civilization, the behaviour of man becomes more and more subjected to a rational order. In all primitive races definite provision is made for an essential irrationality in man, which "civilization" does not officially recognize. This takes the form of orgies held at certain seasons of the year, though no one need imagine that the life of the primitive is one long orgy. On the contrary, he is just as much set about by *tabus* as the civilized man—in some instances even more so. But there are special times when *tabus* are thrown aside, and the tribe joins in ceremonies and dances involving a tremendous outpouring of the emotions. At one time these festivals were held throughout Europe, and the Continental carnivals of the present day are their pale relics. But wherever the restraining influence of Protestantism has made itself felt, these emotional safety-valves have been entirely closed with results both extremely good and extremely evil.

Among the irrational desires of man—and particularly of man in any advanced state of civilization—is the desire for blood and death. This desire is always emphasized when a large proportion of the population is either idle or subjected to monotonous forms of work which stifle the mento-emotional nature. Imperial Rome had its Circus Maximus, where crowds flocked to see the crudest spectacles of death. The degenerate Spanish Empire produced the love of the bullring, and in India (home of the greatest extremes of good and evil on earth) is found the most pronounced form of this death-worship—the cult of Kali, the bride of Shiva, which is the adoration of final annihilation under the symbol of the female principle. We are accustomed to regard these orgies as signs of barbarism, but, revolting as they are, it is probable that the historian of the future will look upon them as comparatively harmless beside the hideous, impersonal slaughter of modern warfare. For it seems that this slaughter is less the result of hatred than of the damning-up of man's irrational desires.

Many things are possible in time of war which would otherwise be denied. Murder, which ordinarily would be punished, is condoned; unusual opportunities are offered for sexual promiscuity; and a release is found from the hum-drum isolation of everyday life in the adventurous fellow-ship of the Army. Emotional outbursts in the form of hysterical mass meetings become almost commonplace, and the attitude of "let us drink to-day, for to-morrow we die" rouses man's emotional capacity to its highest level. Thus while primitive races relieve their emotions by a safety-valve, modern man allows the boiler to burst. Certainly the gigantic scale of modern warfare is directly due to our knowledge of machinery, but machinery was produced by the same tendency which closed the emotional safety-valve—the desire for progress, order, efficiency and rationality, carried to its furthest extremes.

But the idea of man, in his present stage of evolution, as a rational being is a conceit of the mere surface of our minds. However much he may order the externals of his life, however much he may cultivate "good behaviour," in the depths of his being the primitive, unreasoning forces of his nature remain as mighty as ever. In time of war they break from their prison and make havoc until they subside with exhaustion. No one, however, is suggesting that man should cease to order his life and attempt to cultivate good behaviour. There is a picturesque phrase about throwing out the baby with the bath-water; the prevention of War by the giving up of such tiresome things as morality, discipline and good manners would no doubt provide an excellent excuse for a perpetual "good time." Doubtless it would prevent War in any violent form, but I can imagine nothing more dull than a permanent freedom from discipline. It would be like a diet of strawberries and cream, and we would, from necessity, very soon be swinging over to the ascetical fare of plain water and dry biscuits. But just as a perpetual debauch would be not only dull but productive of a disagreeable asceticism, so also a perpetual attempt at good behaviour is both dull and productive of such highly repulsive excesses as War.

What, then, is the solution? Are we to spend half our time in ascetic discipline and half in sensual enjoyment? Are we to mould our lives so as to be not very good and not very evil? It is rather difficult to imagine what the latter alternative would be like; certainly it would be dull, and we should probably be aching for some extreme behaviour so as to beautify the landscape of our existence with valleys and mountains through boredom with a vast, flat plain. There remains the former alternative. I think most of us will admit that that, too, is rather dull. It does not get us anywhere, either to one extreme or the other. It is the monotony of a pendulum, swinging its measured distance throughout eternity. But the pendulum has an arm; the weight is at one end, and at the other is the pivot which remains unmoved however far the weight swings. Suppose one could shift one's centre of consciousness from the weight to the pivot, and so find a position which is neither good nor evil nor a compromise between the two—a Higher Third, which is above and between the pairs of opposites. Jung speaks of this in his commentary to the *Secret of the Golden Flower.* "But if the unconscious," he writes, "can be recognized as a co-determining quantity along with the conscious, and if it can be lived in such a way that conscious and unconscious (in a narrower sense instinctive) demands are given recognition as far as possible, the centre of gravity of the total personality shifts its position. It ceases to be in the ego, which is merely the centre of consciousness, and is located instead in what might be called a virtual point between the conscious and the unconscious. . . . There develops a personality who, so to speak, suffers only in the inferior parts of himself, but in the superior regions, to carry out the future, is singularly detached from painful as well as pleasing events."

Any of the pairs of opposites can be substituted for the words "conscious" and "unconscious," "painful" and "pleasing." We might also say that if equal recognition can be given to both the rational and irrational elements in man, we can develop a centre of being which is detached from both good and evil? Do we perform acts of charity and commit murders with utter impartiality and equanimity? Do we sit smiling on the pivot of the pendulum and watch our weight (which is our outward personality) swinging to kiss our fellow men on the one side and smite them on the other? If we pull it too far in the kissing direction it will eventually return with tremendous force on the other side; if we pull it too far in the smiting direction it will return again with a nauseating kiss. Do we witness these things unmoved? Do we just let it swing a medium distance? Or do we stop it swinging altogether? To do that would be to return to the inanimate existence of stones. It would be altogether without purpose—a refusal to solve a difficulty, a shameful escape from the task, an utter denial of life. And even then, it would be difficult, for spiritual suicide is but another extreme of the pendulum's swing. It is the worship of Kali, the opposite of the fiercest desire for life and consciousness. Whichever way we move we find that we can never escape from an opposite, and while there are opposites the problem remains unsolved. For the pendulum must always return.

This is the most difficult of all problems, and at this point I hazard only the most tentative answer to the question of the pairs of opposites. I shall be glad if all those who have any ideas to offer on the subject will write to me, so that we may clarify the problem among ourselves. I do not fully understand my own answer, so I can only present it in the form of an analogy. When man has shifted the centre of his being from the weight of the pendulum to the pivot he can do something with it which he can never do while identifying himself with the weight. You can prove this by holding a piece of string in your hand with a weight on one end. You can do one of two things with it. You can let it swing to left and right, though you can never make it stay at either extreme. On the other hand, you can make it travel in a *circle*—and in this way *the extremes vanish*. To execute this circular movement is a difficult task from the weight end. If you attach the pivot end to a nail on the wall, it will be a tiring performance to move the weight round the nail. It will be an impossible performance if the string is sufficiently long. The string between man and Buddha is *very* long. But a weight with a considerable length of string can be revolved with ease from the pivot end—and this is what the Enlightened Ones do with the pendulums of their lives.

They revolve their weights, their personalities, in the same direction as the universe itself is revolving. Lesser beings do not revolve; they swing one way or the other. Sometimes they swing with the universal cycle, sometimes against it, which makes them alternately happy and miserable. If they swing against the universal pendulum, its weight hits them and they suffer. If they swing with it, they cannot keep up the effort *unless they shift the centre of their being to the universal pivot upon which all of us are hanging. There is only movement—ultimately beneficent movement, for the knocks which it gives us if we go against it only serve to rouse us to the treading of the Path which leads to harmony with the cycle of Life.*

# THE TRUTH THAT IS MORE THAN TEACHING.

## An Appeal to Buddhists on the occasion of the World Congress of Faiths.

From *Buddhism in England*
*July–August, 1936*

●

This summer, London is to be the scene of a rather unusual gathering. Early this month representatives of every important religion in the world will be meeting for a great Congress of Faiths of which the main object is "to discover what the various Faiths can contribute towards the establishment of World Fellowship," and "to seek for methods of expressing that Supreme Ideal of Human Life which every man of whatever race or creed is seeking in his heart."

Therefore this seems to be a fitting occasion to consider the subject of unity in religion and to examine some of the reasons why, even among Buddhists, there are innumerable sectarian squabbles which prevent us from working together like reasonable human beings.

All schools of Buddhism are agreed that Life is a Unity, and that the apparent separateness of one being from another is illusion. However different we may appear to be on the surface, ultimately we all have our roots in a common source which you may call Life or Reality or whatever other name you may prefer. This is such an important Buddhist principle that I have often wondered at the things which divide us into conflicting parties and which cause believers in this great truth to quarrel among themselves. All conflict must take place on the plane of separateness, in the superficial and illusory aspect of Life where the fundamental Unity is not perceived. In the real aspect there can be no conflict, for there it is realized that the many are One. I believe that such conflict might be overcome if we could accept the fact that in Samsara—the world of form and separateness—it is in the very nature of things to disagree. In all the universe there is no one form that is in every respect the same as another, for all things, while they are essentially One, are unique in their outward appearance.

Therefore quarrels are caused by looking for agreement where it cannot exist, and the man who quarrels with his fellows is he who seeks to impose his own form upon others. But in Samsara unity can only be achieved by agreeing to differ. For difference is the very nature of Samsara, and unity cannot be achieved by trying to make separate forms the same as one another, but only by realizing that all forms have a common essence. For instance, if a bird is to be a bird, it would be ridiculous to expect the wings to be like the beak, or the claws like the tail. And yet many of us seriously expect such impossibilities to be achieved when we try to make others conform with our own patterns and plans. For the human race, in the same way as a bird, is an organism of which every part has a separate and distinct function or *dharma*, and the whole cannot be expressed in its parts unless each part is unique in its form and method of work.

Just as the human race is a total organism, so are the followers of the Buddha of whatever sect or school. It is unfortunate, therefore, that within this great religious body there should be numerous conflicts and quarrels which prevent it from working as a harmonious whole. There is the conflict between Mahayana and Theravada, between the various schools of thought about the Anatta doctrine, between theists and atheists, and between the Self-power and Other-power sects of China and Japan, to mention only a few.

These conflicts prevent Buddhists from sincerely acknowledging one another as brothers, and destroy the effectiveness of a common purpose within the greatest religious community in the world. Of course, it would be too much to expect people not to quarrel, for the seeds of strife are planted deep in human nature. But it is not too much to expect the more conscious and intelligent members of this community to refrain from doctrinal squabbles and to realize that there is a deeper and infinitely more important bond between man and man than mere similarity of belief.

We must accept the fact that, even among Buddhists, beliefs are bound to differ. For all belief in doctrines is a matter of intellect, and intellect is that faculty of the mind which discriminates, which forms ideas and concepts. All forms, whether mental or physical, are of Samsara; thus they will differ in greater or lesser degree with each individual, for, as we have seen, in Samsara there can be no two things of the same pattern. Therefore I am convinced that it is a mistake to try to achieve unity among Buddhists or between the members of any other religion by attempting to construct a common creed or even a minimum basis of generally accepted beliefs. *We can be united and yet have different opinions.* This may sound strange, even impossible, and so it would be if there were not in Buddhism a Truth that is more than teaching, more than a set of ideas about the universe.

The error which is at the root of all conflict is too great a reliance on forms. No one, unless he spent too much reverence on mere concepts, would quarrel with another because of his form of belief, or be offended because someone disagreed with his own. If someone attacks my property and so offends me, my feeling of offence can only arise through attachment to property—which is not a Buddhist virtue. What applies to property must also apply to beliefs, concepts and doctrines, for these are the property of the mind. *Tanha*—selfish clinging—can apply just as much to ideas as to money, for both are *anicca*, impermanent, and *anatta*, without essential reality. For a concept (even the concept of Karma or Anatta) is a form and as such is subject to the same conditions as all other forms. Thus even the Dhamma is a part of Samsara, and for this reason the Buddha likened it to a raft for crossing a stream, a raft which must be left behind when the stream is crossed. Therefore if the Dhamma cannot enter Nirvana, it is certainly a part of Samsara.

One should always be careful to avoid that simplest yet most dangerous of mistakes—the confusion of belief with Truth, the identification of the raft with the opposite bank of the stream. Beliefs are ideas *about* Truth and not Truth itself, for the formless Nirvana cannot be described by the forms of Samsara, and as all forms are illusory and impermanent, he who *clings* to beliefs is lost. He who would attain Nirvana must give up all clinging, for only in this way can he achieve the Enlightenment which is freedom from forms. That is not to say that he destroys all forms, but that he is no longer attached to them, that he no longer depends upon them for his peace of mind. Therefore let us make less ado about beliefs; no one ever travelled far on a road by clinging to its surface, and he who travels fastest, he who runs, touches it least with his feet. But how, then, shall we know that we are on the right road? Must we not depend upon the road if we would reach the Goal? Paradoxically the answer is: That road is the best upon which we feel we need depend least, for that road leads to non-attachment, to freedom from dependence. Further than this, non-attachment is that road, for Buddhism is essentially the art of setting the mind free from the forms which it uses. For the doctrines of Karma, Anatta, Dukkha, Rebirth and the rest are all teachings about the nature of Samsara; they are warnings to us to be careful of the snares of Samsara. But the Truth which is more than all these teachings can only be known when we depend neither upon Samsara nor on ideas about it or about anything else. Therefore why should intelligent Buddhists quarrel over the various merits of certain sets of ideas and doctrines? For the real question for them is not in which set of doctrines to believe, but how to pass beyond all doctrines. Let them ask not, "How shall we reconcile our beliefs?" but "How shall we cease to depend on beliefs?" For the essence of Buddhism is the attainment of Enlightenment through freedom from all objects, forms and concepts—yes, even the concept that we must depend for our salvation on becoming free from objects, forms and concepts! Ultimately Buddhism goes as far as that, for even he who is attached only to Nirvana knows not Nirvana. If this is our ideal we shall become the laughing-stock of the world if we behave like the pundits of whom Omar Khayyam said:

> *Myself when young did eagerly frequent*
> *Doctor and Saint, and heard great argument*
> *About it and about: but evermore*
> *Came out by the same door as in I went.*

---

# LETTERS I RECEIVE
## IS THERE A SELF?
### *By the Editor*

From *Buddhism in England*
*Sept.–Oct., 1936*

●

For some reason the doctrine of *anatta* is the occasion of endless controversy. The remarks of Mrs. Rhys Davids produce storms of protest, and in the past few weeks I have seen several Buddhist periodicals containing somewhat polemical articles on the subject. It has been said that three-quarters of controversy is due to inadequate definition or understanding of terms, and doubtless this is no exception to the rule. Naturally it is very difficult to discuss things intelligently unless we all know what we are talking about, but the real trouble with this particular discussion is that it has little or no relation to practical life. I do not say that it is not a very interesting discussion, in the same way as a crossword puzzle or a game of chess is interesting. Certainly it is a peculiarly delightful and in every way legitimate form of intellectual gymnastics, and so long as we recognize that the result of it does not matter one way or the other, it must be regarded as a very excellent and entertaining amusement. Nowadays people are somewhat prone to treating sport as a religion, with the result that it ceases to be sporting. Sport is really doing things that do not matter for fun, and man's faculty for this is one of the things that make him superior to animals. But it only remains superiority so long as he recognizes that those things do not matter. Thus a man who hits a ball about with a stick for fun is a delightful being, but one who does it as if his life depended upon it is a dangerous lunatic. The same principle applies to the intellectual amusements. It is certainly great fun to discuss the existence or non-existence of the self, but it ceases to be fun when we take it into our heads that the discussion really matters. It then becomes lunacy, because there is no possible means of deciding which party is in the right.

Of course the matter-of-fact person will at once ask, "Surely it matters very much whether I do or do not exist?" But unfortunately it is not quite so simple as that because we first have to define what we mean by "I." In the philosophy of the East we find mention of at least two different kinds of self. One is the little creature "the size of a thumb" who is said to exist somewhere inside the body—a creature who is both personal and immortal. The other is the Self of the Upanishads, the Self which is the same for everyone, existing in all things alike, and this is impersonal and immortal. The first of these corresponds approximately to the Western notion of the soul. There is really no need to define it philosophically, because everyone knows exactly what it means. It is the feeling, the intuition, that I am I, separate from you and from everything else. And therefore the problem is, does this thing which says I am I exist or does it not? If it does exist, is it immortal? And further, is one's intuition of it incomplete in the sense that it is really much greater than one thinks, that it includes the whole universe instead of just that area of space which is bounded by one's own skin?

It is certainly a very entertaining problem, but it does not matter in the least because we have no means of knowing whether, objectively, the "I" exists or not. We cannot examine ourselves to find out if we are really here, because we cannot examine the thing that examines, and that is the great limitation of all scientific investigation. The scientist may probe into the psyche of other human beings and declare that on analysis he cannot find anything in the shape of a self. Unfortunately he cannot probe into the thing that probes. However, the doctrine of *anatta* is included in the Buddha's teaching, and if we believe that the Buddha was the wisest of men, he must have had some reason for including it. Is the answer that he intended us to believe in our non-existence, because, apart from all questions of objective truth, that belief is a working hypothesis conducive to the good life? Was the Buddha a pragmatist, holding that the effect of a belief upon one's manner of life is more important than the truth of that belief?

But it has been said that a man believes a thing when he behaves *as if* it were true, and it is rather difficult to imagine a man behaving as if he did not exist. Presumably he would make a noise like the legs of a snake and run away. But not even the most extreme upholder of the *anatta* doctrine would go so far as to say that if it implies one's complete non-existence. The principle of *cogito, ergo sum* (even if untrue from the standpoint of Absolute Truth) must always hold good for practical purposes. If we disbelieve in it, our disbelief is a mere intellectual perversity having no relation to life, for we cannot reasonably act upon our disbelief. But here again it is important to note that this is not fundamentally a question of belief or disbelief in anything; the living of the Dhamma does not require assent to any proposition which is foreign to our experience. The Dhamma is concerned with life here and now at this very moment; it has no immediate relation to metaphysics, and however rational the doctrine of rebirth and the non-existence of the personal soul may be, they are undeniably metaphysical. In our present stage of evolution discussion of them must always be mere intellectual gymnastics, because we have no means of testing their objective validity.

What, then, does *anatta* mean in reference to ordinary experience? To understand this, it must be taken in conjunction with the two other "signs of being"—*anicca* (impermanence) and *dukha* (suffering). It is important to remember that the Buddha spoke of these three signs of being not as doctrines, not as "revealed truths," but as facts of ordinary experience. *Dukha* does not mean only "suffering" in the Western sense of the word; if its meaning were as narrow as that, it would be absurd to say that all life is *dukha*. We experience happiness and misery in turn, and though the two are frequently mixed, we cannot deny that life is composed of *both* pleasure and pain. *Dukha* is rather "limitation"; it signifies confinement, discontent, the transiency of happiness, the imperfection of our lives, as well as actual suffering and pain. And this is not a doctrine requiring belief or disbelief; it is a fact of experience, and we are as familiar with it as with the hotness of the sun. The same is true of *anicca*. We *know* that all things are subject to change, and no proof is wanted. If, therefore, these two signs of being are facts of ordinary experience, should not the same thing be said of *anatta*? And the answer is, Yes. For are we not perfectly familiar with the fact that the identity of forms disappears? To every form, whether man, beast, flower or stone, we attribute an identity. When we meet Mr. Jones on Monday, we recognize him again on Thursday because we identify him as the same Mr. Jones. He has not become Mr. Postlethwaite or Mr. Featherstone. The Buddha did not deny the fact of identity, but he said something about it which is perfectly obvious to everyone. That was that identities not only come to an end but are in a constant state of flux. When we meet Mr. Jones again on Thursday, we know quite well that he is not really the identical Mr. Jones we met on Monday. In the first place, he may have changed his mind about lending us a five pound note; he has certainly changed in body, for his tissues have absorbed nourishment and some have wasted away; he may have had experiences which have made him a "different man." All these are changes in the identity called Mr. Jones. Therefore, when the Buddha said that all things are *anatta*, he meant that identity is not an abiding principle in any form of life. If everything did retain its identity life would stop dead, for change is really a constant movement towards losing one's identity. As soon as we are born, we begin to die, and our identity is always running away from us.

The trouble is, however, that people are always trying to run after their lost identities. The baby who does not want to be weaned from his mother is running after his identity as a suckling; he resists the loss of his suckling *atta*, and does not want to give up his old self. But if we are to go forward, we must give up our old selves every minute. In fact we are *compelled* to give up these selves, whether we like it or not. What makes the difference between the enlightened and unenlightened man is that one accepts this giving up gladly, while the other does it against his will and usually tries to deceive himself into the belief that he has not done it. Try to imagine yourself back in the identical state of consciousness and experience which you were in two minutes ago. You cannot do it. You are different. And if you think about it long enough, you will find it hard to believe that the "you" which got out of the train two minutes ago is the same "you" which is now walking down the street. It is not the same you. *Sabbe sankharam anatta.*

But what is this "you"? What is the something that two miuntes ago experienced getting out of the train, and now experiences walking down the street? Certainly it may have changed in that two mintues, but what is it? Is it the self? Is it the immortal soul? Is it the unchanging essence of the universe? Those questions cannot be answered, for the simple reason that it cannot look at itself to find out. Some lunatics imagine that if they turn round quickly enough they can see the backs of their heads. But man has eyes only in one side of his head, and a characteristic of all things is that while one side is in the light the other is in the dark. It is that dark side which we are perpetually seeking, consciously or unconsciously. For why does the achievement of desire turn to ashes? Because we find that we can add to ourselves nothing that we have not already. We may possess a kingdom, but it adds nothing to us. It does not make us any worse or any better, for all that we know of it is our own reaction to it. Whatever possession or knowledge we may acquire, it has no influence on the way in which we react to it. We gain from such things solely in accordance with our capacity to gain from anything. A long-desired fortune may weary us when achieved, for it can add nothing to our powers of enjoyment. If we can enjoy little things, we can enjoy great, and if we are bored by little, we shall be bored by what is great. For all things under the sun are mirrors in which we see our own reflections; when we catch them after a long chase, we find that we have only caught ourselves. And so we are like dogs chasing their own tails in the belief that they may be something good to eat. When we find that what we have sought with so much energy is only ourselves after all, it irritates us, for the "self" is such a curious and elusive creature. We find it everywhere when we do not want it, but when we do want it, it always runs away. We turn round to try and catch it, but it is behind us again like the backs of our heads. Thus whether we are trying to run away from it or trying to run after it, we are always chasing it. In the outside world we catch its reflection—but the thing itself we can never catch. We cannot even be sure that it exists.

It was for this reason that the Buddha deemed discussion of the nature of the self unprofitable and not conducive to Enlightenment. For Ignorance (*avidya*) is precisely this tail-chasing process. It leads nowhere, except in a circle. It is just this going round in little circles in pursuit of ourselves which is selfishness, the heresy of separateness, the folly of belief in *atta*. It is the Wheel of Samsara. The Buddha advised us not to trouble about it. We shall know what the self is and whether it is only when we no longer chase it. The secret is to stop running round in circles and—walk on!

---

# LETTERS I RECEIVE
## KARMA, OR
## "YOU HAVE WHAT YOU WANT"
### By the Editor

From *Buddhism in England*
*Nov.–Dec., 1936*

●

From letters which have found their way to me and from many articles which have recently been published in journals connected with the philosophy of the East, it seems that there is a somewhat widespread misunderstanding of the law of Karma. There appear to be two principal ways of misunderstanding Karma. The first is found in the idea that it is some sort of cosmic and impersonal system of reward and punishment, based on eternal laws of justice which in some way correspond very conveniently with human ethics. It is thought that when a man commits a misdeed, quite independently of his own wishes, the universal wheels are set in motion, and after a certain period the exact and fit retribution returns to him. It is rather like those machines into one end of which we place a cow, and in due course receive at the other a pair of boots, a gallon of milk, several joints of beef, ten dozen straps, two horn spoons and a bag of bones. This theory differs only in trivial respects from the idea of the schoolmaster-God, cherished by the more primitive forms of Christianity; the difference is that this God is simply made impersonal, and that His rewards and punishments cease to be eternal.

The second, and more insidious, misunderstanding is found in the entirely logical but wholly stultifying idea that Karma involves the doctrine of determinism. It is argued that if Karma is the law of cause and effect, then nothing can come into being without some cause, and that whatever does come into being can only come from *one* particular cause (or set of causes). The corollary of this contention is therefore that any given cause (or set of causes) can and must have only one as distinct from several alternative effects. Thus whatever we think or do has some cause of which it is the inevitable effect. That cause is rigidly conditioned by previous causes, until we are found to be fettered in "one infinite chain which none can break, nor snap, nor overreach." It is said that every action has some motive; that that motive results in that action because it is the strongest of several possible motives; that that motive is the strongest because. . . . Which reminds one of the delightful verse:—

*Big fleas have little fleas*
*Upon their backs to bite 'em;*
*And little fleas have lesser fleas*
*And so ad infinitum.*

No one can deny for a moment that this theory is completely logical, that its reasoning is perfect in every respect; but the trouble is precisely that it *is* so very logical. It has all the precision of a finely constructed machine, and all its lack of intelligence.

Surprisingly few people, however, are even aware of what the word "Karma" means. It is derived from the Sanskrit root *kri*—"to act" or "to do," and thus the word itself means "action," although the purely English translation, "doing," is in many ways better. Thus when we say that something which happens to a person is his Karma, we mean that it is his doing. And it is his doing in a very immediate and personal sense, for at this moment we are the sum total of all our past actions. The whole doctrine of Karma can be explained by extending the German proverb, "Man is what he eats" to "Man is what he does"—using the word in its widest sense to include thinks, feels, desires. The Buddha taught that all existence proceeds from *Trishna*, a possible translation of which is "desire," and if we follow out this principle we shall discover exactly what is meant by the law of Karma. For there is a saying, "You have what you want." And let us be careful here that we know what we mean by the word "want." If you are sufficiently rude to say to someone, "What you want is a good thrashing," you do not mean what you say. You mean, "What you *need* is a good thrashing," and there is a subtle difference between the two. Therefore, when we say, "You have what you want," we mean that your present circumstances are exactly what you desire and have been brought into being simply by the power of your desire.

This may seem entirely contrary to experience, for the

immediate answer of most people would be that they certainly have not got what they want. But we can never be sure of how much we know about our own desires. Few indeed are the people who really know what they want, and those have a remarkable capacity for getting it. Desire, however, is a strange force, for it is like the iceberg—one part above water and six below, one part conscious and six unconscious. Thus we can never really understand the phrase, "You have what you want," unless we can appreciate that conscious fear is often enough the expression of unconscious desire. This is a doctrine which many people resist with fury; they are highly indignant at the suggestion that they do not know their own minds, that they do not know just what they like and what they do not like. However, in their indignation they are making the proudest of all claims; they are claiming that they have carried out the precept of the Delphic Oracle, "Know thyself," and that is the attainment of the Supremely Enlightened alone.

But the relationship between fear and desire is easily understood if we remember first that the instrument which desire uses for achieving its ends is Imagination—the image-building power. All are familiar with instances in which they have allowed something which they feared to dwell on their minds. They have woven phantasies around it, they have absorbed themselves in its contemplation, they have thought of it day and night. And why? Because they took a morbid pleasure in doing it. In other words, because, although they would be ashamed to admit it, they wanted to. They wallowed in the self-pity which their phantasies produced; they nursed their fears, and ran back to them at every unoccupied moment, like a mother going to her ailing baby at every odd moment between her domestic duties. If someone tries to persuade them that their fears are groundless, they will either argue stoutly against him or reluctantly admit that he is right, and return promptly to their contemplation once again. Indeed, there is no pleasure like worry. The trouble is, however, that because the imagination has been allowed to work on these fears, in longer or shorter time it creates them in actuality. For "all that we are is the result of what we have thought; it is founded on our thoughts; it is made up of our thoughts. If a man speaks or acts with an evil thought, suffering follows him as surely as the wheel of the cart follows the hoof of the ox which draws it."

What is an "evil thought," and why does suffering follow it? The thought is not judged evil by some impersonal tribune of cosmic law and punished accordingly; it is not evil *because* it transgresses certain ethical principles. Evil came first; ethics afterwards. It is evil because it desires a condition of pain. The evildoer inflicts pain on another because he fears it in himself, but in his cruelty he identifies himself to some extent with the sufferer; he revels in the pain which he causes; he satisfies his own desire vicariously. He would find no pleasure in being cruel if he had not a vivid phantasy of what that pain would be like when inflicted on himself. A remarkably interesting study of this sequence of desire, fear and evil will be found in Keyserling's *South American Meditations*. His philosophy is at one with the Buddha's in tracing all life to "Original Hunger" (which might be a good translation for *Trishna*); from this arises "Original Fear." He writes:—

> *Life would absorb into its body the entire universe, and thus eat its way out of all danger. Thus even the nightingale daily devours several times its own weight; thus it is the eternal dream of human understanding to swallow the World. Nevertheless, Life in its nethermost depths knows that its hunger is unappeasable, and that Nature's overwhelming power is irresistible. And from all this arises Fear.*

And again:—

> *Out of Original Fear follows Evil. . . . All torturing is the expression of dimly felt helplessness: the impotency of making the victim suffer the full measure of the fear the torturer himself feels in his heart of hearts.* (Italics mine.)

But we must go further than this and say that he desires his fear.

For here we may read more deeply into the Buddha's teaching, and understand that we suffer not only because we desire, but also because we desire suffering. Our Karma is suffering because we wish it; it is no punishment; it is simply a kind of pleasure found in a more easily recognizable and conscious form in certain neurotic cases, where it is known in psychological jargon as "masochism." In a less intense form this is the familiar experience of taking a pleasure in doing what you don't like, or making a martyr of yourself. It is difficult to understand just *why* we desire to suffer, and more difficult still to explain how we change our desires, both conscious and unconscious, for the better. The first step is obviously to know them; the second to educate them in much the same way as one educates a taste for pictures. Acquaintance wth great art gradually ousts the liking for inferior art, which would seem to show that there is a divine principle in man which ultimately responds to what is divine in both art and life. This principle will not be forced because it is essentially free; it is subject to no compulsion. We have to *let* it grow like a glorious flower, and discipline ourselves by taking the weeds out of the way. Yet, strangest of all, the flower needs filth—manure—for its roots. As "Interpreter" pointed out in an article in the first number of this volume, the lotus rises up from the slime, and filth is just as essential to its life as sun and air. But he said also that evil was to place the flower in the slime and the roots in the light.

And this brings us to the fallacy of the determinist interpretation of Karma. We have already seen that this interpretation is entirely logical. In terms of pure reason it is quite impossible to make out any case for Freewill. Accordingly, from a strictly rational point of view, life is a machine; beauty, intelligence, love and virtue are all the outcome of complex mechanical processes—the inevitable effects of a chain of causes going back into infinite time. If all human thoughts and actions are the inevitable results of certain causes, it is therefore interesting to enquire into the cause which results in the belief in determinism. It seems as if it were closely allied to the desire for suffering, for bondage, for limitation. If masochism is the conscious love of pain, determinism is the conscious love of bondage. We say "love" because almost all determinists argue for their doctrine as if their lives depended on it. It appears, therefore, that determinism is a form of neurosis (Freudians, please note); it is a supremely reasonable creed, but the trouble is that of all reasonable people lunatics are by far the most reasonable. No ordinary lunatic ever does anything without a very closely thought-out reason; his smallest and most inconsequential actions, for which the sane man offers no reason whatever, have a specific purpose. When the sane man twiddles his thumbs, he just twiddles his thumbs; but when the lunatic does it, it is so that his thumbs may grow large and conspicuous, believing, as he does, that he is Imperial Caesar, and that when he puts his thumb up in the arena there must be no mistake about it.

However, because the desire for suffering will be found to include the desire for bondage, it is true that most of us have no Freewill at all, or precious little. We do not allow ourselves to be free; we tie ourselves up in Karmic effects until, consciously or unconsciously, our minds are hopelessly limited. But in terms of logic, freedom can never exist. That is because the logical faculty is essentially a mechanical faculty. If man uses this faculty alone for understanding the universe, then it is only to be expected that he will view it as a machine. The logician claims that his particular faculty is the highest of all faculties, but that is simply because he does not know any higher. His thoughts are limited by his instrument of perception. He may ask us to prove that there is any other instrument of perception, but, unfortunately, it seems that one can only shake one's head and say, "Poor fellow!" It is as hard to convince a logician that there is a higher faculty than logic, as to convince an idiot that he is not in fact Jesus Christ or a poached egg. Both are splendidly isolated by the barriers of rationality, those tough, iron walls through which nothing human can penetrate. Their Karma is Fate, because they make it so; but if you choose. Karma need not be Fate, for in itself it is just your own doing.

---

# LETTERS I RECEIVE
## EDUCATION FOR PROGRESS, WITH A CAPITAL "P"
### By the Editor

From *Buddhism in England*
*Jan.–Feb., 1937*

●

A reader has sent me an amusing cutting from *The Times*—a letter to the editor from Mr. J. C. Dent, the headmaster of Westminster City School. "Progress," he writes, "unless it is a complete illusion, consists in increasing the range and quality of a man's desires; and in spreading throughout mankind generally a desire for that increase." This somewhat doubtful definition would perhaps have been a little less doubtful if used in connection with the desire for wisdom, or for any sort of quality which makes progress something more than a mere accumulation of possessions. Unfortunately it was used in connection with what are termed "the necessities of life," concerning which the writer says, "what is accepted by one class of society as a necessity is envied by another as a luxury." The reader who sent me this cutting comments, "Can we wonder that modern youth suffer such grievous illusions when their teachers hold such dreadful views?" Of course, there is this side to the question: that one must do all in one's power to encourage people to buy things, because that is good for industry and solves the unemployment problem. And that is a very pleasant idea provided (*a*) that one has the money to buy them, and (*b*) that the solution of such problems is the aim of education and the meaning of Progress.

Naturally there are many kinds of progress, but only one of them is really entitled to be called Progress with a capital "P." If you can make two blades of grass grow where one grew before, that is progress in terms of quantity. If you drink Napoleon Brandy in place of methylated spirits, that is progress in terms of quality. But remember that a misguided use of either may lead to unfortunate consequences. Thus whatever the number or quality of things we may have or desire to have, it makes not the least difference to the way in which we use them. A desire for Chinese paintings may have more quality than a desire for Edwardian furniture; it shows a higher degree of taste, and, indeed, the same may be said of the desire for virtuous and vicious actions. But moral desires are not in question here. What was being discussed in this letter was the possession of things, of "necessities of life," and it was written because some equally misguided person had spoken of poverty as a condition favourable to the growth of sound character. Thus we are confronted with two opposite views of Progress. The first, common to a vast number of modern men and women, is that Progress consists in having and fulfilling desires for more and better things. The second, found only among a few, has this important asset: that it conceives Progress as growth of character, but it considers that this can only come precisely from a lack of "things," from poverty, from "going through the mill."

Obviously the solution to this conflict of views may be found in the Middle Way, and this provides an unusually clear illustration of the fact that the Middle Way does not mean a mere compromise between extremes. If this were so, we should say that the Middle Way consists in having neither too few possessions nor too many, that in quality they must neither be too good nor too inferior. That, however, would be a lukewarm and lifeless solution to the problem; indeed, it would not be a solution at all, because, as we have seen, the number or quality of one's possessions makes no difference to the way in which one uses them. Thus the Middle Way is not only between extremes but also above them, for it shows that progress in wisdom has nothing to do with either wealth or poverty except in so far as it shows itself in the use one may make of them. A poor man may appear to be wise, but if wealth kills his wisdom it is not real wisdom. Often enough a man will neglect his friends and develop vicious habits after "coming into money," but that is less a reflection on the evils of money than the evils of man. The converse is also true. Often we see one who is happy and content while rich become a grumbler in poverty. In both instances we see that their "wisdom" depends on their circumstances. Thus if character is to be educated by poverty, who shall say that it will stand the test of wealth?

But poverty does not necessarily call forth the best in man. It does not follow that because most of the great saints and sages have chosen to be poor, all poor men are therefore saints and sages. On the contrary, wherever there is a community abjectly poor, there is cruelty and immorality of every kind, and that has not only arisen in these times of the cinema, hire-purchase and other methods of increasing men's desires. Long before advertisers ever attempted to persuade the milions that luxury was within their reach, the poor quarters of every great city harboured vice; one has only to look at Hogarth's pictures to understand that poverty and nobility of character are not inseparable, and never have been. Nor must it be imagined that poverty and vice are only found together in the slums of great cities. Much sentimental romance has been written about the poor but honest countryman by those who have always lived in towns. But in those quaint and curious little houses with tiny windows which look so picturesque from the outside one often finds the equivalent or worse of the city slum. There, too, vice flourishes in the same way, save that it is less apparent. Yet it would not be either fair or true to make any sweeping generalisations about the relationship between material and moral conditions. For to say that poverty necessarily breeds virtue is just as untrue as to say that it necessarily breeds vice. We simply note the fact that where there is great poverty and where there is great wealth, there one is likely to find great evil. It does not necessarily follow from this that either is a bar to wisdom; what does follow is that neither is more of a bar than the other.

Thus if one imagines that education, if it is to be of any value at all, is concerned mainly with "things," whether in scarcity or abundance, the whole point is missed. One school of thought would teach children how to do with little, another how to do with a lot; the trouble with the first is that some men have riches thrust upon them, and they are a karmic responsibility not to be denied. Precisely the converse is true of the second. Both make the mistake of trying to produce wisdom by circumstances instead of circumstances by wisdom. Closely allied with this error is another which in the West (and in much of the East) is making education a pure farce. And this is the error of teaching children to cope with material things rather than spiritual and moral things. The aim of much modern education seems to be to produce successful men of business instead of successful human beings. It is said that they must be taught something of "use," something which will help them to "get on in the world." Thus delightful but quite "useless" subjects, such as Religion, Hebrew, Latin, Greek, or maybe Sanskrit, Pali or Hebrew are replaced by Economics, Shorthand, Typing, Accountancy, Science, and other *literae inhumaniores*. The result is that our youth tends to become merely clever. It is like educating technique and neglecting art. The child becomes an efficient manipulator of the machinery of modern civilization, but his understanding goes little further; he has not been shown how to direct that machinery with wisdom.

Such "useless" subjects as dead languages and ancient history are thus of far greater importance than the purely utilitarian, and for two reasons: firstly, that they pass on the tradition of an old culture which a new civilization must feed upon in the same way as a tree feeds upon a soil of dead matter. Moreover, this tradition contains not only supreme literature and art, but that legacy of spiritual wisdom which the ancient sages seemed to see more clearly than their modern counterparts. Secondly, that their study exercises the faculties of the mind and improves the judgment in such a way that any new subject can be mastered rapidly and with comparative ease. In all commercial and scientific subjects one is occupied solely with quantities; in languages, in literature, history and religion one is concerned with qualities, not only material but moral and spiritual. Perceiving this fault in our education, a great scientist of the present day—Prof. Whitehead—writes: "When you understand all about the sun and all about the atmosphere, and all about the rotation of the earth, you may still miss the radiance of the sunset." Thus you may know everything *about* life; you may measure and weigh it and give its parts all manner of names; but still you do not necessarily know life; you do not taste its quality.

Thus Progress, if it is to be more than an acquisition of "things" and of cleverness, can only mean progress in wisdom. Material goods and knowledge about the world, in whatever quantity and of whatever quality, may be used for base and immoral ends if wisdom is lacking. And of all men, the educationalist must be the first to realize this, for in the modern world he wields a far greater influence than the old source of spirituality—the Church. Nowadays, nobody need go to a church or join any religious community. Almost everyone, however, goes to school, and that is now the only place where teaching has (or can have) a universal hearing. Hence, with the decline of the Church the educationalist inherits a tremendous responsibility, and it is fortunate that there are still a large number of important schools free from the control of the State. For while State schools may be compelled by law to give the type of education required by a deluded public, the independent schools are still able to give the world what it ought to have as distinct from what it thinks it wants. Their influence is still strong enough to arrest this false utilitarianism if they work together. This, however, will be difficult, although its necessity seems almost painfully obvious. So much so that many might well call these remarks platitudinous. Nowadays, however, platitude is frequently a name given to an inconvenient truth to make it look absurd, for there is a widespread dislike of the obvious. The obvious is often a little annoying, so we look for truth in obscurity; and by making out that the problems of the world are much too difficult for anyone to understand we conveniently manage to shelve them.

# NOT ONLY BUT ALSO

From *Buddhism in England*
*March–April, 1937*

●

There is truth in the old saying that familiarity breeds contempt, and perhaps one of the greatest tests of a religion
is that though one may study it unceasingly it never becomes
familiar. There comes a stage in one's pursuit of Buddhism
when those fundamental principles which one learnt in the
beginning, the Four Noble Truths, the Eightfold Path and
the Three Signs of Being, seem to be a limitation on thought,
to be dull and lifeless. One imagines that, in so far as pure
intellect or even intuition can grasp their meaning, one has
fully understood them, and the mind cries out for more
nourishment, for new teachings which will offer fresh ter-
ritory for the adventure of thought. This is a natural and
proper stage, for after exploring further one suddenly sees
the old principles in a new light. After studying other
religions and philosophies, one realizes the immeasurable
profundity of the Buddha's wisdom—a wisdom in which
most of us are just dabblers. At this realization one marvels
at one's own ignorance and at the immense arrogance of
those who can dismiss his teaching as mere nihilism, or for
that matter as mere anything. For at first sight the principles of original Buddhism seem perfectly easy of compre-
hension; its whole system is set forward in a series of
tabulated formulae as if it could be mastered with the comparative ease of a Latin Grammar. But the depths of the
Buddha's understanding seem infinite, and though one may
imagine that one has found some other philosophy greater
than Buddhism, after working through it one comes upon

Buddhism again, only at a deeper level. And from this new point of view the ordinary differences of opinion concerning *anatta*, the Unity of Life, and the existence of God seem to be as far removed from reality as the famous remarks of the blind men concerning the appearance of an elephant. They seem to have no more to do with Buddhism than with book-binding.

Thus one becomes somewhat hesitant in expressing any opinion on a teaching of which one is just realizing one's abysmal ignorance, but there is always the chance that even the tentative statement of a new understanding may help others to penetrate just a little further. Or, on the other hand, it may prompt those who have gone further still to speak of their own understanding and so increase the general enlightenment. It must be stressed, however, that even the widest differences of opinion on so vast a subject should be expressed with the humility of ignorance rather than the pride of knowledge. But true knowledge is without pride.

One of the first and most difficult bars to the understanding of Buddhism in the West (and even in the East) is language. Even among those who speak English argument may be occasioned simply because different people use the same words with a variety of meanings. The difficulty is therefore increased when it comes to the understanding of Pali and Sanskrit words for not only were they evolved among people with a psychology far removed from our own, but also they are capable of expressing more subtle shades of meaning. For example there are those three crucial words *dukkha, anicca* and *anatta*, the Three Signs of Being, usually taken to mean that life is characterized by Suffering, Impermanence and Absence of Soul, that is to say, of any individual principle in man that is real, much less eternal. From this we are given to understand that the object of Buddhism is to escape from suffering and impermanence by understanding that there is no "I" which suffers or changes. There being no actor, it follows that there is no action, and that the whole phenomenal universe is a mere figment, a shadow without substance on the face of Nothingness. On the other hand, there are those who say that the Buddha could never have preached so hopeless, not to say illogical, a teaching, maintaining instead that though the "I" which suffers is illusory, there is behind the false a true "I" which is the Self not only of the individual but of the whole cosmos. It would be so easy to pin the Buddha's words to one or other of these interpretations, but it was not so easy to pin the Buddha himself. A certain Vacchagotta once tried to obtain a definite Yes or No on this point and received only a Noble Silence (*Samyutta Nikaya*, iv. 400). For unless the Buddha had compromised and said No or Yes, it would have been almost impossible to explain to that obtuse person that before one can say whether Self does or does not exist, one must not only know very clearly what is to be understood by "Self" but also by "existence." Furthermore, the Buddha's teaching is no mere matter of words and definitions, for even his own most dogmatic assertions can only be regarded as hints, as glyphs into which each disciple will read just as much as his understanding permits.

*Dukkha*, it is said, means Suffering, and the Buddha expressly stated that his doctrine was concerned with one thing, *dukkha* and deliverance from *dukkha*. The obvious interpretation of this would be that Buddhism is first and foremost a method of what is vulgarly termed "saving one's bacon," or rather of avoiding the responsibility of having any bacon to save. Life is a misery, an intolerable burden, therefore get rid of it as quickly as possible by committing spiritual suicide. It is as if a king was appointed to rule a kingdom and said, "Oh, this is too much like hard work" and promptly abdicated, the kingdom, in the meantime, reverting to anarchy. Or perhaps Buddhism teaches that there is neither king nor kingdom, and that it is mere ignorance to suppose that there was ever any question of responsibility at all. But is there not a passage in the scriptures which speaks of a kingdom, a city which has to be most vigilantly watched? This city has a gate corresponding to each of the senses—a city far more difficult to govern than any ordinary city, for this is the realm of one's own mind. The Buddha appears to have taken the responsibility of its government very seriously indeed, and in the *Samyutta Nikaya* (ii. 103-4) he speaks of the Path as an ancient road leading to a lost city which is to be restored to its former glory. Even if that is mere figurative speech, one would hardly use a prosperous city as a simile for well-regulated spiritual suicide. Moreover, however intolerable the burden of life may be, it is ridiculous to imagine that any but the most depraved mentalities would prefer an eternity of oblivion to an eternity of mixed pleasure and pain—if those were indeed the *only* two alternatives.

Let us then leave the dreary prospect of eternal oblivion. Perhaps the Buddha really meant that we should evolve some kind of super-consciousness in which we become identical with the universe, in which we become nothing in particular but everything in general. This was certainly a doctrine prominent in India at his time, that is, if Western interpretations of the Upanishads are not wholly false, which is likely enough although outside the scope of this article. In this event suffering would be an illusion because it is only something which pertains to individuals. Individuals are unreal from the viewpoint of the One Universal Self, and therefore if one's consciousness is identified with that Self, suffering is unreal. The implications of this teaching are only slightly removed from mere nihilism—if we accept it at its face value. For it implies that the whole universe of form might as well not be there; that it is without meaning, without interest, and that the only thing of worth is a No-thing, a colourless, formless, infinite consciousness which has nothing to be conscious of. But it will be said that it is conscious of the Infinite, a sublime mystery which requires a special sense of appreciation. The trouble with the Infinite seems to be that it is only half the truth, and one of those half-truths which may easily be worse than falsehood. Someone has wisely said that there is nothing infinite apart from finite things, and perhaps we have in that saying a key which will unlock the first door of that inconceivably vast palace of the Buddha's wisdom.

There seems to be something about the interpretations of Buddhism considered above altogether inconsistent with that tremendous title *Buddha*—Supremely Enlightened. They are so shallow, so reminiscent of the vague generalisations made by those who have never penetrated deeply into their subject. It is so easy to proclaim the doctrine of "Nothing But", to say that life is nothing but this, or nothing but that, for this is the practice of almost every tyro in every field of study. When, however, he has progressed far enough to realize his ignorance, he comes instead to the doctrine of "Not Only But Also," which is another name for the Middle Way. Thus to every reliable observer, life is characterized not only by suffering but also by happiness, for the whole existence of the world of form depends entirely on the existence of opposites. We should not know pain unless we also knew pleasure, and the same may be said of living and dying, hot and cold, day and night. Hence, as Buddhism is the Middle Way *par excellence*, let us assume for the moment that *dukkha* means neither pain nor pleasure, nor an indifferent condition between the two. Let us call *dukkha* as "discord" or "lack of harmony," and then ask if it does not refer to a state of discord in relationship between pleasure and pain, implying a conflict between the two opposites. This conflict exists only in man's mind, for it is he who sets the opposites at war by striving for the perpetuation of one and the abolition of the other. It is precisely this conflict which is at the root of man's misery, of his spiritual disease, for he is seeking something which simply does not exist, which is *maya* in the real sense of that term. For there is no such thing as pleasure apart from pain, and *dukkha* would seem to be the illusion (*maya*) of seeking pleasure as a thing-in-itself (*atta*).

This principle may also be applied to the *anatta* doctrine. Because man does not understand *anatta* he tries to hold himself apart from life as a separate entity; he tries to appropriate to himself various other entities, and in this he is like one who attempts to separate the beautiful parts of the human body from the ugly with the result that he kills both. For surely *anatta* means that any individual thing considered in and by itself has absolutely no meaning, no use, no life, no autonomous soul. Did anyone ever see a finger working without a hand? Or a spoke running round without a wheel? Or a hair growing without a head? For if we consider those two opposites, the part and the whole, we see that they can no more exist without each other than pleasure without pain. That they are opposites we know well enough, for each one of us distinguishes sharply between the self and the not-self, subject and object, "I" and the universe. But separate self from the universe and it has no existence—it is *maya*. The converse is also true, and this is where we have to distinguish between Buddhism and the "All-is-Nothing-But-One" doctrine. The whole has no existence without its parts. No one ever saw a hammer without handle or head, or a cube without any sides, and even the Platonic Idea of a cube, the abstract prototype cube, requires prototypical sides. That is to say, if you take a chariot to pieces and then say, "Where is the chariot-soul?" the answer is, "In the mind of the man who made it." But that mental chariot is inconceivable without its mental parts. Thus *maya* is a term applicable to any one opposite considered apart from the other, and when the Mahayana sutras say that the opposites are *maya* they imply that they are meaningless, illusory and non-existent apart from the Reconciling Principle which relates them to one another. And this principle is called *Dharma*, or *Tao*, or *Logos*; it is the Meaning, the *raison d'être* of the opposites just as the child is the meaning and *raison d'être* of man and woman. Hence so far as oneself and the universe are concerned, the object of Buddhism is surely to follow the Middle Way, to become absorbed neither in oneself (which is *Trishna*) nor in the universe (which is no-thing), but to give full attention to the Meaning which reconciles the two. This reconciliation is love (*karuna*), the higher reflection of the love of man for woman, which, fulfilling itself, is directed beyond and between the two opposites to the child. To express it in as concrete a way as is possible: forget yourself, forget the world outside you, and go straight ahead, but don't remember either by *trying* to forget. . . . After all, if you have concentrated on this article that is what you have been doing all the time. You forgot yourself, forgot the printed letters, and remembered only the Meaning which was born of your thoughts and mine.

---

# LETTERS I RECEIVE
## SIMPLE LANGUAGE
### *By the Editor*

From *Buddhism in England*
*March–April, 1937*

•

Many people write or tell me at Lodge meetings that they find Buddhism so very complicated and so full of strange technical terms. The other day a lady told us that she found it almost impossible to understand what we were talking about, to which one of our older and wiser members replied, "Well, the only difference between us is that *you* are more candid." That remark, however, did not come from one who might be described as "muddle-headed"; he often writes in this journal, and what he says is anything but confused. For the deeper one's study of Buddhism, the more one realizes how very little one understands. In the words of Chuang Tzu: "He who knows he is a fool is not a great fool." The fact remains, however, that it is of little help to the beginner to offer the more abstruse metaphysics of the Mahayana or elaborate explanations of the Four Jhanas or the Paticca Samupada. For the beginner invariably tells us that he wants Buddhism explained in simple language, which apparently means that he does not want to be overwhelmed by the terminology of pandits, by vague references to "transcendental Reality," "noumenal ontology" or "alaya-vijnana."

But what is simple language? Does it consist in economy of words? The *Tao Te Ching* is a model of such economy, but who will say that he understands it? Does it mean ordinary words of not more than three syllables? But what are ordinary words? It may be said that they are the words used by the great masses of the people, but here we can only ask, "Which masses and which people?" What is common speech in East London may perhaps be more or less unintelligible in Lancashire, not to mention New York. Perhaps then it means the language of what we call ordinary educated and intelligent people (implying people like ourselves). Yet I have often seen such people argue for hours without understanding each other in any sense whatever. Indeed, it has frequently been my experience that the more intelligent the company, the more it fails to arrive at any understanding. Take, for instance, the very "simple" phrase, "Without faith in spiritual realities there can be no religious life." All the five important words used are common enough in everyday speech, but if any three people can be found who can fully agree to the meaning of any one of them, I shall be not only amazed but incredulous. And if the simplicity of words consists in their familiarity and brevity, here is a list of fifteen ordinary four-lettered and one syllable words over which we might argue for millions of years:—

| Love | Life | Good |
|------|------|------|
| Hope | Fact | Real |
| True | Hate | Mind |
| Soul | Time | Fate |
| Sane | Form | Self |

For the difficulty is that even when we (perhaps) know what we mean ourselves by these words, those to whom we speak give them widely different meanings. If we were so very simple, in more senses than one, as to tell people that the first principle of Buddhism is that Life is Pain, and the second that Pain is born of Lust, we should be neither explicit nor intelligible. This may be simple language, but it does not convey a simple truth. For there are two kinds of simple language: one is used by such people as the Buddha, Lao Tzu and Jesus Christ, and this is more difficult to understand than the most formidable tomes on metaphysics. The other conveys a meaning which one not only sees but sees through, as when pleasantly vague people produce the devastating remark that Love solves all problems. We have known it to create some exceedingly difficult ones. But the paradox is that profound Truth is complicated because it is simple. We stumble over it because we are seeking it far away, and perhaps the most difficult thing in the world is to perceive the obvious. The remarks of the Zen masters are said to be baffling, yet they refer to such commonplace things as shoes, dishes, spades, the weather, sticks, trees and cups of tea. What is found so strange is that they talk about these things in answer to religious questions. The disciple asks about something which he imagines to be distant and difficult, and the master points to something under his nose. Whereat we feel that the master must be an obscurantist or a lunatic. But almost everyone has at some time engaged in a furious search for the glasses, pen or knife which he was carrying all the time in his hand or in his pocket. And when someone points out this odd lapse of memory we do not scratch our heads (or tap them) but laugh at ourselves for not having thought of the obvious.

Here we may say, in parenthesis, that this is the main reason why religion is not the serious and solemn affair which so often masquerades under its name. For essentially it is the same as the joke about the man looking all over the house for the shoes he is wearing or the dog spinning round in a wild chase after its own tail. Certainly it is a solemn business both for the man and the dog, but religious experience itself, the actual awakening to the truth, is such that a Zen master has said of it, "Nothing is left to you at this moment but to burst out into a loud laugh." But the mind of man, and especially of educated man, is so easily led away by the pride of knowledge that the obvious becomes merely contemptible. The things which lie at our feet are called "ordinary" and "commonplace" as if these words were synonyms for "dull." It is said that the deepest shadow is nearest to the lamp, and in this shadow are all manner of wonders and mysteries. We can only call ordinary things dull when we never really look at them, and simple things platitudinous when we never study them. Thus for "intelligent" people the difficulty is to be simple, and by this I do not mean what is often called "leading the simple life" for this is just another way of being complicated. To don a loin-cloth and feed on beans in the wilderness, and to imagine that such practices are necessarily conducive to religion is, in any event in the West, just another form of spiritual pride, of the love of being peculiar, of the contempt for what is usual. In the words of St. Jerome, "Beware of the pride of humility; and having renounced the desire to attract by thy fine raiment, seek not to call forth attention by thy rags." And beyond this there is an even more subtle trap: the pride of the religious man in being ordinary, in making himself conspicuous by being normal.

Thus, when we are asked for simple language, we are not really being asked for simple language at all. The readers of *Buddhism in England* would no doubt be a little surprised if, instead of articles on Buddhist philosophy, they were suddenly treated to something so simple as a few hints on cooking or carpentry. If the Editor were a Zen master these surprises might be expected. Nor are we being asked for articles full of those dangerous little words of four letters. In fact, we are not being asked for any particular kind of article at all. For when someone wants Buddhism explained in simple language, he means his OWN language, and if the Editor and his contributors are to satisfy in this way they must have the Gift of Tongues. By this I do not mean that they must be able to write in every language from Esquimaux to Arabic. That would be comparatively easy; the British and Foreign Bible Society has done as much already. The Gift of Tongues is the art of putting oneself so much *en rapport* with another person that one uses words in the same sense as he understands them. To return to cooking and carpentry: it is well for those who wish to explain Buddhism to find analogies for it in every form of human activity, so that it can be represented to one's cook or one's carpenter in the terms of their respective arts. Hence in talking with another, let him first do the talking so that his language may be learnt. It is almost useless just to talk *at* people; one might as well waste one's Swedish on a Hottentot or one's knowledge of the differential calculus on the professor of Early Greek History. One must always begin with what is called the Socratic method of asking questions—a method almost invariably used by the Buddha himself.

Unfortunately it is a little difficult to do this in a periodical which appears only once in two months. It would be hard enough if it were a "daily," but at the same time our aim is to try to present a central Truth under as many forms as possible in the hope that *sometimes* they may come near to *someone's* language. In this we have the advantage that Buddhism is a religion of tremendous variety and that among its many sects is a way of life suited to almost every general type of human being. In the words of Dr. Suzuki: "Buddhism, being a great world religion, has eighty-four thousand ways of teaching at its command, any one of which is available on any occasion. One single word casually dropped from the lips of a master, or his gesture such as the raising of the eyebrows, or the pointing of a finger at a flower, is sufficient to open the mind of the intelligent disciple. Buddhism performs this miracle when necessary, that is, when conditions are thoroughly matured. . . . The business of (Buddhist) philosophy is to deal with concepts, which is really the most roundabout way of reaching the truth. Practical religionists all avoid this."

---

# LETTERS I RECEIVE
## THE EXPERIENCE OF MYSTERY
### By the Editor

From *Buddhism in England*
*July–August, 1937*

●

Perhaps the greatest advice ever given to those who tread the path to Enlightenment was the Zen master's answer to the question, "What is the Tao?" "Walk on!" Unfortunately so many of us are much more inclined to walk off, even to the extent of making jumps into the air. In other words, life moves and to attain harmony we must keep pace with it; to stop for a moment to regret the past, to put off the future or to retain the present is to be thrown out of time. For life passes on, and those who lag create about themselves a turmoil like a log caught up in the weeds by the side of a stream. But those who move forward in time attain that stillness which is perfect motion; the stream carries them and the turmoil ceases—hence the Christian paradox that in the service of God is perfect freedom. But there are so many leaping salmon in the human stream, jumping up from the water at the elusive objects of the upper air. Perhaps they are attracted by the glories of the sky, preferring them to the familiar water. But if only they would not create so many ripples they would see that the water holds the sky's reflection. For this world is the counterpart of the worlds beyond; man is the universe writ small; and every littlest thing of this world is a symbol of eternal principles.

Therefore it is rather disturbing to find so many who discredit this ordinary world that we know with our five senses. Someone wrote to me saying that she was very anxious to attain "Cosmic Consciousness," and could I please help. So much is written and said in occult and "spiritual" circles about the development of senses which can see beyond ordinary life; our senses, they say, deceive us and with occult perception we could discover the truth behind this mirage of form and substance. It does not often occur to them to ask why, if our physical senses deceive us, our occult senses should not deceive us also. Furthermore the question arises, "If there are deeper worlds within this world, do we become any the wiser just for changing our realm of perception?" But for the vast majority of people, even for the majority of religious people, extraordinary states of consciousness, conditions of occult perception and the rest are simply means of leading one astray. For the Buddha said, "In this very body, six feet in length, with its sense-impressions and its thoughts and ideas, I do declare to you are the world, and the origin of the world, and the ceasing of the world, and likewise the Way that leadeth to the ceasing thereof." (*Anguttara Nikaya*, ii. 46.) And here are two Zen stories which demonstrate the same truth. The disciple asked, "What is the Tao?" And the master replied, "Usual life is the very Tao." On another occasion a disciple asked,

"What is *satori* (Enlightenment)?" The master answered, "Your everyday thoughts." Moreover there is that well-known saying of Zen master Rinzai:

> *The truly religious man has nothing to do but go on with his life as he finds it in the various circumstances of this worldly existence. He rises quietly in the morning, puts on his clothes, and goes out to work. When he wants to walk, he walks; when he wants to sit, he sits. He has no hankering after Buddhahood, not the remotest thought of it. How is this possible? A wise man of old has said, If you seek after Buddhahood by any conscious contrivances, your Buddha is indeed the source of eternal transmigration.*

I have just been reading Miss Evelyn Underhill's famous work *Mysticism*, and was astonished to find that her opening chapter was based on the peculiar theme that mystical understanding involves the knowledge that this "worldly existence" is only a shadow-play, that sense knowledge is a distortion of Truth and that its familiar forms are only the symbols of what lies beyond. Certainly they are symbols, but they are not *only* symbols. In the word "only" there is the suspicions of a sneer. Now in sneering there is pride; there is also a tinge of what is known as the "inferiority complex," which simply means pretending to be superior to something to which you inwardly know yourself to be inferior. As a rule, those who in any way deprecate the ordinary world of the senses are those who have not come to terms with it; and those who have come to terms with it do not deprecate it. In the sayings quoted above from the Buddha and the Zen masters there is no trace of pride; they are the words of those whose eyes have been opened to the miracle of a world from which so many would-be mystics seem anxious to run away. But there's no mysticism in exploring other worlds, in attaining mere knowledge. If we are to understand mysticism as the art of bringing oneself into harmony with life, as perceiving and living its deepest meaning, then this world is sufficient for us. Attempts to see beyond the senses come under a totally different department of human activity, namely Science, whether physical or psychic. This is a perfectly legitimate undertaking so long as we do not imagine that it increases our spirituality. It is simply the accumulation of facts about the universe, and it has been said that the important thing is not facts but their significance. Lao Tzu once said that without going out of his door he knew the whole universe. That is to say, in the world in which you live you have the secret of all possible worlds; when you know one you know all, for all are based on the same principles. Therefore spiritual wisdom is less in accumulating experiences than in perceiving the significance of any one experience, and for that purpose our ordinary everyday experience is enough. For the secret is that the Enlightenment which we seek by such curious and roundabout ways is precisely what we experience at this very moment, whether it is sitting in a chair or having breakfast. As Hui Heng might say, the difference between a Buddha and ordinary person is that one realizes this and the other does not. For this reason a Chinese poet said:

> *How wondrous and how miraculous this,——*
> *I draw water and I carry fuel.*

Or in the words of Hakuin;

> *This very earth is the Lotus Land of Purity,*
> *And this body is the body of Buddha.*

For mystical understanding involves a great sense of wonder and reverence for the most common experience. As a rule vast knowledge of the mysteries of the universe increases pride; to lay bare all mysteries is to be in danger of becoming bored, and Van der Leeuw has wisely said that "the mystery of life is not a problem to be solved, but a reality to be experienced." If you try to discover the secret of beauty by taking a flower to pieces, you will arrive at the somewhat unsatisfactory conclusion of having abolished the flower. For beauty is beauty just because it is a mystery, and when ordinary life is known as profound mystery then we are somewhere near to wisdom. Here is a new connection between mystery and mysticism, a connection which is sometimes indignantly denied. So you will say, is the important thing just to cast aside all curiosity and embrace the maxim that where ignorance is bliss tis folly to be wise? Of course the catch is that every degree of wisdom has its counterpart in folly, and the two are so alike that the wise man is wise simply because he can distinguish them. The highest and lowest notes of the musical scale are both inaudible, and the ignoramus and the sage are both faced with mystery. The difference between the two is that even if you explained the mystery to the sage it would still remain mysterious, whereas the fool would simply be disappointed and disillusioned. For the fool would imagine that the explanation, the taking to pieces, the analysis, had spoilt the mystery; the sage would see that it had not even begun to explain it. The fool would think that he had thereby become wise; the sage would know that he was still a fool, and, in the words of Chuang Tzu, "He who knows he is a fool is not a great fool."

Therefore if the sage is told that this world is no more than a maya, a phantom, conjured up from the Primordial Essence by deceptive senses, he is not very much impressed. If a doctor explains the transformations undergone by food in his stomach, he does not cease to enjoy his dinner. If a scientist informs him that thunder is not the music of the gods but mere electrical disturbances, the thunder is for him no less wonderful. For what is especially interesting about explanations is that they do not explain; and what is especially dangerous about them is that if they are taken seriously enough and far enough, they simply explain things away. And even if one does resort to the ultimate madness of explaining all things away, there remains still the impenetrable mystery of who is it that explains and why?

---

# LETTERS I RECEIVE
## THE MAN AND THE MEANS
### *By the Editor*

From *Buddhism in England*
*Nov.–Dec., 1937*

•

The other day I recommended a friend to read that great classic of Buddhist Taoism, *The Secret of the Golden Flower*, which Richard Wilhelm translated from the Chinese for the first time some few years ago. A few days later he wrote in a rather disturbed frame of mind, for he had come across an exceedingly uncomfortable saying. It was this: "When the wrong man uses the right means, the right means work in the wrong way." "If this is true," he said, "I cannot see that there is any hope for any of us. No path of spiritual development is of any use, for every such path is a 'means' and everyone who feels in need of a path must recognize that he is in some way 'wrong.' No one would ever dream of seeking spiritual enlightenment unless he was convinced of his own wrongness; yet this saying would imply that even if he finds the right path it can be of no benefit to him until he reaches its end, which, because he is wrong in the first place, he cannot do—which is absurd." "It is," he wrote, "rather like being told that you cannot have a university education until you have first obtained a university degree."

It is hardly surprising that he was disturbed, for he had touched on what is perhaps the most fundamental problem of religion. A point of interest was that he did not once question the truth of the saying, for it is one of those things which a moment's consideration will show to be an absolute, unavoidable and irritating fact like the fact that you cannot lift yourself up by your own belt. This is soon apparent when we understand what is meant by the "wrong man." Clearly it means one who is wrong, foolish or evil in his inmost desires, who is selfish, who acts from the wrong motive. Even if he chooses the right path he cannot help choosing it for some selfish end; because of his inherent wrongness, he aims at spiritual unselfishness for the sake of his own pride, or in the belief that it will in some way deliver him from the limitations of circumstance. The fundamental problem is, therefore, of motive, and for this reason the Buddha put Right Motive at the very beginning of his Eightfold Path. And yet, it must be asked how can we have right motive until we have trodden that path?

Obviously our fundamental desires are the deciding factors in every enterprise that we undertake. This is particularly true in the sphere of spiritual activity, for the whole aim of religion is to remove wrong desire, to cleanse the heart in order that Enlightenment may make itself known. It exists within us all the time, but in most of us it is hidden by dark clouds. Thus there comes a time when everyone who attempts to follow some path of spiritual development realizes that all his efforts are in vain if his underlying motives are impure. For he has to ask himself the awkward question: "Why am I treading this path?" Because I want Enlightenment. And why do I want Enlightenment? Here we have to be careful about our answer. Only too often we shall have to confess that it is because we are afraid of the world and wish to find some power which will enable us to overcome it, to become such great masters of life that we shall no longer feel the agonies of frustrated desire. Or again, it may be that we feel ineffective in comparison with our fellows and wish to have some means of making ourselves superior. If we come to the conclusion that our true motive is one or both of these, we may possibly try another course. We may decide that we must accept the limitations of circumstance without trying to overcome them, that we must admit and remain satisfied with our inferior position. But then we must ask ourselves again just why we are making this act of acceptance. Nine times out of ten we shall find that we are only trying to achieve the same end in the opposite way, that we are accepting our limitations in order, paradoxically, to escape from them. Acceptance may be the right means, but again it works in the wrong way because acceptance is not our real motive.

Much is said in modern psychology of the evils of trying to escape from life, by which is meant suffering and limitation, for naturally we do not try to avoid the things which give us pleasure. But psychology does not give us much help beyond this destructive criticism; it does not tell us how *not* to try to escape, although it pretends to do so. It teaches the doctrine of acceptance, which is all very well so long as it is recognized that acceptance may simply become the tool of the desire to escape, which is always an essentially selfish desire. The same truth has been expressed in the saying that "'Nirvana is not for those who desire it, since Nirvana is the absence of desire." The question is naturally asked, "How, then, do we not desire Nirvana?" And again we must ask ourselves why we want not to desire it. The answer must be, "In order that we may have it," which brings us back to the point where we began.

"If the wrong man uses the right means, the right means work in the wrong way." How do we find the right man? Why do we want the right man? Because we are the wrong man. Those who are persistently honest with themselves are always led to this strange *impasse*, this point where they seem to be revolving in circles, vainly trying to achieve the impossible. In this state they begin to despair of salvation, for in all religious effort they see only the hopeless attempt to run away from the one thing from which we cannot escape, seeing that it is the very thing that runs away—oneself. And when they learn that trying not to run away from it is only running in the opposite direction, they understand that nothing can be achieved by trying. The self cannot change itself any more than the blind can lead the blind; all attempts to be different are vain attempts to avoid what *is*, and to try not to avoid what *is* is only an indirect means of avoiding it. This is rather like the Zen koan about the goose in the bottle. In time the goose grew so large that it could not get out. Now the man did not want to break the bottle, nor did he want to hurt the goose. How can he get it out?'' Is not this koan a symbol of the ultimate paradox to which religion must eventually lead?

At this point our minds may be troubled by serious doubts. We shall be wondering if religion is not, after all, an absurdity. For the moment we begin thinking about our own thoughts, feeling about our own feelings, and desiring about our own desires, we become involved in the morass of infinite regress, the endless circling of the dog in chase of its own tail, or the perpetual efforts of a lunatic to kiss his own lips. This, we may say, is wholly unnecessary. What is the use of working ourselves into this hopeless condition which may so easily lead to madness? Animals have no religion, and before we began to think about these things we just behaved like animals and went ahead with the ordinary business of life, eating, sleeping, and playing without having another thought about it. Perhaps it would have been much better to stay in this condition after all. But we are men and not animals, and man has this peculiar faculty of self-consciousness which is the source of all the trouble. His personality seems to be divided; there is the self and the self which is aware of the self, and these two divisions are by no means at peace with each other. Like Siamese twins, they are inseparable and yet wish to go in opposite directions. We have no evidence at all that there are two selves; it is more likely that there is just one self which is hopelessly confused by the one thing which it cannot understand—itself. For it is self-conscious; it knows that it exists but cannot see what sort of a thing it is that exists.

But it is not wholly self-conscious, for this is revealed in the very fact that it tries to change its own desires and control its own impulses. It looks upon those desires as something almost external, something which it can clutch and move. It is as if a man were trying to walk by moving his legs with his hands, not realizing that he can make his legs move by themselves. What is true of the legs is true also of the mind; it is not something apart from ourselves which we can control and restrain, as it were, from without. There is a Zen story which illustrates this point peculiarly well. A disciple came to Bodhidharma and said, "Master, I have no peace of mind. Pray pacify it." Bodhidharma answered, "Bring out your mind here before me and I will pacify it." The disciple was sorely puzzled and said, "But I cannot find my mind to bring it out." "Then," replied Bodhidharma, "I have pacified your mind." There is yet another story which shows the same truth in a different way. A disciple asked, "How can I be delivered from the wheel of birth and death?" The master replied, "Who is putting you under restraint?" Indeed, who is? When you walk into trouble do not blame your feet.

# THE MONKEY-MIND
# IN RELIGION

From *Buddhism in England*
*Jan.–Feb., 1938*

●

One of the most disturbing features of religious thought to-day, whether among Buddhists, Christians, Hindus or Theosophists, is the enormous amount of pure materialism dressed up in spiritual guise. By this I do not mean moral materialism, such as the sensuous pursuits of decadent priests or the use of religious forms for selfish ends. Nor should the term materialism be understood in this sense as the denial of a life after death, of the existence of God or of eternal values transcending time and space. For the particular form of materialism in question is something much more subtle than this, something which is found in almost every department of philosophy and religion, something which is, in our time, the most potent enemy of true spirituality, the more so because its presence is unnoticed. Part of the difficulty is that we are wholly vague as to what we mean by such elusive terms as "matter" and "spirit" and their even more elusive adjectives "material" and "spiritual." It has been said that spirit is simply a finer form of matter, and, especially in occult circles, this saying is the cause of a most lamentable confusion of thought. For the so-called occultist is often under the impression that he is being spiritual in the highest sense of the word when he is concerning himself with the study and manipulation of these finer forms of matter, when he is developing his senses of raising his consciousness so that he can perceive and control them. But in fact he is still being purely material, for matter does not cease to be material when it takes on finer forms, when it becomes invisible to our ordinary senses. Strictly speaking, the occultist of this kind is dealing with psychic things, and under the heading "psychic" we must place all such phenomena as telepathy, clairvoyance, projection of the astral body and the development of those powers which are known in Buddhism as the *siddhis*. Even the word "psychic" is unhappy in this place, for it comes originally from the Greek word *psyche*, meaning the soul. But it has been used so constantly in connection with these phenomena that it is now impossible to separate it from them, and we can only be clear on the subject if we agree to define as psychic just those material things which are unperceived by our five senses in their present state of development. Thus there is no difference of kind between material and psychic substances; there is only difference of degree. Besides occultists of this kind, there are others who are victims of the same confusion, but in a less obvious form, and I think they may be placed under two general headings.

The first are those who consider that there is something spiritual and religious in beliefs or even knowledge about the visible or invisible structure and destiny of the universe. They hope to arrive at spirituality by studying the laws of the universe, maintaining that for every material law there is a spiritual counterpart. This is true enough if we agree to call this counterpart not spiritual but psychic. It is true also that the outward forms of spiritual development are analogous to many material processes such as the conception and birth of a child, the motion and nature of the wind, the growth of a flower or the inner workings of the body. This we understand from observing the behaviour of spiritual people and from their own words which liken spiritual attainments to material processes. But these are only the *outward forms;* they are the *what* and the *how* of spiritual development, but never the *why*, and it is only this last that belongs to the realm of true spirituality. No one can obtain the spiritual gifts of a sage by copying his outward behaviour; for this is only copying what the sage does, and is not necessarily doing it for the same reason as the sage. If the motive for the sage's behaviour is love, it may well be that the copyist's motive is nothing more than self-aggrandisement.

This brings us to our second category—those who believe that spirituality can be attained simply by shaping their lives in accordance with a pattern, simply by imposing upon themselves a technique. The mere observance of a rule of life can no more produce spirituality than figs can grow on thistles, or a beautiful symphony can emerge from a purely mathematical arrangement of notes. There are no rules for producing spirituality any more than there is a specific method of creating in oneself love for another person, any more than one can read in a book how to make oneself a Beethoven or a Shakespeare. Certainly we can say *what* a Beethoven symphony is, but we cannot say *why* it is beautiful. The musician may try to explain its beauty by its accordance with certain rules and standards of musical expression. But question him further, and he will be quite unable to say just *why* those rules and standards are beautiful. It simply happens that we like them; the innermost core of our being shouts a joyous "Yes!" when it hears them. But words can tell us no more than *what* it shouts at; why it shouts remains an impenetrable mystery. One might indeed write music which accorded in every respect with those rules and standards and yet fall a long way short of Beethoven's genius. For this is simply copying; it is following slavishly in the paths which others have trodden, and this is the very antithesis of spirituality. It is just that materialism which we have described as the besetting danger of religion in this age—and for that matter in any age.

For in just the same way the slavish copying of someone else's religion—whether the Buddha's, the Christ's,

Patanjali's, Krishna's or Lao-Tzu's—can only lead to a dead end. This is why the teachers of Zen have discouraged reliance on scriptures, on moral rules on ritual as means of producing Enlightenment. These things may be necessary for ordering the lives of those who neither desire nor care about spiritual attainment, but he who strives for Enlightenment must be ready to accept the dangers of giving up these props and crutches, for he must be prepared to die for his Goal. For they are no more than the mechanism, the technique, the means of expression of true spirituality, and without spirituality they are like a brush without an artist. For ethics, exercises in meditation, prayer or self-sacrifice can no more effect spirituality by themselves than a brush can jump up off a palate and paint a masterpiece. They can make a well-ordered life, but this is not necessarily a spiritual life. This may seem a far-fetched analogy unless we remember that spirituality is something essentially *creative*. In just the same way as a mastery of musical technique will not of itself make a Beethoven, a mastery of moral technique will not of itself make a Buddha. In this respect religion offers an exact parallel with art, music and literature. For there is all the difference in the world between the reason *why* a Buddha will be moral and why a copyist will be moral. The one is a free and creative genius using a limited technique in order to express, as far as possible, his genius in the world of form and limitation. The other is a slave who is no greater than his technique; he relies on it, depends utterly upon it, and is used by it instead of using it. He is like a carpenter who is no greater than his hammer, who expects it to show him the right way to knock in nails.

The essence of spirituality is creative freedom. It is compelled to pay regard to the regulations of technique if it is to be expressed at all in this limited world; but it always feels technique to be a poor instrument and inwardly rebels against its insufficiency. But in this it is a thousand million miles from the copyist who seeks Enlightenment within technique, who expects these limited rules to reveal the supreme secret by themselves. This, perhaps, is the reason behind the strange dynamic antics of Zen teachers and of the true mystics of all time. In every Zen book will be found warnings against the danger of copying these antics which seem to laugh at all the rules of logic. But when the Zen master hands his disciple a cup of tea in answer to a question about Buddhism, he is not trying to be obscure. He is performing a creative, free and spontaneous act; he is expressing the creative power of the universe which pulses in his own soul. He is not acting in accordance with a precept, handing his disciple a cup because an old book says this is the right thing to do. For in the spiritual man all thoughts and deeds proceed spontaneously from this centre of power. It is impossible to tell anyone how to attain this state, except to say, "Just go straight ahead with life. Don't stop to imitate. Just live, and one day the secret will reveal itself quite unexpectedly, for if you live fully, life itself will show it to you. For of a sudden you will find to your surprise that you have performed an unpremeditated, spontaneous and above all *genuine* act—not a forgery. But if you go about *expecting* this revelation you will not find it, because the irritating joke is that you have it all the time without knowing it. At every moment you are expressing this great creative power, but you hinder its expression by trying to copy someone else's *style* in the belief that it will give you his genius." That is why all mystics tell us to seek Enlightenment not in books but in our own hearts—and mark the word "own." It is lying there all the time, and just because it is the thing nearest to us (which indeed *is* us) it is the thing least known. It only comes to light when we *use* it, when we learn to see with our own eyes instead of asking another to tell us what he sees. No one can tell you how to see with your eyes except to say, "Look!" No one can tell you how to use your legs except to say "Walk!" Spirituality is a faculty given to every man just as much as speech and sight and movement; it is undeveloped just because we do not make ourselves, through use, aware of its "muscular centre." You cannot walk without first becoming aware of the power in your legs; you will get nowhere by trying to move them with your hands! But this is just what the copyist is doing; he copies the sage just as the monkey copies man and imitates his efficiency without developing, through use, the power of thought.

Spirituality, therefore, develops through use, and not through the use of its means of expression, monkey-wise. The only thing we can say to the man who wants to become a great musician is "Just use your technique creatively. Create musical sounds! Sing music from out of yourself!" In the same way to the aspirant to spirituality we must say, "Use the forms of life creatively. Live life from out of yourself. Let each act be something new, but do not make a fetish of novelty. And above all remember that as you live you are creating the universe anew out of nothing in every thought and deed. If you stop creating for a moment, your universe will return to nothingness. And if you copy instead of creating, you will not have a universe at all!"

But does this mean that, for the beginner, all technique must be abandoned? Furthermore, can we make any final distinction between technique and life itself? For is it possible to live at all without technique? Breathing, eating, walking—all these things require a certain degree of technique, and perhaps we should never have dreamt of any kind of spiritual attainment at all unless we had first learnt the technique of speech. Again, to revert to our musical analogy, it must be asked whether Beethoven would ever have discovered his own latent genius if he had not first been drilled in the technique of music. Perhaps it is true that although religious technique will not of itself produce spirituality, it will clear the way for its approach. This is true enough, but the danger is that we should become slaves to technique, and this is especially liable to happen in religion. For unlike music or painting, true religion is not a *particular* activity. There can be no painting without canvas, brush and colours, but vital religion can exist and manifest itself apart from meditation, prayer, ethics and dogma. For spirituality is precisely creative and spontaneous *living*, and this can come through a whole multitude of techniques most of which may not seem to have anything to do with religion as generally understood. For this purpose chopping wood can be as effective as any ritual, seeing that the hallmark of spirituality is that it is universal. Freedom and limitation are ultimately inseparable, but spiritual freedom is not bound to a particular set of limitations. Spirituality is limited in so far as life itself is limited by its countless forms of technique—but no further. Therefore when we say that slavish devotion to technique is the antithesis of spirituality, we refer to the idea that Enlightenment can *only* be found through one or other of the techniques generally understood as religious, to the idea that we are being spiritual only when our lives are limited by specifically religious or ethical forms.

On the contrary, these forms are worse than useless unless we can see beyond them, unless we can bring forth our spirituality through any other kind of activity of which we may be capable. For true religion dies if we try to fit it into "water-tight compartments," and the spiritual man rejoices in and acts creatively through and with any means of expression at his disposal. So also, he who would achieve spirituality must remember that the spirit is life and that he has the means of penetrating its secrets in every task and action that comes to hand. He must avoid apeing the religion of others, realising that the technique of the spirit is the whole vast technique of life and not just that particular assembly of meditation, ethics, doctrine and ritual called religion. For religion in this sense was never intended to be anything more than an aid to life. To become absorbed in it and to neglect life altogether is wholly to miss the point; it is always preparing to live and never actual living. Therefore the mistake is to confine spirituality to any particular physical, mental or moral form; it is embodied in every form, for every form partakes of life and is produced by the creative energy of the universe.

But the trouble is that the religions of the world are thronged with such a vast number of "seekers," combing through a host of doctrines and practices to find the One Royal Road to Truth, trying to confine Truth's immense life without a set of definitions. Herein is materialism and an idolatry of ideas, an attempt to rise to the stature of the great masters by wearing their cast-off clothes. But the secret is not to devote one's life to religion, for this is to become shut in a particular box. Rather it is to devote one's religion to life, expanding from the particular to the universal, to the knowledge that the spirit rises anew and unceasingly in everything that lives and moves. Furthermore to "seekers" and copyists and all who put their means into obscure holes and corners to see what lies right before them in the open we would address the tremendous words of Zen master Rinzai:—

> *"Do not get yourselves entangled with any object, but stand above, pass on and be free! As I see those so-called followers of Truth all over the country, there are none who come to me free and independent of objects. . . . They are all ghostly existences, ignominious gnomes haunting the woods or bamboo-groves; they are elfish spirits of the wilderness. They are madly biting into all heaps of filth. O you mole-eyed! . . . What do you seek in a neighbour's house? You are putting another head over your own! What do you lack in yourselves? O you followers of Truth, what you are making use of at this very moment is none other than what makes a Buddha. But you do*

*not believe me and seek it outwardly. Do not commit yourselves to an error. There are no realities outside, nor is there anything inside you may lay your hands on. You stick to the literal meaning of what I speak to you, but how far better it is to have all your hankerings stopped and be doing nothing whatever!''*

# WAR

I shall not fight. No cry of England's need

To guard each ravished jewel in her crown;

No boast of war's adventure, of renown

That waits the winning of the office-freed;

No urge uprising from a social creed,

Nor woman's word, shall drag me down

To strike a blow for human greed,

And watch the heart of Abel bleed.

Let those who know not splendidly defend

Our England's banner on the field of woe.

I shall not fight, for I shall know

That he who meets me at the bayonet's end

May wear the semblance of my country's foe,

Yet will he be my brother, and my friend.

UPASAKA.

# THE UNIMPORTANCE OF WAR

From *Buddhism in England*
*May–June, 1938*

•

It is well known that those who are most afraid of great heights are those most likely to lose control of themselves when looking over the edge of a precipice. Their very fear of falling is the power which hurls them over the edge, and in this familiar fact there is a moral which must be applied to the various bugbears which from time to time become fashionable in human society. Whether or not human beings would be happy without some particular spectre to haunt their minds is a question which we cannot at present consider, though everyone is no doubt familiar with people who are not happy unless they are miserable, who get a certain "kick" out of imagining that they are the most unfortunate people in the world, who can never feel that life has any zest unless they can believe themselves threatened by some dire event. Whether this peculiar trait is characteristic of society as a whole I do not know. Thus it is not easy to say whether the present and very prevalent terror of war is something which society would be happy to have removed or not. We only know that it undoubtedly exists.

Whether the race as a whole either consciously or unconsciously desires war is a problem wherein we have no statistics to help us. Presumably this article will be read by those who believe themselves innocent of any desire for war, and who, moreover, would do anything in their power to prevent its happening. In this they may be prompted by an urge to serve humanity and promote civilization, or else by fear, though if fear is the motive one can only assume that their efforts will be more of a hindrance than a help. The possible steps they may take to avert war may be divided into three groups. Firstly, there are those who believe that war can only be prevented by intimidating potential war-makers with the might of armaments. Secondly, there are those who prefer to shame the war-maker by turning to him the other cheek, believing that to resist him by his own means is to sink to his own depraved level. Thirdly, there are those who desire by various forms of propaganda to fight the "ideology" of war and to make those who espouse it seem , in the eyes of the world, ridiculous, criminal, or mad. Each of these three has its own particular sanity and its own particular madness, but whether sanity or madness preponderates depends not on the kind of action taken but on the motive from which it springs.

Therefore, for this reason and another I believe it more profitable at this time to consider not how we shall try to prevent war, but what our attitude to it may be, whether it comes or not. For we have to realize that, at this stage, there is really nothing we can do either to prevent it or to cause it, unless, of course, we can summon the wits, the money, and the will to do something very alarming indeed, such as purchasing a fleet of private aeroplanes to deposit bombs and propaganda in certain carefully selected spots. Why no philanthropic millionaire has done this I cannot imagine. Much might also be done by some grimly determined secret society such as Dennis Wheatley's "Millers of God," but as a rule the people who have the necessarily vast sums of money at their disposal lack the imagination to do anything so desirable. However, so far as the ordinary man and woman are concerned there is really nothing that can be done immediately except to buy a hermitage in the Himalayas or some other remote spot. But this again is expensive, although I am told that quite a number of people are doing things of this kind, storing their Shagri-las [sic] with canned food against the coming storm. They may be regarded as escapists and cowards, but since war itself is an act of cowardice and military courage for the most part a matter of running away from one's own fears, I do not think they are to be especially blamed. They may be cowards, but they do at least know what they want. After all, war is, if we are to believe human history, just as much a natural phenomenon as a thunder-storm, a flood or an earthquake. If you believe you can save your homes you stay behind and fight the fires or help to stem the water. If you know you can't you just go to a safe place; to stay behind would only be sentimental foolhardiness showing a lack of responsibility. For everyone is responsible for his own life to the community; if he knows the community can be benefited by putting his life in danger or even by losing it, then, if he dies, he dies responsibly. If, however, he knows that the loss of his life will help to save neither the lives nor the homes of the community, then if he deliberately goes and gets killed he commits suicide, which is usually and sensibly regarded as a crime. Talk of "standing by one's post" or "going down with one's ship" is, under the circumstances, irresponsible and pernicious nonsense. One is only justified in doing this kind of thing when it serves the general good.

But now everyone knows, or should know, that in modern warfare defence is something which has practically ceased to exist. Attack has always been the best form of defence; now it is the only form, and unless you choose to fly up in an aeroplane and bomb other people's cities, you will just have to stay at home and be bombed. And even if the bombs, or the gas, or the flames, or the invading hordes don't get you, the subsequent plagues or famines certainly will. Therefore most people have got to make up their minds either to be killed or to get right out before anything happens. Hence responsible people who have the welfare of the community at heart should instantly acquire distant and secret retreats and transport as many people to them at an appropriate time as their means will allow. This is nothing less than what every Government will do with itself when the time comes, and they, after all, are said to be the most responsible people in the community. When the trouble is over, they will appear again in what is left of the public and start again. Naturally, only a few people will have either the means or the sense to do this, and therefore their retreats will remain comparatively remote and secret. They will not be escapists any more than anyone else; they will just be blessed with good karma. In any case, no one was ever called a coward or an escapist because he left his house when it seriously caught fire. When my kitchen curtains blow into the gas-stove and set the room alight, my cook is not considered a glorious martyr if she is burnt to death while standing resolutely at her post with an emptied fire-extinguisher. If, however, she had been so surrounded with flames that she could not leave the kitchen, that would be quite another matter.

Therefore we have to face the fact that most of us are in such a position that we cannot remove ourselves to safety in the event of war. I think we also have to recognize that there is nothing we can do immediately to prevent it from coming; we must just hope and continue to behave like civilized people. Now I know many people who would regard this as the most abysmal pessimism, for they all believe war to be the greatest evil which could befall us. Anyone who does not work himself to a skeleton to prevent it (however ineffectually) is to them an irresponsible slacker. These people, who exist in enormous numbers and in various degrees of enthusiasm, regard war as the bugbear of bugbears, the utter end of civilization, beside which all other evils are as pale shadows. War to them is the end of everything and hence the thing most of all to be avoided. But let them consider for a moment. After all, war is only death and perhaps a highly unpleasant death. Certainly it is a great deal of death, but this is a matter of quantity and not value; in spiritual matters, it is value that counts. Without doubt war involves other evils besides death, if death is actually an evil. It releases the basest passions of which man is capable, for "whom the gods wish to destroy they first make mad." But all that can be expected of any one of us is to see that our own basest passions are kept under control; though we may not be able to prevent the gods from destroying us, we can at least make sure that they do not steal away our souls. In war the madness is far worse than the death, but if you have a good control of yourself, you have only the death to fear.

Nevertheless, the prospect of death inflames many of us with varying kinds of madness, and the prospect of much death with more madness still. But this is only because our sense of proportion is absurdly distorted and because we have not learnt to accept the changing aspects of nature. To some extent, this is the fault of our education, at least so far as our sense of proportion is concerned. But if we learn anything from Buddhism it should teach us one thing—that bugbears such as war are of very little significance. To those of us who would be inextricably involved in any future war it has two important messages. The first concerns our sense of proportion.

For why all this fuss about war? You are going to die; civilization is going to disappear. So what? Is this any special cause for misery, and is the acceptance of the fact pessimism? I think not. Empires and civilizations have vanished many times before, and of ancient Egypt we have a good deal less than bombs may leave of London, Berlin and Paris. Of Atlantis, if indeed it existed, we have hardly a trace, and yet humanity survives. For physical catastrophes cannot touch the spirit unless we let them, and even then only for a brief time. It may take two hundred years for civilization to rise again, but what is a *mere* two hundred years? And is this physical civilization of ours really such a great treasure, whose loss would be the end of all things? Rather I would say that if it is capable of blowing itself to pieces, it deserves to be blown to pieces. Next time it may learn better, and even if it doesn't there is infinite time in which to try again. Indeed, the wisdom of the East gives us a vision of the soul's past and future beside which Armageddon is an almost imperceptible glow. And yet it does not lose the proportions. A single mistake in the life of the spirit may throw you back a million years on your path, whereas a world war can only put you back three score and ten at the most; before eternity this is just the littlest fraction of a moment. The wounds of earth will heal, and in time you will return once more to start life again. Do you doubt this? Well, I cannot prove it, but if you try believing it you will find that it affects you as no other belief will. Even so, you will in time outgrow it; that is not to say that you will reject it, but rather that you will grasp its true meaning, which is this: that time the infinitely long is the same as time the infinitely short. To see eternity you may have at first to see life and death in perspective; after that you will be able to see it in every passing moment. At first you may feel that to obtain the sense of eternity you will have to bide and behold the passing of immeasurable time; but afterwards you will see that you can slip into eternity through any moment, for the eternally long is one with the eternally short. But to slip through the moment requires a certain knack which comes with practice, because the moment is an elusive creature. To begin with, it cannot be measured; it is so much shorter than a second that before we can begin to think of it as here and now it has already passed. At the same time we can never get away from it, for our very thinking and our trying to grasp it partake of it and exist in it. For the universe exists only in the moment; the world of yesterday is not and cannot be; the world of tomorrow is not, and will never be; the world of to-day is, and will never cease to be. To-day is therefore eternity, for it is not the moment that moves but only its measure. Time stands still, but the stars and planets go racing on their courses. Yet however much the planets race and in whatever way they behave, even if they rush together and beat upon each other, even if blazing comets are hurled out of the void and whole systems dissolve into dust, they cannot affect the stillness of Time or break the persistence of the eternal Now.

This brings us to the second message of Buddhism in regard to misfortune. If you never lose your hold on this eternal Now, you find yourself in harmony with life. Hui Neng says: "If we allow our thoughts, past, present and future, to link up in a series we put ourselves under restraint. On the other hand, if we let our mind be attached to nothing at all times and towards all things, we gain freedom." This freedom is just walking on with the Now, which is to become one with the creative impulse of life; for at this moment the whole universe is being created. It did not come into being at some point in the infinite past, nor will it cease to be at some point in the infinite future: it is born now; it dies now; it begins and ends with the moment. This is perhaps a metaphysical, or even mathematical, way of stating a fundamental principle of spiritual psychology. It is that you live in this eternal Now, that you *are* it and that by no possible contrivance can you get away from it. Therefore it is written: "Have perseverance as one who doth for evermore endure. Thy shadows live and vanish, but that which in thee *knows*, for it is Knowledge, is not of fleeting life. It is the Man that was, is and shall be, for whom the hour will never strike" (*Voice of the Silence*). The realization of this brings the most unbelievable freedom of spirit, releasing energies of the soul hitherto undreamed of. Loss and gain become things of no account because you have nothing to gain and nothing to lose; you can stake your life without turning a hair, and at every point you find yourself free to go left or right, backwards or forwards, just as you choose. For you yourself have become the eternal Path, and carrying it with you you can never depart from it whichever way you turn. This is called responsible irresponsibility, for the sage is a law-abiding vagabond.

In the words of Chuang Tzu: "The perfect man is a spiritual being. Were the ocean itself scorched up, he would not feel hot. Were the Milky Way frozen hard, he would not feel cold. Were the mountains to be riven with thunder, and the great deep to be thrown up by storm, he would not tremble. . . . The revolutions of ten thousand years leave his unity unscathed. The universe itself may pass away, but he will flourish still."

---

# THE ORIGINAL FACE
## From the Zen Sermons of Wu Tao-kung

From *Buddhism in England*
*May–June, 1938*

●

An old master used to hit people on the mouth when they asked what his religion was. How understandable! But perhaps he should have controlled his feelings a little better. Yet it may be that I am too kind-hearted, talking along like this instead of lifting you off your feet and throwing you out of the room. What is my religion? What can you want with a religion? Is it not after all like looking over the whole Empire for your own face? Heaven and earth perform their functions every day without fuss: butterflies have more beautiful clothes than even Pien-lu could make; no music excels the sound of the waterfalls at Chechiang; and even Confucius could not arrange his life as well as petals are arranged round the stem of a peony, but have *they* a religion?

But man, having involved himself in the ten fetters and the fourteen afflictions, finds in the innumerable objects a certain reluctance to adapt themselves to his convenience.

How sad! Now tell me, have you any fault to find with the world of ten thousand things? If you have a fault will you please show it me? A wise man of old has said that the man who finds the fault is the man who put it there. But he does not know he put it there, and so blames the ten thousand things. Do you blame the ten thousand things, or do you blame yourself? If the former, then you are like a deaf person who blames his neighbour for not talking loud enough; if the latter, someone may tell you you are a wise man. But are you? I tell you no praising, no blaming! Praise yourself, and you are like Lung-chao who made a fine stew out of his own tongue; blame yourself, and you are like the demons who eat the filth off their own bodies. So much for all your talk and sadness about your own evil minds! Do you go to the Buddha to get rid of your evil mind? Why not give me your evil mind, and I will give it a good washing. If you cannot give it me, how do you know you have got it?

The object of the ten good deeds (*paramitas*) is to get rid of the evil mind and to make ordinary men into Buddhas. Does anyone here want to become a Buddha? If so, he shall have a knock over the head with my stick. Trees and grass are all Buddhas, and man is supposed to be greater than they. So how should you want to become a Buddha? Having climbed to the top of Mount Lu you still say you are not an inch off the ground. But whether you are on the top of the mountain or in the rice-swamps by the river you still cannot get away from it. Trees and grass are Buddhas and have never known what it is like to think they are not Buddhas. Ordinary men are Buddhas but seem to have forgotten it. Buddhas are Buddhas and have never been anything else. But you want to remember what you have forgotten. Let me first ask you a question: What is this forgetting, and who is it that wants to remember? If a Buddha forgets he is a Buddha does he cease to be one? And if a Buddha wants to remember that he is a Buddha, is he not like the idiot who, when eating a bowl of rice, wondered if he was there to eat it and could not understand why it did not drop straight on to the seat of his chair?

I tell you the Buddha is none other than your own original face. You carry it about with you wherever you go. Going to the Northern River, you cannot catch it; running to the Southern Lake, you cannot get away from it. Therefore what is the use of all your ten merits, all your toiling and trying, all your sutra-reading and worrying about the silly tricks of the old masters? Here in this place everything is clear as the vastness of heaven. Drinking tea, eating rice, sweeping up leaves, sleeping at night, taking a walk, who has ever lost it? And yet you want me to talk to you about Buddhahood. With all the ten thousand things existing around you I wonder you can hear me speak for the noise all the Buddhas and Bodhisattvas are making. I am sorry I cannot shout any louder, but I am an old man and you must excuse me.

---

# CAN WE HELP OURSELVES?
## A Lecture

From *Buddhism in England*

●

The study of religion or even of all religions can so easily lead us such a long way from religion. For religion itself is something intimately bound up with life, so much so that one hardly knows where to draw the line between the two. A specific religion such as Buddhism or Christianity is really a set of ideas and symbols *about* life, and these ideas and symbols are just tricks or cunning devices to make us see things which are so obvious that we don't notice them.

Nothing, for instance, could be more obvious than one's own face, and yet in one way it's the most mysterious thing about us because we can never actually see it. We have to go and look in a mirror if we want to know what it looks like. Now when you go and stand in front of a mirror you know, as a rule, that what you see is just your own reflection and it doesn't cause you very much surprise. You understand, in fact, that the mirror is just a trick, a clever dodge for making you see yourself. But if you didn't understand the ways of mirrors and had never seen one before, well, you might get rather a shock. There is a story of an old man and his wife who used to live on one of the islands off the West Coast of Scotland. Their island was slowly being washed away by the sea, and at last they had to leave their home and go to live on the mainland. When they came to their new house, the old man went up into the bedroom and saw a curious smooth and flat object on the dressing table the like of which he'd never seen before. He walked up to it, looked into it and suddenly stepped back in amazement. "Loch!" he exclaimed, "'tis feyther!" Well, he got rather worried about it and didn't think his wife ought to see it. So he put it under the bed. But he was so intrigued and puzzled by the thing that from time to time he would go up to the bedroom during the day to have a look at it. At last his wife began to notice that there was something funny about him, and she couldn't account at all for his constant visits to the bedroom. So one day while he was out at the local pub, she decided she would go upstairs and have a look round on her own. And after a while she pulled out this thing from under the bed. When she looked at it she nearly wept. "Ah me!" she sighed, "a might ha' known it: 'Tis anither woman, and loch, ain't she ugly!"

Well, in rather the same way the ideas and symbols of a religion seem to us so entirely strange, and often enough our notions about them are quite as curious as those of that old Scotch couple. The early stages of religion are concerned mainly with gods and other supernatural powers. We pray to them, we conceive them as external personalities who can, if they choose, bestow all heavenly and earthly blessings upon us, or, alternatively, all manner of punishments and adversity. But in time we begin to understand that we must seek God in ourselves, that wisdom must be sought from within, that heaven and hell are of our own making, and that all the spirits and demons and angels of primitive religion are symbols of the vast potentialities for good and evil of our own souls. Even so, we have as yet a long way to go. For at this stage it is so easy to fall into a subtle trap, because the concrete, external gods of the primitive have been replaced by other gods which are more misleading because they are less obviously naive. These new gods are not conceived as external realities at all. On the contrary, they masquerade as inner realities, for they are no other than our own ideas about life and religion. Thus, instead of seeking wisdom from gods which we really understand as gods, we seek it in ideas which we discover in books, hear at lectures or think out for ourselves. But these ideas are just as much cunning devices, just as much mirrors, just as much external deities as Jupiter, Mars, Minerva and the rest. You may chase ideas for ever and become no wiser; you may work out all their implications in an unending universe of thought which you might explore to the end of time. If you wish, you can easily get lost in this universe, for the more you explore, hoping to find the place where wisdom is hidden, the further you are led away from the place where it actually is, which is right under your own nose, here and now in this ordinary life.

There are others who seek this wisdom not so much in ideas as in peculiar states of consciousness. They somehow imagine that if they can depart to the astral plane, or visit the world of departed spirits, or awaken psychic forces in the body, or develop new powers of perception, they will find the wisdom which seems to be absent from this ordinary world and unknowable through these five ordinary senses. Now I have no doubt that there are astral planes, that we can speak with departed spirits, that we can exercise occult powers, that we can see things which underlie the world of the senses on finer planes of matter. But here again, if we are going to imagine that any of these admittedly diverting pursuits are going to give us wisdom or an understanding of religion, then once more we are just running after the old gods. For all these investigations have no more to do with religion than with botany. In fact, they have probably a great deal more to do with botany than with religion, for they are essentially scientific pursuits, and unfortunately, it is seldom recognized nowadays that science and religion are two things as entirely different as an inch and a joke. For one is a question of quantity and the other of quality or values. By means of an inch you may understand size, and means of a joke you may appreciate the comic. And whereas you may presumably have a joke about the inch, you cannot possibly have an inch about the joke. That is to say, although you may have religious science, in the sense of a scientist who can find religion in analysing milk, you cannot have scientific religion. For religion is something applicable to every possible form of activity; but it does not consist in, nor can it be qualified by any particular form of activity. Thus there are many activities to which it would be unreasonable to apply science, although I regret that some people seem anxious to do so. If, for instance, you desired a scientific explanation of why you enjoy the music of Mozart, of what precisely made it seem beautiful to you, you would be confronted by considerable details of nervous responses, sense mechanisms and what not which would simply explain its beauty away. Science is purely a question of measurement, analysis and mechanism. To measure a quality is like combing a bald head; to analyse it is like expecting a post-mortem to reveal the secrets of a woman's beauty; to mechanize it is like expecting a pencil mounted on wheels with a clockwork engine to write words of wisdom. Thus scientific investigation may increase our knowledge, and though knowledge may be power, it is no wisdom. It does not follow that because you know this world, the astral world and all possible worlds, you are therefore capable of leading a religious life in any one of them, much less all. The Hermetic maxim says, "As above, so below," which is to say that all these worlds are based on the same fundamental principles, and that when you know one you have the key to all. Yet, knowing those principles, you have no more than knowledge, which is simply an instrument, a tool, a useful gadget. And a carpenter is not a good carpenter on account of his amazing faculty for buying immense quantities of tools.

Religion, therefore, is not concerned with the acquisition of knowledge and experience; it is rather a matter of our response to and use of even a little knowledge and of any experiences that happen to come our way. In the last resort we need no more for it than our ordinary, everyday experience, conveyed to our minds through our five senses. For here is life as we know it; yet how little we know it, for we have to have a cunning device called a religion to enable us to live it aright. Even so, it is astonishing how easily this device leads us astray, and perhaps we can somehow find out just how it does this. Therefore I want you to consider with me for a while a rather horrifying picture. In some ways it is rather an amusing picture; I suppose it depends how it strikes you. But the picture I want to show is that of ourselves in search of Happiness, Truth, Enlightenment, God, Wisdom, or whatever you like to call it.

Presumably all of us are here to-night because we are in search of this mysterious thing, and presumably most of us have the idea, common to all mystics, that in some way or other we must find it within ourselves. That is to say, no one else can give it to us any more than another person can eat our own food for us. We cannot find it by going to any particular place or state of consciousness. If there are any orthodox Christians here, they may look at it in rather a different way. For them, God is the source of all wisdom and by reason of Original Sin we cannot find it for ourselves. Therefore wisdom must come through opening the soul to the Grace of God. In this the Christian is very nearly right, but for a reason which cannot quite be shown at the moment. If he does not object too strongly, let us leave the Christian on one side for the moment and consider those of us who are trying to work out our own salvation, who either disbelieve or do not care about any supernatural power which could simply give us wisdom for the asking. Most people in this category would say with the Indian mystics that man's real and inmost Self is God, and that our task is to realize, to make real, this fact in our lives. To put it another way, man is God in potentiality, and religion is the task of developing the potential into the actual. Thus in the end the Goal is to attain complete unity with God, the Absolute or the Universal Self. Personally, I prefer a more matter-of-fact name for this God. Let us say, shall we, that all of us want to discover the mystery of life, to know what life is and so to live in harmony with life. I think, if we talk about it in this way, it brings us a little nearer to fundamentals, for, as we have already seen, religious terminology has a way of leading us away from the thing which religion is really about, and that is life itself. Even so, life is rather a bad word because it has two meanings which are rather apt to get confused. One is life as opposed to death, and the other is the life which is a perpetual process of living and dying. Life in this latter sense is also something just a bit more than living and dying, in the same way as the whole is greater than the sum of its parts. It is also the meaning, the *raison d'être*, the cause and the effect of living and dying, just as the child is the meaning, the *raison d'être*, the cause and effect of man and woman. Neither man nor woman can exist for long without each other, and there is no point in having two sexes unless there can be the child to give them a point. The same may be said of life and death, and of all other pairs of opposites. Therefore I want a term for that life which is not only living and dying, but also their meaning, *raison d'être*, cause and effect, the source of their mystery and wonder, of their rhythm and movement. It is just that mysterious life which exists in ourselves and everything else, which ultimately *is* ourselves, and which we are all so anxious to discover.

Well, if you will excuse me, I will take my word for this mystery from a place at the other side of the earth called China. The word is untranslatable in any case; it is sufficiently unfamiliar not to involve the chaos of cross-purposed associations which always arise when we use familiar words like God and Spirit. This Chinese word is Tao. The first thing to remember about Tao is this: that as Tao is, in a sense, life, everything which happens, everything we think, do, or say, simply *is* Tao. Therefore, whether we like it or not, we can't help living in harmony with the life or the Tao. We may feel that we lack something, whether possessions or wisdom, and so go in search of it. But it is Tao which is searching through us, and there is nothing in the way of possessions or wisdom that can be added to Tao, for Tao includes everything. This is why religion can be expressed in the paradox, "Become what you are." Or as a Buddhist sage put it, "Ordinary men are all Buddhas, and the only difference between a Buddha and an ordinary man is that the Buddha realizes that he is a Buddha, whereas the ordinary man does not." Yet although in reality we are in perfect harmony with life, we feel that something is wrong. But that is only because we do not realize that we are in harmony. We do not understand that each one of us is in fact the all-sufficient Tao, and therefore we seek this Tao in external things, whether in possessions or ideas. And while we seek it in some ways, we try to run away from it in others. Since we do not realize our identity with the Tao we fear that certain things such as loss and death can take something away from us. But loss and death are themselves included in Tao, and cannot take anything away from it. For the Tao is presented to us in all forms and in all experiences, and because we are the Tao, to run after them is running after ourselves, and running away from them is running away from ourselves. Pursuing it we cannot catch it; fleeing it we cannot escape it. Indeed, one is reminded of the words of the Psalm:—

> *Whither shall I go from thy spirit?*
> *Or whither shall I flee from thy presence?*
> *If I ascend up into heaven, thou art there;*
> *If I make my bed in hell, behold, thou art there.*
> *If I take the wings of the morning,*
> *And dwell in the uttermost parts of the sea;*
> *Even there shall thy hand lead me,*
> *And thy right hand shall hold me.*

Yet here are all of us searching, searching for this Tao—and what a wild, mad picture it is! We are trying to find wisdom, and we might as well try to lift ourselves up by the seats of our own trousers. Some of you have no doubt tried to practise the teaching of the *Bhagavad-Gita*, to separate yourself from all your thoughts and deeds, and to realize that your Self is the eternal essence which is not affected by the forms of the world. But haven't you found that this is rather like trying to see your own eyes, and that you just go round in circles? You divide yourself from your thoughts, but is not that very dividing itself a thought, and why not divide yourself again from that? And then again, why not divide yourself from the thought that you were dividing yourself? Yes, you could go on like this forever in an infinite regress leading to the ultimate madness. But you would not be understanding Krishna aright; you would simply be chasing yourself round in circles indefinitely. That always happens when we try to face that tremendous problem, "What am I?" And there is its allied problem: If I am what I am, how can I make myself different; how can I increase my wisdom? To put it in another way: If I am in a state of darkness because my Higher Self is identified with my lower self, how then can my Higher Self free itself? It can't lift itself up out of the morass of the lower self—unless perhaps there is something higher even than it, some fixed and firm branch or hand above it to which it can cling. Indeed, what a strange position we are in when we try to help ourselves; if you think about it long enough you can easily go mad with distress and hopelessness.

Now it is just at this point that our friend the orthodox Christian is entitled to interrupt. "There," he will say, "I told you so all the time. Man cannot help himself, and only God can help him. For God is the firm branch above to Whom we can cling and lift ourselves out of the mire of sin. That branch is offered freely through Christ to all; its name is Divine Grace, and we have only to desire it sincerely, only to lay ourselves open to it in all humility, confessing our own wretchedness, and at once we shall find it." Well, personally, I am inclined to feel that the Christian is very right, but not quite in the way he thinks he is. I have no doubt at all that his solution is wholly effective for a certain type of mind, for the mind that can believe in a personal, external and transcendental God. But this very belief seems to me to complicate the situation unnecessarily. Moreover, while it will bring some to true salvation, others it will simply lead astray into the realm of ideas and feelings *about* Truth, and not to Truth itself. Furthermore the problem of the objective and external existence of God is a scientific and not a religious problem, resting ultimately on knowledge. Such a God may or may not exist, but His existence is something outside our everyday experience. Is there not, perhaps, yet another Way, requiring only the experience of ordinary life, a Way which brings us to a condition similar to the Christian salvation in its essentials, but differing in its theological and philosophical details?

Indeed, there is such a Way, but how can I or anyone put it into words? The moment we stop to think about it, it is lost. It is right here before us at this moment, standing perfectly plain and open, and every one of us is travelling serenely along it—did we but know it! But how shall we see it? I talk about seeing it, yet every word I utter is a black devil to hide it from our eyes. But do not be too unkind to these devils, for if your eyes are open even these are all the perfect Tao and are all walking along this Way with us. If we must give this Way a name, let us call it the Middle Way, because it is neither pursuing the Tao on the one hand, nor fleeing from it on the other. To seek for the Tao is to be like the dog which chases its tail; to flee from it is like the dog running away from its tail. Yet this is really Tao chasing Tao, and Tao running away from Tao, and there has never been any mistake at all. Just the same thing happens when you try to catch hold of the present moment; try to keep it, and before you can so much as wink an eyelid it has become the past and has altogether vanished. The more you think about this present moment, the more elusive it becomes; you cannot say just when and where it is, for before you can utter the word NOW! it has already gone. Yet, paradoxically, you have been living in it and moving forward with it all the time. It never waits for you to catch it, but you can never separate yourself from it. You see, it is the moment, or better, the movement of Tao. All you have to do is to go straight ahead with it. Do not worry about whether you are going along with the Tao or not; you are doing it all the time in spite of yourself. If you suddenly understand that it is no cause for pride; rather you should laugh at yourself for not having seen it before. And is not this just what the Christian says about the Grace of God? It is offered freely to you in spite of yourself, and if you find it, it is not your doing but the work of God and all the praise should be accorded to Him alone. You see, all this is just like the story of the idiot who went all over the world in search of his head, which he had never lost. There is nothing special for you to see, nothing special for you to learn; just go straight ahead. You cannot find the Tao by pursuit; you cannot avoid it by flight, and whether you pursue or avoid, or whether you just walk straight on, it is simply Tao that pursues, Tao that avoids, Tao that walks straight on. Thus you are no more held away from the freedom of the Tao than your eyes are separated from your eyes. Well, there you are! Just look right ahead and see what you see.

A Buddhist sage was asked, "How shall we escape from illusion?" He replied, "Who is holding you back?" In truth there are no obstructions, and if you can really open your eyes just for a moment, you will see that this every-day life and experience which ordinarily seems so oppressive, so limiting, is nothing other than the supreme religious experience. In getting up in the morning, in dressing, in going out to work, in sitting in the train, in washing your hands, in greeting a friend in the street, there are no restraints; in all this the Tao is just moving freely along its unhurried way. Does the present moment seem like a lightning flash? Does time go too fast? That is only because you are running after it. The Tao runs when you run, because the Tao is you. And yet there was really no running at all, for Time is in itself neither fast nor slow; thus Time is Tao, and you are Tao. And perhaps you are now tempted to ask, "What IS Tao?" I need hardly give you the famous answer of the Chinese sage. It was just this: WALK ON!

However, I am just wondering whether I ought not to apologize for inflicting on you my attempts to describe the indescribable. Some of you may be thinking that I do not understand what I am talking about, and perhaps you are right. And some of you may have been having your doubts about this thing called Tao. You may be thinking, "Well, if everything is nothing but Tao, how dull! A universe in which there is really only one thing must be as flat and uninteresting as an infinite desert." Of course, you are quite right. All of us know only too well those philosophies, which, seizing the hammer of intellect, batter the universe into a solid lump of homogeneous mud called the one essential Substance, proclaiming all diversity, all individuality, all personality to be a vain illusion. But please do not think that Tao is this One unindividuated substance, that because I am Tao and you are Tao and everything is Tao therefore I and you and all created things are just nothing, just unimportant and insignificant phantasies. If you can put up with another paradox, we should say rather that while there is certainly only one Tao, Tao is not only one thing. For it *is* this One Substance which exists undivided in all separate things, yet at the same time it is just those very separate things; it is each one of them in all its uniqueness. Thus Tao is both the One and the many, and here again we see that the Tao is the Middle Way; it belongs to neither extreme alone, neither to unity alone, nor to diversity alone. If, therefore, we are to realize the Tao in our lives, please do not imagine that this in any way denies the value of personality and of that variety which is wisely said to be the spice of life. I am afraid that so many of the philosophies and religions of the East have got themselves a bad name over here because they are supposed to be so radically impersonal and to deny absolutely and entirely the value of individual things. But that is only a surface impression, for the profoundest philosophies of the East always recognized a stage beyond mere unity, mere absorption into the One Reality, involving the disappearance of the whole objective world of form. Thus the Chinese Buddhists have a saying, "If the many are to be reduced to the One, to what is the One to be reduced?" Again, there is another saying: "To him who knows nothing of Buddhism, mountains are mountains and waters are waters. But when he has learnt a little of the teaching, mountains are for him no longer mountains, and waters no longer waters. (That is to say, all separate things become merged into the One Reality.) But the saying con-

tinues: Yet when he is thoroughly enlightened, then mountains are to him once again mountains, and waters once again
waters."

You see, however far away we wander, we are always
brought back again to this ordinary world where I am I and
you are you, where this table is this table, and that is all there
is to it. And, as we have seen, in the last resort our everyday experience of walking, sitting, talking, thinking and eating is the supreme religious experience. Is this rather
disappointing? Do we not imagine that the supreme religious
experience ought to be something much more wonderful
than this? But, think for a moment; what could be more
wonderful than the surprising fact that we are alive? And
can you really conceive anything more astonishing than the
fact that you can laugh and breathe and sleep and speak and
see? The philosopher and scientist may try as hard as they
like to reduce all this to a "nothing but," to nothing but illusion, nothing but mechanism, nothing but a "fortuitous congress of atoms." Yes, if you analyse everything down to its
elements and beyond in order to explain it, you must finally
explain away all things. And even then you have to face the
ultimate problem of: Who is it that explains, and why? And
that at once sets you off running round in circles to try and
find out what your self is. It has been said that the mystery
of life is not a problem to be solved, but a reality to be
experienced. Perhaps it was for this reason that a Buddhist
poet once wrote:—

*How wondrous and how miraculous, this,—*
*I draw water and I carry fuel!*

For the whole point of the Tao is that it is a mystery;
you can never turn round and look at it, because it *is* that
which turns round, namely, yourself. Indeed, we are "fear-
fully and wonderfully made," and perhaps the most wonderful thing of all is that in spite of ourselves, in spite of
our stupidity, our sins, our illusions, and our egoism, we

are never separated from the Tao for one moment. Nothing that we can do can put us out of accord with Tao, or, as the Christian would say, no amount of sin can prevent God from loving us. In fact, in order to attain salvation, to find harmony with life, we do not have to do a single thing; there is nothing that we can do, except, perhaps, to recognize that we are saved as we are in spite of ourselves, to acknowledge this mystery with reverence and gratitude, and then pass freely on our way. That is what is meant when we say that the whole thing is right here before us in our ordinary life, and that all we have to do is just to go straight ahead with it. The only trap is that it's no good just going straight ahead with it *in order* to obtain this realization. You can't obtain it; you've already got it, and you only think you haven't because you try to get it. And when you know this, what else would you do than just go on with your life as you find it in the joy and freedom of the spirit? Every one of us has that freedom whether we know it or not, and no one prevents us from seeing it but ourselves. In short, we are making a great fuss about trying to lift ourselves with our own hands out of a prison from which we are already free. Under these circumstances one feels rather like saying with another Buddhist sage: "Nothing is now left to you but to have a good laugh."

# BUDDHISM ADVOCATED AT A CHRISTIAN RELIGIOUS CONFERENCE

From *Buddhism in England*
*March-April, 1933*

●

A most striking example of the difficulties and problems with which the Christian religion finds itself confronted today was demonstrated at a Conference of Public School Boys which was held at Haywards Heath (England) on June 10th–13th of last year (1932). The Conference was organized by the "Teaching Church Group for Adult Religious Education," and was presided over by the Archbishop of York.

The Conference took the form of Lectures and Group Discussions, the subjects of the Lectures being:—

*Christianity as a Reasonable Faith: His Grace the Archbishop of York.*

*The Christian Moral Standard: Rev. Canon Grensted.*

*Prayer: Rev. Canon Grensted.*

*Vocation (I): Rev. C.H. Smyth; and (II): Mr. G.K. Tattersall.*

The Group Discussions included the six questions detailed below, each question being discussed by two groups.

I. *Do you think modern science makes a religious view of life easier, or more difficult?*

II. *What is the relationship between creed and conduct? What have you to say about the "necessity of dogma"?*

III. *Why should we pray, when God already knows our need?*

IV. *How far should the individual accept the authority of Christian tradition in matters (i) of belief, (ii) of conduct?*

V. *What truth is there in the alleged contrast between the "Religion of the Church" and the "Religion of Jesus"?*

VI. *How far should Church-going be considered obligatory? What do you take to be its purpose?*

Mr. Alan Watts, a member of the Buddhist Lodge, London, took part in this Conference, and whilst the discussion under heading No. 5 was in progress, he brought forward the subject of Buddhism. It had been suggested that the Church should follow the example of Christ in giving fresh impetus to mission work, and to this Mr. Watts objected, asserting that the Church had no business to try to do away with religions which were just as good as Christianity, as for example, Buddhism. There followed a long argument as to the comparative merits of Christianity and Buddhism, in which varying opinions were expressed.

When the report of this group was read before the whole Conference, an objection was raised to the statement of Mr. Watts, who then made the following reply:

"I trust the Conference will not think that I am wasting its time, but the subject of Buddhism is one that merits the attention of all Christians owing to the great revival of that religion now in progress. The Christian opposition to Buddhism has arisen from the misinterpretations of Buddhist scriptures made by scholars of the late XIX century; for instance, many westerners are under the delusion that Nirvana, the Goal of Buddhist endeavour, means annihilation of the soul, and that the Buddha is a god and his images idols. All this is utterly untrue. The Buddha was an ordinary man whose teaching may be summed up in a line of Arnold's *Light of Asia*: "Foregoing self, the Universe grow 'I.'" The story told by the Archbishop about Sir Walford Davies* and his class of working men is strictly Buddhistic; the tune is the Universe and we are the singers—if you want to sing well, forget yourselves and think only of the tune—if you want to live well, forget yourselves and think only of Life, the Ultimate Reality. Nirvana is the Christian "Kingdom of Heaven"—not annihilation, but Understanding of Reality.

"In the personality of the Buddha we find stoic-calm combined with Christ-like compassion—here indeed is the highest form of man—and he reached this state without anything we should understand as prayer. It can be done—the Christian God is not necessary for the perfect life. Both Buddhism and Christianity are manifestations of the same spirit which strives for perfection through conquest of self, and though Buddhism is often criticized because of its corruptions, it must not be forgotten that Christianity also is corrupt."

---

* *The story about Sir Walford Davies referred to above is this: Sir Walford was teaching a class of working-men how to sing. First of all, he gave them a song which they all knew, and they sang it so lustily that it sounded abominable. Then he gave them a song which they did not know, and he had to call in his choir in order to show them how to sing it. Then he said to them: "Now whatever you do you must not try to sing this song. Just let yourselves sing it and listen to the tune: think only of the tune, and don't try." And the result was that they sang it excellently, because they no longer "forced" it.*

This was replied to by Canon Grensted, Professor in the Philosophy of Religion at Oriel College, Oxford, who submitted that the personality of Christ was to be preferred to that of the Buddha because of what he suffered. He admitted that the story of the Buddha's life was one of the most beautiful in the world, and that he had a great respect for his teachings, but at the same time he could not help feeling that his renunciation was not quite so great as that made by Jesus. Citing the story of the "Agony in the Garden," he said that there was something about the essential humanity of Christ's prayer, "Let this cup pass from me," which the Buddhist would consider rather weak, though he himself thought it the sign of a Divine suffering which the Buddha had never had to undergo.

Mr. Watts comments: Quite why the suffering of Christ should have been greater than that of any other person who was crucified he did not explain unless it were through his deep compassion for the sufferings of the world—but did not the Buddha also feel this? And which is worse, the mental agony of leaving one's wife and child—more dear to one than anything else—or the physical agony of crucifixion? Who knows?—but Christ's claim to supremacy in this respect is not quite so obvious as it might seem.

Mr. Watts's address aroused a great deal of interest, and he was asked numerous questions as to the teaching of Buddhism on God, Fate and Free-will, Grace, etc., and also, what did he think was the essential difference between Buddhism and Christianity, and why did he prefer the one to the other.

Mr. Watts tells us that one of the outstanding features of the Conference was the highly tolerant spirit displayed by the managers of the Conference, and he adds that it was gratifying to see that the "Christianity" advanced by the speakers, was an infinitely more enlightened type than the crude conceptions we are accustomed to hear taught as "orthodox."

# SOME EXPLANATORY NOTES

*The origins of the above Conference date back to an address given by the Archbishop of York to the Head Masters' Conference, in December, 1930, on the subject of Adult Religious Education. From this resulted a Conference of headmasters, chaplains and parish priests in 1931, at which the suggestion was made that a conference of Public School Boys should be held, at which masters were to be excluded and only boys in their last term at school invited. The above Conference was the result. A report of the Conference has been published, but it is much to be regretted that it consists only of "Impressions" made by one of six visitors who acted as Chairmen to the discussion groups. A detailed report, not necessarily a verbatim one, would have been a most interesting and valuable subject for study by all who are interested in the attitude of modern youth towards the subject of religion.*

Appendix I

# BOOKS REVIEWED BY ALAN WATTS
# IN *BUDDHISM IN ENGLAND*: 1934-1938

●

**Essays in Zen Buddhism (Second Series),** by Prof. D.T. Suzuki. (London: Luzac, 1933)
*Nov/Dec 1934*

**Outlines of Buddhism. An Historical Sketch,** by Mrs. Rhys Davids. (London: Methuen)
and:
**The Book of Gradual Sayings, 111.** Translated from the **Anguttara-Nikaya,** by E.M. Hare, with an introduction by Mrs. Rhys Davids. (Oxford U.P. for the Pali Text Society)
*May/June 1934*

**Islamic Sufism,** by Sirdar Ikbal Ali Shah. (London: Rider, 1933)
*July/August 1934*

**Essays in Zen Buddhism (Third Series),** by Dr. D.T. Suzuki. (London: Rider, 1933)
*Nov/Dec 1934*

**An Introduction to Zen Buddhism,** by Dr. D.T. Suzuki. (Kyoto: Eastern Buddhist Society, 1934)
*Sept/Oct 1935*

**Buddhist Meditation in the Southern School,** by G. Constant Lounsbery. (London: Kegan Paul, 1935)
*Jan/Feb 1936*

**Manual of Zen Buddhism,** by Daisetz Teitaro Suzuki. (Kyoto: Eastern Buddhist Society)
*March/April 1936*

**A Dictionary of Religion and Religions,** by Richard Ince M.A. (London: Arthur Barker, 1935)
and:
**A Survey of the Occult,** ed. Julian Franklyn. (London: Arthur Barker, 1935)
*May/June 1936*

**A Guide to Philosophy,** by C.E.M. Joad. (London: Gollancz)
and:
**Ancient Buddhism in Japan,** by M.W. de Visser. (Leyden: Brill, 1935)
*July/August 1936*

**Faiths and Fellowship. The Proceedings of the 2nd International Congress of the World Fellowship of Faiths.** (London, 1936)
*Sept/Oct 1936*

**Zen Buddhism and the Japanese Love of Nature,** by Daisetz Teitaro Suzuki. (London: Luzac)
*Nov/Dec 1936*

**The Web of the Universe,** by E.L. Gardner. (London: T.P.H., 1936)
and:
**Self-Realization Through Yoga and Mysticism,** by Josephine Ransom. (London: T.P.H., 1936)
*Jan/Feb 1937*

**What is Your Will?** by Mrs. Rhys Davids. (London: Rider, 1937)
*March/April 1937*

**The Ten Principal Upanishads.** Put into English by Shree Purohit Swami & W.B. Yeats. (London: Faber, 1937)
and:
**The Venture of Faith,** by Sir Francis Younghusband. (London: Michael Joseph, 1936)
and:
**The Gnosis or Ancient Wisdom in the Christian Scriptures.** No author given. (London: Allen & Unwin, 1937)
and:
**War Dance. A Study of the Psychology of War,** by Eric Graham Howe. (London: Faber, 1937)
*July/August 1937*

**The World's Need of Religion,** Being the Proceedings of the World Congress of Faiths in Oxford, 1937. Preface by Sir Francis Younghusband. (London: Nicholson & Watson, 1937)
*March/April 1938*

**World Vision.** by Leslie J. Belton. (Lindsey Press)
*March/April 1938*

**Shinran & His Religion of Pure Faith,** by Gendo Nakai. (Kyoto: Shinshu Research Institute, 1937)
*March/April 1938*

**Sage Ninomiya's Evening Talks,** trans. Isoh Yamagata. (Tokyo: Kyo Bun Kwan, 1937)
*March/April 1938*

**The Aryan Path.** Sept. 1938. Special Hind Swaraj Number. (Theosophy Co. (India) Ltd.)
*Nov/Dec 1938*

# LECTURE SERIES BY ALAN WATTS

## Essential Lecture Series I

Ego
Nothingness
Time
Death
Cosmic Drama
The More It Changes
God
Meditation

## Essential Lecture Series II

We As Organism
Myself: Concept or
    Confusion?
Limits of Language
Intellectual Yoga
She is Black
Landscape,
    Soundscape . . .
Seeing Through the Game
Play and Sincerity

## Essential Lecture Series III

Birth, Death, & the
    Unborn (I & II)
Philosophy of Nature
Man's Place in Nature
Baseless Fabric of This
    Vision
Tribute to C.G. Jung
Historical Buddhism
Yoga Cara

## Philosophy

Veil of Thoughts
    (Parts I–IV)
Early Chinese Zen
    Buddhism (Parts I–IV)

## Meditation

Philosophy of Meditation
    (Parts I–IV)
Sonic Meditation
    (Parts I–IV)

To receive the above lectures on audiocassette please send thirty-five dollars for each series to the address below, or send $150 for the entire five series set. A complete Alan Watts bibliography and tape list will be included with each order. For VISA, MasterCard, or COD orders phone (415) 663-9102.

**Alan Watts Electronic Educational Programs**
Box 938
Point Reyes Station, CA 94956

# ALSO AVAILABLE . . .

**The Essential Alan Watts**
The last original work by Alan Watts, this is a collection of his own basic tenets and several classic essays including "Work as Play" and "The Trickster Guru." $6.95

**OM: Creative Meditations**
Based on a series of his talks, this book is an outstanding introduction to the teachings and philosophy of Alan Watts.    $6.95

Available at your local bookstore or directly from the publisher. Send your check or money order (plus 75¢ per book for postage; California residents please add 6½% state sales tax) to: CELESTIAL ARTS PUBLISHING, P.O. Box 7327, Berkeley, California, 94707.

# A WORD FROM THE PUBLISHER . . .

CELESTIAL ARTS is the publisher of many fine books in the subject areas of psychology, spirituality, health, and New Age thought. For a copy of our free catalog, please write to the address above or phone (415) 524-1801.